JAPAN

TRANSLATED FROM THE GREEK BY

GEORGE C. PAPPAGEOTES

BERKELEY / 1982

CHINA

BY NIKOS KAZANTZAKIS

WITH AN EPILOGUE BY

HELEN KAZANTZAKIS

CREATIVE ARTS BOOK COMPANY

ACKNOWLEDGMENT

I should like to acknowledge my indebtedness to Mr. John Chioles, Mr. E. W. Hathaway and Mrs. Helen L. Stephenson for their valuable collaboration in this translation. Specifically, to Mr. Hathaway for editing and improving stylistically the English of my translation of the first chapters of Japan and of China, to Mrs. Stephenson for most of Japan, and to Mr. Chioles for the rest of the book. I should also like to thank Mr. Chioles for his translation of the canto, "Hideyoshi," by Nikos Kazantzakis into English blank verse. I should also like to express my gratitude to Mrs. Helen Kazantzakis and Professor Robert Austerlitz of Columbia University for their aid in the transliteration of Japanese and Chinese names, words and phrases in this book.

—G. C. P.

CREATIVE ARTS BOOKS
ARE PUBLISHED BY
DONALD S. ELLIS

■ CONTENTS

PROLOGUE

■ PROLOGUE

■ WHEN I CLOSE my eyes to see, to hear, to smell, to touch a country I have known, I feel my body shake and fill with joy as if a beloved person had come near me.

A rabbi was once asked the following question: "When you say that the Jews should return to Palestine, you mean, surely, the heavenly, the immaterial, the spiritual Palestine, our true homeland?" The rabbi jabbed his staff into the ground in wrath and shouted, "No! I want the Palestine down here, the one you can touch with your hands, with its stones, its thorns and its mud!"

Neither am I nourished by fleshless, abstract memories. If I expected my mind to distill from a turbid host of bodily joys and bitternesses an immaterial, crystal-clear thought, I would die of hunger. When I close my eyes in order to enjoy a country again, my five senses, the five mouth-filled tentacles of my body, pounce upon it and bring it to me. Colors, fruits, women. The smells of orchards, of filthy narrow alleys, of armpits. Endless snows with blue, glittering reflections. Scorching, wavy deserts of sand shimmering under the hot sun. Tears, cries, songs, distant bells of mules, camels or troikas. The acrid, nauseating stench of some Mongolian cities will never leave my nostrils. And I will eternally hold in my hands—eternally, that is, until my hands rot—the melons of Bukhara, the watermelons of the Volga, the cool, dainty hand of a Japanese girl. . . .

For a time, in my early youth, I struggled to nourish

my famished soul by feeding it with abstract concepts. I said that my body was a slave and that its duty was to gather raw material and bring it to the orchard of the mind to flower and bear fruit and become ideas. The more fleshless, odorless, soundless the world was that filtered into me, the more I felt I was ascending the highest peak of human endeavor. And I rejoiced. And Buddha came to be my greatest god, whom I loved and revered as an example. Deny your five senses. Empty your guts. Love nothing, hate nothing, desire nothing, hope for nothing. Breathe out and the world will be extinguished.

But one night I had a dream. A hunger, a thirst, the influence of a barbarous race that had not yet become tired of the world had been secretly working within me. My mind pretended to be tired. You felt it had known everything, had become satiated, and was now smiling ironically at the cries of my peasant heart. But my guts—praised be God!—were full of blood and mud and craving. And one night I had a dream. I saw two lips without a face—large, scimitar-shaped woman's lips. They moved. I heard a voice ask, "Who is your God?" Unhesitatingly I answered, "Buddha!" But the lips moved again and said: "No, Epaphus."

I sprang up out of my sleep. Suddenly a great sense of joy and certainty flooded my heart. What I had been unable to find in the noisy, temptation-filled, confused world of wakefulness I had found now in the primeval, motherly embrace of the night. Since that night I have not strayed. I follow my own path and try to make up for the years of my youth that were lost in the worship of fleshless gods, alien to me and my race. Now I transubstantiate the abstract concepts into flesh and am nourished. I have learned that Epaphus, the god of touch, is my god.

All the countries I have known since then I have known with my sense of touch. I feel my memories tingling, not in my head but in my fingertips and my whole skin. And as I bring back Japan to my mind, my hands tremble as if they were touching the breast of a beloved woman.

When Mohammed came knocking at the door of a faithful sheik, he wanted to talk about war. Zeinab, his friend's wife, ran to open the door for him. But just as she opened the door, the wind blew and her robe rippled and revealed her breast.

Mohammed was dazzled. He immediately forgot all the other women he had ever loved. He raised his hands and gave thanks to God. "Thank you, Allah, for having made my heart so fickle."

This same grateful prayer I myself spoke in Port Said as I stepped onto the Japanese steamer that was to take me to the Far East. I forgot at once all the countries I had loved before, all my licit and illicit geographical love affairs, and turned my entire self toward my new amorous adventure, toward the faraway land with its slanted Mongolian eyes and the motionless, hard, mysterious smile.

Let us, too, thank Allah who has made our heart so changeable, and let the fresh wind blow and show us a little of the breast of the Orient.

—N. K., 1938

PART I:

JAPAN–1935

■ SAKURA AND KOKORO

■ When I started for Japan I knew only two words of her language: *sakura,* which means cherry blossom, and *kokoro,* which means heart. Who knows, I thought to myself, perhaps these two simple words will be enough. . . .

Until recent years when she threw off her kimono and revealed the cannon and the swords behind her cherry-blossom trees, Japan used to glimmer in our imagination with her polished red wooden sandals and the chrysanthemums in her kimono and the ivory combs in her spreading blue-black hair and her silken fan inscribed with a sentimental *haiku:*

> O sweet flowers of the cherry-blossom tree,
> Reflecting yourselves every spring upon the
>   waters;
> I stood up to cut you, but I only wet my
>   embroidered sleeves.

Fuji stood perennially snow-clad at the back of our minds, and the three-stringed samisen, invisible, sighed quietly, slowly, with restrained, reticent sadness. Landscape, kimono, woman, music, twilight . . . all these kept weaving back and forth inside us, made harmonious by her seriousness and grace.

Japan has been the geisha of the nations; she has kept smiling over the distant waters, full of pleasure and mystery. Marco Polo called her Zipangu, the beautiful, the pleasure-loving, the golden, and she fired all imaginations, fired the imagination of Columbus, who set out for her sake, taking to the ocean with three caravels to seek her out. Had not his ancient teacher, the great geographer Toscanelli, written him that this island was made of gold and pearls and precious stones? The roofs of the houses and the doorways were of gold, he had said. How, then, could the greedy Genoese sleep? He set out on his journey for plunder, but he did not find Zipangu. The barrier of America was raised between them. Fifty years later she was found by another adventurer, the Portuguese Ferrão Mendez Pinto, whose ship was endangered by her rocks. Docked in her waters, he sold his merchandise dear, heaping gold and silk in the hold of his ship. The rude sea wolves were amazed at the riches of Japan, at her noble civilization. They used to relate with admiration that no one there ate with his fingers, as they did in Europe at that time, but with two little sticks of wood or ivory.

The adventurers came hungrily running from all sides, and the missionaries came running too with their religious wares. The first of these was the gentle St. Francis Xavier, who continued to affirm for the rest of his life that this new land had been the great consolation of his heart. He even went so far as to say that the Japanese were the most virtuous and the most honest people in the world; they were good, they were without guile, and they put honor above all other virtues of men.

After a few years churches were built, thousands of Japanese were baptized, commoners and aristocrats worshiped the new Buddha, Christ. However, along with their Christianity the Europeans brought to this virgin land their guns, their syphilis, their tobacco, their slave trade. Western civilization began to spread its roots—merchants without conscience, Frankish pirates, abductors of women, drunkards—and thousands of Japanese were loaded into galleys and sold as slaves in the distant bazaars. And something even worse: as the Japanese Christians increased in numbers, they forgot the tolerance and gentleness of their race and began to persecute. Buddhist monasteries were burned to the ground; those who did not wish to be baptized were boiled in caldrons . . . until the Japanese could stand it no longer, and one day in 1683—blessed be the day—a horrible massacre cleansed the soil of Japan from Christians and Europeans.

I was leaning out over the prow of the ship watching the dark-green waters part as we entered the Suez Canal. The exotic journey before me would last for over a month, but in heart the slender, sea-beaten body of Japan had already begun to take shape.

Three Japanese cooks with white chef's caps sat on their heels close by looking at a flowerpot in which was growing a microscopic flowering rhododendron. They did not speak, but in a moment one of them extended his finger and began to count the roselike little flowers, gently touching them and then the petals one by one. Then he drew back his hand again, spoke one word, and the other two bowed as if they were worshiping the flowerpot.

Love, silence, concentration—how far we were already from the shameless shrill voices of Port Said and the vehement superfluous gestures. I was thinking what a barbarous impression would have been made on these taciturn souls by the Spaniards and Portuguese who came as Europe's first emissaries, and how the Japanese spirit must have felt relieved when the ports were closed and silence and tranquillity could again reign over the pointed, many-colored roofs.

The ports had remained closed to the white barbarians for two centuries, but one morning in the summer of 1853, the American Admiral Perry appeared in the Japanese world. He carried an ultimatum in a golden box, and asked that the Japanese ports be opened to American ships. The admiral left the golden box with the letter to the native dignitaries, the samurai, and said that he would return in a year for their answer.

There was great turmoil in Japan. No, we should not let the barbarians infect our holy ground again. The ancestors rose up in their graves and cried out. But next year the admiral returned with his warships, threw a few shells from his cannon, and the Japanese understood. There is no safety; how can we fight those white demons? They have iron ships, they have cannon, their ships advance into the wind without sail, by devilish machines, and all the forces of evil are on their side; there is no safety. They opened their ports. And then there was presented to the enchanted eyes of the Whites that superb spectacle: forests of blossoming cherry trees in springtime, thousand-colored chrysanthemums in autumn, gentle, diminutive women, silks, fans, strange temples, statues, paintings, an unexpected world full of joy and grace.

The small-souled, tired Pierre Loti came and depicted this ever-virginal land as fragile bric-a-brac, soulless but full of grace; the women dolls, the men pygmies: take away their kimonos and nothing is left. Then came the romantic Lafcadio Hearn and presented Japan as an eternal idyl, all soul, disciplined pathos, mystical smile. "Do you wish to learn what the heart of Japan is? It is the flower of the mountain cherry tree, spreading its fragrance in the morning sun." Sweetness, finesse, silence, men who die smiling, women all obedience and silent depths. . . . Great authors have cast their eyes upon this land and it is difficult to see it without being carried away by their vision. They have thrown over the thin-spined body a kimono embroidered with the most exotic flowers of their imagination.

Let us raise the kimono a little and see. When I left, I knew only two words of Japanese, *sakura* and *kokoro*, but now that I am on my way, if I want to make complete contact with Japan, I suppose I shall have to add a third —a word I do not yet know how to say in Japanese. In English it is terror.

ON THE JAPANESE SHIP

■ THE DOORS OPEN the wrong way; the sailors are short, yellow, taciturn; they wear white gloves to keep their hands clean; strange letters—like fallen trees, doors, scaffolds—gleam coal-black on a brilliant snow-white background. And everywhere, behind the doors, under the stairs, between the ropes, glittering slanted eyes are upon you. You are frightened, as if you had entered a jungle. This is the *Kasima Maru*, a Japanese ship.

A multitude of races: Englishmen and Englishwomen playing shuffleboard on deck or drinking fizzy drinks in the bar; Japanese gazing silently at the land we have left behind us; a German loaded down with cameras and binoculars. A Frenchwoman; a Russian; British missionaries bound for India to peddle their two prime wares, Christ and Britain; a Polish violinist talks ceaselessly in broken German. Already we are all privy to his secrets, although it is only our first day on board. He is on his way to Tokyo to open a violin school and bring out Stenka, his faithful and devoted honey-blond girl friend who has been living with him for nine years. He shows us a handful of pictures and we learn all the secrets of her body. From the saloon comes a horrible screeching as if the gramophone were a cageful of cats that had suddenly been let loose and had now come jumping out all the windows.

I walk on deck. I smoke my pipe, my faithful fellow traveler. Wisps of conversation drift by and get caught in my ears: small talk about women, Shanghai, music, Christ, Mussolini, and the tooth of the Buddha, which we will see in Ceylon. The Frenchwoman lies on her back in the sun showing off her silk stockings. Noise. Confusion. Chaos. You cannot yet distinguish the faces, you cannot form opinions. The first glances, the first words, the first encounter. Everybody is out prospecting for the fellow traveler whose company will suit him best and to whom he can cling until the thirty-two endless days of the voyage are over. A slight panic seizes the passengers; they all quail before loneliness, that cruel tiger.

The sea is calm, viscous. The desert is on both sides of us. Steam rises from silent sandy places, slightly wavy, ash-colored, with yellow fringes. My old craving to walk straight ahead day and night without ever turning my head leaps up again as I behold the endless sands. A slight intoxication, and an intense, mysterious yearning to get lost in the desert. Not wine, not woman nor any idea has so lethally and sweetly moved my mind.

But since I haven't the courage to get lost in the desert, I should like to remain silent for the entire trip. A Pythagorean cure! To be cleansed of all the words I have heard and spoken, to let silence spread cool and green like crawling ivy inside me. But the crowds of humanity will not let you remain silent. They want to cling, to lean like sheep, neck to neck. They are afraid of silence. Only prattle can strengthen their hearts.

We enter the Red Sea. Oppressive heat. We breathe with difficulty. The women shed their clothes, the Englishmen drink iced lemonades, the Japanese wave their fans. A faint sweetish-peppery odor of sweat and decay. The Pole talks on. His voice is drawling and repugnant, yet without wanting to we all turn our ears and listen. His ancestor, he says, was a gigantic peasant who followed the king. One day the axle of the royal carriage broke. His ancestor put his finger in the wheel to replace the axle so the carriage could go on. His finger was eaten away but the king made him a count.

The German leans over, anxiously regarding the Red Sea. It isn't red at all. It's blue. Why? He had left the Baltic because he had read of the wonders and marvels of tropical lands. He would lean over the bow of the ship expecting to see sharks with open mouths, schools of dolphins, strange sea birds, and at night to see waters so brightly phosphorescent you could read by the light of the sea. And now! Only a few ordinary sea gulls and the sea blue by day and black by night. "And the cherry blossoms?" he asked me one evening, terrified lest the cherry blossoms too might not be real, might only exist on paper and bloom only in the brilliant posters. I calmed him. At this very moment, I told him, over there in Japan, the branches with their silken skin are getting ready, the sap is ascending, the buds are swelling, and by the time we get there all the inner preparation will be finished and the sacred flowers will be bursting from trunk to crown on every cherry tree, exactly as in the travel posters.

Gradually the confusion lessens, individuals come to the fore, the amorphous mass begins to jell, the first homogeneous groupings begin to take shape, habits can be discerned. Everyone joins a group. The Englishmen now spend endless silent hours throwing rings of rope over little poles. Only occasionally is their silence interrupted by wild, inarticulate cries. A Viennese dancer with bleached hair is going to Java to join her husband. Her voice is harsh, full of passion, like a cat on the rooftops. She talks about her Bubi, her curly haired little dog that was killed during the Socialist revolution in Vienna. All the horrible killing, the clash of two relentless and bloodthirsty ideas, reduced to the sentimental little story of a dog that died.

The Japanese passengers fall into two groups: the first- and second-class passengers, who speak English and play shuffleboard, and the third-class passengers, who play with their cats for hours, look at the flowerpots or the sea and eat their rice with those two miraculous little chopsticks.

I talk with a quiet old Japanese who sits cross-legged at the stern watching the green wake of the ship. His English has a heavy Japanese accent, but I manage to understand him. He tells me of the superhuman grandeur of the Mikado. "During the Russo-Japanese War," he said, "an admiral appeared before the Mikado weeping, 'Your Majesty, I bring terrible news. Our greatest ironclad battleship has been sunk.' The people outside the palace wept. The admiral trembled. The Mikado, calm and unmoved, replied, 'Yes, it has been sunk.' Nothing else.

"A few days later, the admiral ran joyfully up to the Mikado, 'Your Majesty, I bring wonderful news, the Russian fleet has been sunk!' The people were jubilant with joy and shouted and cheered outside the palace, the admiral was elated, but the Mikado, still imperturbable and composed, replied, 'Yes, it has been sunk.' Nothing else."

The Japanese looked at me with his small, sparkling eyes and remained silent for a while. Then he turned back to the sea again and whispered a Japanese word I did not know, "*fudoshin!*"

"*Fudoshin?*" I asked. "What does it mean?"

"To hold your heart immovable, unshaken in the face of joy or misfortune. It is a Japanese word. No other language has it. Made in Japan."

That same evening, a blue-black bird came from the mountains of Africa, flew around the masts, passed over our heads two or three times crying, "Tsee-oo, tsee-oo!" and flew off again toward Africa.

For many days now, my two great joys on board this ship have been my conversation with the old Japanese and the coming of the blue bird.

■ EASTERN PORTS

■ Bougainvilleas in flower, unspeakable filth, harsh voices, squabbles, yellow flashes from eyes, tankers smelling of tar, fish and rotten fruit, brazen, shameless adolescent girls with precocious swelling breasts, boys and old men who come after you promising untold delights, and over everything the acrid smell of human sweat; the whole harbor exudes the aroma of a beast aroused in heat. Eastern ports, such have they been since the beginning of time.

I thank God that I was born and have been able to be in ports like these, and experience the most mordant human stench, and hear words I ought not to have heard, and feel how sweet they are, and not only sweet but also holy, the forbidden fruit of oriental ports.

Heavily painted girls—eyes, lips, fingers, toes—sit silent and motionless at the water front like a display of round and fragrant fruit, watching the ships that cast anchor. In the loins of a clay figurine from Knossos a small piece of magnetic iron was found embedded: you feel that these oriental women, these eternal sirens, are equipped with a well-known invincible magnet which they use to draw in the ships. They sit there, munching melon seeds or peanuts or fragrant chewing gum and making crackling noises —calm, serene, they ruminate like cows. They know there is no need to move or shout or wave their handkerchiefs to welcome the sailors. The magnet waits immovably and draws the ships to it.

Barcelona, Marseille, Naples, Constantinople, Jaffa, Alexandria, Tunis, Algiers—the women of the water front, these suntanned sirens have been sitting for centuries around the Mediterranean seducing the sailors. And not only the sailors. Everything takes on the mysterious aroma of their sweat. Everything here, fruits, men, ideas, morals, has come from the same muddy, lukewarm waters, from the much-traveled, many-colored caïques who come to anchor at their bosom and their dark, salty-skinned sailors made wild by their long fasting from wine and woman.

Bananas, melons, dates, carob beans, citrons all have a deep and mystical bond with the civilization that has grown up in their shadow and breathes their fragrance. Fruits, men, ideas, morals—all have a family resemblance. You must broaden your heart to comprehend, you must steel your mind to resist, if you are to withstand the aroma and the stench; you must impose iron discipline upon your impulses, otherwise the sight of an oriental port would be unbearably repulsive, or else it would enthrall you with its deadly enchantment. A narrow, pure, cold, virtuous soul will not feel anything here. In the ports of the Orient the bounds of virtue are different, and vice has other and far wider privileges. Suddenly in these ports you feel with untold bitterness that "virtue" is against human nature.

■ COLOMBO

■ WE HAVE COME through the Red Sea already and are out on the Indian Ocean. We have not seen land for days. A cloud of lassitude has descended upon the masts and has settled down over the deck like a fog. Heavy heat. We suffocate. We think of the stokers down in the hold and feel cool. Sometimes a dolphin, well nourished and sleek, flips up to breathe; sometimes flying fishes leap like arrows close along the viscous waters. All the passengers have lost their strength from the heat and stay in the shade, flaccid and gasping for breath; you can feel the decay in your nostrils.

Only two Moslems from India maintain their dignity and their rhythm. Every morning when the sun rises and every evening when it sets they kneel on ruche mats and say their prayers. Their religion gives them a rhythm that is truly of the sun, and you feel that their souls are like sunflowers, obeying the course of the sun. Even if all the rest of us here on the ship should rot, disintegrate, these two faithful Moslems will hold out, resist putrefaction.

Thus the days and nights pass, monotonous, full of decay. But one evening all the faces are aglow, for by dawn the next day we shall have reached Colombo, the famous port of Ceylon.

Dark purple clouds, dull carmine sun, sluggish, sodden light. We slip slowly into the harbor as if afraid of awakening the city, which sleeps like a Turkish odalisque. The morning star still shines above us and seems about to drop like dew upon her breasts. The first morning light catches the tops of the minarets, and a few of the cupolas take on a rosy tinge. The sea gulls wake up, a flock of crows flies overhead. A sweet hour, a mystic, erotic moment, as the prow glides quietly into the city.

From the dark depths of the harbor come tall slender boats like gondolas, one behind the other, with long boxes on them, like coffins. On each boat, standing on top of the coffins, are three chocolate-colored men, half-naked and wearing white belts, gently moving the long oars.

The sun rises, the houses laugh with light, we hear voices and quarreling: the city wakes up. We jump to land. I walk up and down the water front. The streets open up before me like a fan and I rejoice in not knowing which one to choose. Behind the miserable "magnificent showcase" of the English section I can make out the broad leaves of the banana trees and the peppery aroma of native flesh. I ride in a ricksha, a light two-wheeled carriage: the man-horse with the wide soles runs. The European section is already behind us, we have escaped from it. Flowering trees, magnolias, wisterias, jacarandas, jasmine, papyrus. . . . My nostrils, my eyes, my ears all open up, my heart wells up and blooms and spreads over the inside walls of my chest like a bougainvillea.

We have escaped from the white, restless, wily men. Here the bodies are chocolate; chest, thighs, calves, feet are bare; the women smell of musk, their loins are brilliant with green, yellow, orange cloths, and their soul sits cross-legged in their suntanned breast, looking out at the world from the cool cave of their entrails.

In the middle of the street on a low altar sits a Buddha, small, sly, engaging, who gazes at the passers-by and smiles. A thin man in a yellow shirt kneels before him and looks at him intimately. A girl with white bracelets on her ankles goes up the steps and puts a handful of red flowers at the Buddha's small feet. Beyond the altar, under a palm tree, some girls are lying. They roll over, yawn, chew betel nut. Their lips are painted a dark orange.

Warm people, black eyes, long nails painted red, an easy, balanced stride, large white teeth that light up in the narrow, half-lit little shops. A little Singhalese approaches me. His long, spreading hair smells as the wind moves it. He speaks a little English, his chocolate-colored face shines with joy and sweat.

"You like ruby, sapphire, turquoise?"

I knew that on this island they have precious gems, which I love so much and cannot buy. Yet the sound of their names gives me such pleasure that I let him say them over and over again, fast, loud, full of vowels. They fall and crackle on the stones of the road as though my hands had been filled and overflowed. When I was satisfied and had had enough pleasure from the sound of the names, I shook my head to indicate that I wanted no precious stones. Then he offered me silks. Then pearls. Then girls. Then he studied me intently, trying to figure out what could interest me. Suddenly his eyes sparkled:

"You like temple of Buddha?"

I laughed. I spread out my hand and clapped him firmly on the shoulder:

"You've got it! That's what I want!"

At the threshold of the temple, I put a small silver coin in the rosy palm of my guide and he left me. I entered the small temple alone. My eyes became calm and my forehead relaxed. In the dim light I discerned on every side a multitude of statues—bronze gods, wild spirits, green faces, red mouths, sunken cheeks. Surely these are the diseases and passions of man! High in the background, behind a white curtain, Buddha sits with crossed legs and smiles seductively.

On his head were fixed some ten colorful little paper pin wheels. These are the sacred prayer wheels. From the door a slight breeze was blowing, and the wheels turned and turned, spinning out the desires of men.

■ SINGAPORE

■ THE PEOPLE ARE different here. The face of the earth has changed. Here you feel that our race has come to an end. These people laugh differently, talk, eat, cry, dance differently. They are descended from a different animal, they were made from a different clay.

A forest of canoes surrounds us in the port, and in each canoe sits a reddish-yellow Malay with broad cheekbones and small round eyes, holding a single paddle with two blades which he dips into the water right and left, driving his light, arrow-sharp dugout with amazing grace. They play a game, batting rubber balls with the backs of their paddles, and laugh up at us. Two or three Englishwomen with pinkish, excited flesh lean over the side and watch them, panting.

Let us set foot on this land, let us see it. Broad streets paved with asphalt, thousands of small shops, abundant yellow flesh, an unbearable stench from houses and sewers. It takes a highly trained nostril to distinguish the human stench from the sewer stench. Exotic fruits, lots of children wallowing in the mud, serious, silent, like little Confuciuses. . . . And here and there amid the filth a heavenly green tree with clusters of red flowers, like wisterias.

The women wear black pajamas, long tresses of shining black hair hang down their backs; their faces are carved of yellow knotless wood. Some older women totter along on their deformed small, round nanny-goat's feet, while others stride over the stones on their broad bare soles supplely and decisively like men.

One thing that makes a great impression on you is the inexhaustible crowds, like swarms of ants. The streets flow full of them like rivers. You are reminded of the blind ants of Africa that come rolling down like torrents through the villages they devastate. If a man falls in their path only his bones are left after a few minutes. The same thing happens here if a white man falls in the path of these people.

The other thing that impresses you is their eyes, full of fire and intelligence and full, at the same time, of burning hatred of the white man. Often as you walk through Chinese streets you turn your head and shiver to see thousands of eyes staring at you pitilessly.

If you can forget this hatred, the streets with their signs in Chinese characters will give you great joy. The Chinese letters are so expressive: you feel their construction is intuitive, that you do not have to know what they mean in order to understand them. Spirit and letter coincide. You walk and enjoy their color harmonies. White letters on a black ground, golden on green, black on crimson. The colors here in the Orient are so warm and cheerful. They are not aimed solely at the sense of sight but at the hearing, too, and the taste and touch and smell.

The twilight begins to fall like ashes. A thin, greenish crescent appears in the sky behind a cluster of palm trees, and I can watch the evening star roll down from leaf to leaf. The whole square is full of stalls. Men and women sit cross-legged under straw canopies and eat, holding their bowl of rice and the two chopsticks with which they seize the food and throw it into their famished mouths with the skill of a juggler.

I felt hungry, too, and sat down. A Chinese with a long pigtail brought me rice, fish and eggs. The rice smelt like a Chinese, the fish was in a thick and suspicious sauce, the eggs stank. I asked for tea, and they brought me a thick liquid that looked like salep and resin. I got up hungry. O Orient, Orient, I thought, how strong a mind and stomach one must have in order to endure you! And what an intricate and painful task it is to weave all these contradictions of the Orient into a higher synthesis, to find the mystic path of the Oriental oyster that transubstantiates its sickness into a pearl of great price.

Now it is night already and the lamps are lit, many-colored Chinese lanterns hang over the doors and in the balconies. The shops close, the stench dies down, the night flowers come out. The women put on their make-up, smooth down their hair with butter, put on their fresh, bright-colored pajamas and their wooden shoes, red, yellow, green, and go out into the street. Clack-clack, clack-clack, and on they go. Where are they going? To the park.

An immense park, red lights, wild, hoarse radios. Cheap passion. A lot of colorful booths selling cigarettes, peanuts, toys, women. They dance, they sing; the gong rings, and Chinese actresses covered with powder mount the small stage and dance and undulate.

The stars shine above us, the sky is fleecy, silent. And down here on earth, at the back of the park, the big night-club has opened. On the lintel are painted a pair of green dragons with burnished scales, their tongues moving stormily, like a fire. At the door stands the English impresario, brutish, burnt by the tropical sun, reduced to a beast by his diet of liquor and steaks. Under the high, arched door the Chinese cocottes begin to enter, thin as snakes, without breasts, without buttocks—swords. They have on silk dresses, narrow and tight like a sheath, and in divine colors, green like the dragon, orange, blue, black, slit open up to the thighs. At every step the whole leg shows, slender, strong, indomitable, gleaming as if lacquered. And above this reptilian, dangerous body is the terrifying mask of the face, wide like an angry cobra. A motionless, orange mouth. Slanted eyes, motionless too, look at you, indifferent, relentless, the way a snake looks at you.

Inside on the glossy floor they dance. The blond Englishmen howl. Their eyes are blurred. These yellow women keep sucking their blood. As the night goes on, the women become animated and the men debased. By dawn all the white race will be wallowing on the ground and the yellow women will raise their necks and lick their lips like satiated vampires.

The sun has already risen. I feel tired, and both merry and disgusted. A thick, muddy sediment as though I had taken opium and waked with a hangover, remembering the departed paradises with nostalgia and horror. Their streets smell of sewers and jasmine together, their fruits are both nauseating and fragrant at the same time, their women are filled with enticement and death, and, in the same way, their paradises both fascinate and disgust my soul. This, I suppose, is what the Sirens do to a soul that is full of curiosity and dignity and does not want to miss any of the temptations of this earth, but also does not want to be debased. Of the two possible choices—to give yourself body and soul to the Sirens and to rot, to yield not an inch and become a saint—Ulysses' scheme is still the best.

■ THE JAPANESE
CHRISTIAN

■ WE HAVE BEEN sailing along the Chinese coast and are now approaching Hong Kong. At my table on the ship there are six people: a Frenchwoman; a young pianist; next, an astonishing blend of a Neapolitan father and a Japanese mother; the Polish violinist; then an Indian, returning from London, a doctor; and finally, directly opposite me, a fat, elderly Japanese, Kawayama San.

Short, plump, serious. He seldom took part in our conversations. He did not laugh. He did not smoke. He did not drink. He did not play cards. But his hands touched the table, the bread, the fruit, the children, all with a strange, sensual insistence. When he spoke he pursed his lips like a spinster, and the words came out solemnly and tenderly. When he saw anything he especially liked—a fruit, a sea gull, a sunset—he would close his eyes in ecstasy.

All the Japanese caress things with their hands or their eyes, but in him I seemed to discern a tinge of embarrassment: he did it surreptitiously, furtively, hurriedly, as though it were a sin.

We became friends. He drew for me in my notebook pictures of Fuji, the sacred mountain of Japan, as it looks with snow in the winter, as it looks under the clear sky of summer. He spoke about nature with knowledge and sensitivity—the mysterious, ever changing beauty that light gives to the landscape; the different flight of each

33

kind of bird; the fish, and the way they twist their bodies and move their tails and play with the waves, each in its own different way.

Likewise, with passion and knowledge he loved his race, its leaders, its poets, its painters, its peasants, its fishermen. And as he spoke he made a strange gesture. He would press the palms of his hands firmly on his belly and, slowly drawing them upward, would spread them wide open before his face as if he were tearing open his belly and pulling out his entrails and offering them up as a sacrifice.

Suddenly a flash of lightning split my brain. All at once, everything—gestures, words, solemnity, tenderness, surreptitious sensuality—it all made sense. I could not contain myself and I cried,

"You are a Christian, Kawayama San!"

He smiled, closed his eyes blissfully and crossed himself.

I was glad. I had seen Christ in various geographic climes. I had seen him as a poor fellah in rags in the Sudan; as a Lapp in a furry coat of wolfskin in a hut near Archangel. And once on Mount Athos in the Monastery of St. Gregory I had seen a Virgin, yellow and slant-eyed, with thick eye bones like a Chinese woman. And once in my sleep I had dreamt of a Virgin who looked like a Vlach girl and wore a short woolen coat and a necklace of golden coins and red shepherd's shoes with clout nails in soles and heels. She was climbing a mountain and carrying her little child that looked like the Christ-child on her back in a Vlach cradle. And now was my chance to admire the Son of Mary in a kimono in a garden of chrysanthemums and drinking tea with his disciples the coolies.

I kept avidly gazing at this Christian Japanese whom good fortune had sent my way. I longed to see how the religion of perseverance and faith in a future life after death would be transformed by the heroic soul of Japan which is so full of the love of this life.

"I thought," I said, "that the natural religion of the Japanese was Shintoism, the heroic worship of the ancestors. The land of Japan was created by the gods and is continually re-created by the parents who die. Your natural religion is the worship of the Japanese land. As a great ancestor of yours once said, the Japanese has no need to pray, it is enough for him to live on the earth of Japan; in this way he lives within his prayer. How could a religion that denies the barriers of land and race and directs all man's hopes beyond this earth take root in your soul?"

Kawayama San closed his eyes as if sunk in profound meditation. Then he opened them, smiled, and said,

"The Japanese soul is both simple and complex. It is strange, it follows its own paths, and a European who does not know them will get lost."

"I am not a European," I replied, "I was born between Europe and Asia, and I understand."

"I did not mean to offend you," he said, throwing up his plumpish arms in distress. "Now that you are going to Japan to become acquainted with its soul, you should have in mind some of its characteristics, in particular these three:

"1. The Japanese soul accepts foreign ideas very easily;

"2. It does not accept them slavishly, but assimilates them, and it has a great power of assimilation; and

"3. In the process of assimilation, it harmonizes them with its previous ideas so that the new ideas and the old are welded into a harmonious and indissoluble totality.

"Our first true native religion was Shinto, the worship of our ancestors. Suddenly, in 552 A.D., a new religion came to our country from Korea, Buddhism, and we accepted it, but not without resistance. It could not take root in our soul until it had been assimilated and harmonized with our previous religion. How could we accept

Buddha as supreme when we had for centuries had
Amaterasu, our great goddess of the Sun? The old faith
resisted the new. The struggle lasted for about three centuries, until finally our great priest Kūkai came and
found the solution: Buddha and the Sun are one and the
same god. In India he took on the person of Buddha, and
in Japan he became Amaterasu. After this the Japanese
soul accepted the new religion without further resistance.
Why? Because it had been able to assimilate it and reconcile it with its previous faith of Shinto. The same thing
is now beginning to happen with Christianity.

"It is not by its ideology that Christianity appeals to
us, nor by its ethics, nor by its rituals, but because it is
based on the idea of sacrifice. The essence of Christianity is sacrifice." (Here he again performed his gesture of
hara-kiri, and did it with such force and vigor that I
threw back my head lest his entrails should splatter on
me!)

"It's the idea of sacrifice—that is what fascinates us
Japanese and makes us Christians. For sacrifice is the supreme yearning of our race: to sacrifice yourself for the
Mikado, the descendant of our great deity, the Sun; to
sacrifice yourself for your honor, by committing hara-kiri.
And now Christianity takes us one step further, to sacrifice yourself for something even greater than ourselves,
our kings, or our race: to sacrifice yourself for mankind
—that is the ultimate in sacrifice."

"Are there many Christians in Japan?"

"We have 1,708 churches throughout Japan, and there
are 254,000 Christians, or a few more. But we know how
the Japanese soul works and we wait with confidence.
We do not expect dominance but harmonization. Among
the Japanese a new world view never struggles to uproot
the old but strives to be reconciled with it so that both
become one."

He closed his eyes again and remained silent. I went

up on deck and stood leaning over the prow and gazing at the sea. We had already passed the Gulf of Siam and were approaching Hong Kong. Charming little islands, bare like bodies that have been in swimming and are now basking in the sun to get dry. And through them pass the exotic Chinese junks, broad, tall sterns smeared with tar, slender prows reaching out over the waters like thirsty dragons, dark-brown sails spread out like the wings of a huge bat.

We are surrounded by broad, low boats where the families of the fishermen live the year round, propelled by the father with a long single oar attached to the stern. The woman, eternally stooping, washes, mends, cooks or picks lice from her little children. And the big son stands naked at the stern and shouts at us to throw a coin which he will then dive down to the bottom of the sea and seize.

I went into Hong Kong with the Japanese Christian. When we entered the Chinese city I was pleased. Narrow streets; signs on banners with black, red, green pictograms; silent women sewing or cooking, squatting on the sidewalks; mandarins with black silk caps and sparse goatees; coolies gasping for breath and carrying fish, rice, sugar cane; guttural voices; open sewers; nauseating Chinese smells—suddenly, the curtain went up all the way and a Chinese city appeared.

I cast out my eyes like a trawl, and when I had gathered in the whole panorama I turned to my Japanese friend. He took me by the arm, gently but insistently.

"Come," he said to me humbly, "come. Here in Hong Kong we have a large church. Let us go and worship."

"There at the corner," I replied, "I see a booth overflowing with fruit—pineapples, mangoes, papayas, pomelos. I will take that road."

Thus we separated. In the evening, when the lights were already gleaming over the whole mountain and the exquisite scenery of Hong Kong at night was visible, I returned to the ship. At the ship's ladder I met my friend. I was happily holding a basket of fruit; my friend's hands were empty but his face, too, was shining with joy.

"All roads lead to joy," he said, with light malice.

I gave him a heavy bunch of bananas and replied, laughing,

"Yes, but I like the road with the fruit."

■ SHANGHAI—

THE ACCURSED CITY

■ A MUDDY SEA, the Yangtze River carries with it the soil of China and muddies the ocean for miles out to sea. A heavy fog has fallen and the ship whistles in alarm. Everybody leans and stares, trying to pierce through the fog to the famous and infernal city of Shanghai.

I look at the map, divided into zones like a splotchy monster. The red zone is the international Shanghai; the green, the French; the yellow, the Chinese. In 1843, when the port was opened for the first time, Shanghai was a wretched fishing village surrounded by swamps and reeds. The white men came with their demonic activity; they deepened the river, they built wharves, established factories, banks, a stock exchange, skyscrapers, they brought strange machines and merchandise, they created new needs for the Chinese in order to make them their customers. The fishing village ended up as a huge city, and the naïve, happy fishermen became its beaten and famished coolies.

One of my fellow travelers, a Japanese, saw me avidly studying the body of Shanghai spread out on the map and smiled at me slyly.

"Don't be in a hurry to become acquainted with the forbidden fruits of Shanghai. There is no more horrible city. Wherever you touch it, it drips poison."

Someone laughed behind us, hissingly, mockingly. Two drops of spittle splashed my ears. I turned. An Englishman with sunken yellow cheeks and bleary blue eyes had heard us talking and snickered:

"There is no more attractive city in the world!"

He stretched out his trembling hand and caressed the whole of Shanghai.

"Women? Whisky? Dollars?" I asked teasingly.

"Pffft!" said the Englishman contemptuously. "Not women, nor whisky, nor dollars, but 'Chinese princesses' as we call the handsome yellow youths in Shanghai. Soft sofas, the lights turned off, the long pipes lit—the curtain which you call reality falls, and the true world, paradise, is opened before us and we enter. . . . "

The dim English eye lit up for a moment. His thick denture came out of place and his mouth was distorted. I felt the disgust and indignation that always assail me when I see the degeneration and degradation of the human soul and human flesh. I turned abruptly and went forward toward the prow alone.

The fog had already dispersed and the sun had come out. Shanghai lay spread out before us over the yellow muddy waters. Ships flying all kinds of flags, very tall chimneys on the factories, the sky blurred with smoke. At our right, a few still uncontaminated farms show green —who knows whether on my return they will have been eaten up by cement and iron? Without being consciously aware of it, I raised my hand and waved them farewell. A throng of sailing vessels in odd designs, winged dragons with their multicolored sails, pass over the waters like mythical monsters.

The ship threw down its hanging staircase and pawed at Shanghai. Hastily I leaped again to land, strode off across the wharf and thrust myself into the many-colored, many-headed streets. I think there is no greater happiness than to see, smell, taste and touch something for the first time. I hurry past the wide European streets, the banks, the offices, the shops. I leave behind the red-faced Englishmen, the fat French merchants, the tubercular Hindus selling their silks and tea; I leave behind the churches, lodges, hospitals, libraries, clubs—all the hypocritical show windows of white civilization—and I immerse myself in the yellow zone with its yellow crowds, full of mud and filth.

I open my eyes, I can hardly keep from shouting aloud with joy. I never thought I should see the face of the earth so rich, so variegated. A strange intoxication seizes me: to mingle with this dense, thousand-headed mass, to be wound on the same spool and forget whence you have come and whither you are going. Slowly your sight clears and you begin to be able to distinguish things: narrow streets at odd angles, long banners with Chinese characters, green dragons carved on walls and roofs, small shops like cells with bent yellow little men in them working wood, leather, lighting fires, cooking, chopping all sorts of meat—beef, horse, dog.

Lepers with fingers eaten up, stark-naked children with swollen bellies, women with tight black trousers, harsh voices, gaudy colors, odd harmonies, and over everything, unbearable, thick, omnipotent, the Chinese stench. Every man here is a sewer, untold is the filth that he piles up, that his forefathers have been piling up for thousands of years to form the flat, flexible skin of China. I walk slowly, fighting to stave off panic so that I may enjoy this amazing, horrible spectacle without fainting.

It gets dark. Night, the great conspirator, falls. The banks, the factories, the offices close down. The Europeans put down their heads like bulls and wash themselves, perfume themselves, and go out into the streets. The Laotian lanterns in the Chinese neighborhoods light up —red with black dragons, green with yellow scarabs—and down in the half-lit cellars the first moanings of jazz.

The peacocks of the night, the cocottes, wake up. They spread their glittering feathers, they paint their nails. Silent yellow servants transport them in velvet handbarrows. The cocottes get up; when one raises her foot the whole leg gleams for a moment through her slit silk pajamas. Others walk swiftly, traversing the filthy streets with furious long steps, like yellow, slant-eyed archangels. They are in a hurry. They go from nightclub to nightclub, they talk, they laugh, they caress the men for a moment as though they were sick children, they get paid, and again they open the door, again they raise their feet. The brilliance of their flesh flashes in the street like lightning and they go on to other men, sullenly, hurriedly. They drag themselves to another place, they pluck off their feathers, they lose their paint, they put on their make-up and do their hair and continue their nocturnal march.

Half-lit square yards of space, low vaulted doors everywhere, like a monastery, high railings all around—half-naked women lean out and call you. It smells of cheap perfumed soap, toilet water and human sweat. Somebody opens a window and pours out dirty water, you hear some hoarse singing and laughter, and then again the slender, multicolored ghosts leaning on the railings and calling you. Here for a few dollars you can see all the shamelessness and wretchedness of the human race, all the horrors of pleasure, and be disgusted with both male and female (if you are a man). Here you can see how the white men are debased, how the two great poisons of the Orient—women and opium—eat them up and rot them.

The atmosphere of all Shanghai contains something antispiritual, the deadly enemy of meditation, thought and purity. In Colombo or Singapore there is a certain sweetness in this degradation of the white man, and some justification for it in the climate: heat, humidity, you breathe with difficulty, you keep fanning all the time to make a breeze, you see all the tropical trees, you fall into a torpid state, you enter into nirvana, you evaporate into the whole. You become a tree, a cloud, a shadow of a tree and of a cloud. You are lost. But you are lost in being identified with something grander, broader, more eternal than yourself. But here in Shanghai you are debased. You are lost by falling into something meaner, narrower than the soul of man.

Accursed city. A prophet's vision of the future of the world if it continues in its present path. Such would have been Babylon, Nineveh, Thebes in Egypt, Knossos before the barbarians. An insatiable thirst for gold and hasty pleasure, purchased and full of sickness. Nowhere is found human sweetness and the unselfish smile. Men have returned to their ancestors, the boar and the sow. You pass through the European streets of Shanghai and your flesh creeps as if you were passing through a jungle. The faces of the whites are tense, morose, greedy. Hyenas, their eyes filled with slaughter and rapine. They run, climb stairs, knock on doors, bend over, write down numbers, make telephone calls, send telegrams, do business. They are wolves. When the night comes they turn into pigs. Hungry beasts in rut. They are in a hurry. Why are they in a hurry? Because they sense their end.

The vast wall of Chinese hatred stands high around them, the space between them and the wall gets narrower, the wall comes closer to them, like a net. Innumerable small, slanted, burning eyes gaze at the white man and wait. And sooner or later the Great Moment will come. But a just judge, an unbiased mind, equally disgusted by such Whites and such Yellows, cannot but wait, impatient as a hungry vulture, for this Great Moment to come and cleanse the earth of our rotten brothers and ourselves.

■ LAST DAYS

ON THE SHIP

■ LIFE IN A MONASTERY, on a ship, in a closed, isolated space can be truly unbearable if you are not obsessed by a great passion. Or, if, going beyond every passion, you do not reach the supreme calm of the blind man I saw in Shanghai yesterday. He sat in a filthy Chinese coffee shop, full of noise; everyone there was quarreling, or picking lice off himself or haggling over prices. And the blind man was sitting all by himself, ragged, barefoot, with his head erect; and his face shone ecstatically, as if invisible, clear, spring spirits passed above him. If you do not have a vehement passion, or if you have not overcome all passions, confined in a closed space you are lost.

I follow my fellow travelers here on the ship and sometimes pity captures me, sometimes my eye becomes hard and does not want them. After the men had parceled out the women; after the women had parceled out the men, and they had exchanged their wares; after they had put on all their evening clothes; after they had told all their anecdotes, they were left empty. Now they hang on the ropes of the ship, empty balloons. Like trousers, like shirts, like robes, a human wash, flapping and swelling in the sea breeze.

The Englishmen persist, they play a little more shuffleboard, but they are bored. Suddenly one of them stands up, stretches open a mouth armed with gold teeth, and utters an inarticulate animal cry. He is relieved. The

44

Japanese read all the English newspapers over and over, put on all the Buddhist postures of silence and resignation, and reach the last figure of boredom, the yawning. Lying in a row on the deck, like crocodiles, they open their jaws with a crack, rhythmically.

In the lounge, an American dancer, a "girl" who came aboard in Singapore, does exercises. She jumps as if suddenly ennui hit her mind. Her hair is bleached like linen; her eyes washed out, without eyelashes; her painted nails drip blood as if they were the talons of a predatory bird. Her experienced, widely traveled feet go up and down, make signals. She jumps, utters thin cries, rehearses, but no one pays any attention to her. We are already fed up with looking at her spindleshanks and her fat knees. This morning she put on her red- and green-checked slacks, took an accordion and sat on a bench and began to play, as if she played the balalaika, but nobody listened to her. She played, shouted, her slacks shone green and red in the deserted room. I felt pity for her. I tried to approach her, to say a kind word to her, but I became weary. I took again my little Dante, my fellow traveler, and I immersed myself in the *Inferno*.

Boredom—that is what the profound Florentine forgot to put at the bottom of Hades, the jaws that open and yawn. Because the unresigned exile was full of passion, hatred, love, desire, he was in a ceaseless, merciless orgasm and never experienced boredom—the essence of Inferno. The true devil is the ghostly spirit of ennui.

We have learned all the Japanese words we can. *Arigato*, which means "thank you"; *ohayo*, meaning "good morning"; *kobawa*, "good evening"; *Nippon panjai*, "Long live Japan"; *taiyo*, "the sun"; *ts'ki*, "the moon"—but all this gives no comfort.

A dog tied in the prow looks at the deserted sea and howls mournfully. We hear it and shiver, as if it had a human voice. As if it were our voice. In boredom, men and animals become one. I have already begun to discern that my fellow passengers are gradually losing their human expressions. Everyone returns to the primeval, ancestral animal, the totem of his family—one to a pig, another to a parrot, another to an ass. And the women go back to the vixen, to the mare, to the sow. The ship already looks like an infernal monster that carries us on its back. At night it is full of green and red eyes, and its iron guts groan. In daytime it has a bunch of human tongues and speaks. And when it arrives at some port, it begins to whistle mockingly in order to have people come from the mainland to see us.

The China Sea rose and fell wildly. All day it was turbid, yellow, and the hot bath we took in sea water was full of mud. I have never seen such an inimical and repulsive ocean. The hatred of the waves was vast. They frothed, dumb, dark, full of spite, and struck the ship. And she sighed, creaked, raised her head again and moved on. But other waves came towering, silent, yellow, with foaming hatred and kept battering her. There is no salvation, you felt. The day will come when the ship will be wrecked.

The Japanese were playing the phonograph. White women danced with yellow men. Violent American music, enrapturing, full of barbarous enchantment. You felt that the yellow men had already embraced our white women and were fleeing. . . . I drank a small glass of hot sake, a beverage made from rice; I lit my pipe and watched the bi-colored couples who were dancing. From the phonograph a modern crooner sings to the moon. Her voice is thin, metallic, monotonous, like a curse:

> *I painted my face with light rouge—*
> *La, la, la, with light rouge.*
> *And the moon rose in the sky—*

And its face is powdered—
La, la, la, lightly powdered. . . .

I smoked my pipe all alone, happy. "Happiness," I thought, "you whom they seek in the extremely high or in the extremely low, you walk on the soil we walk on and stand beside us like a little woman and come straight into our heart!"

Through the air, we discern far on the horizon the mountains of Japan. After one month's trip, we have arrived at our destination. All hearts are lightened. Blood is alive again, faces take on again their meaningful, human expressions.

My Japanese fellow passengers laugh, begin to joke; one anecdote brings another, a new facet of the mysterious yellow soul is gradually uncovered before me—laughing. Laughter has always been for me one of the greatest, most revealing gods. I know well why the rough and laconic Spartans, who took life more seriously and tragically than all the rest of the Greeks, had erected an altar to the god Gelanor (Laughter). Only the spontaneous, purest laughter can neutralize (not, of course, overcome, because it is never overcome) the horror of life, as long as we live. Tragedy could not have been born (it would have been unbearable for man) had not comedy been born at the same moment. They are twin sisters. Only he who feels the tragedy of life can feel the redeeming power of laughter.

The austere and soft-spoken Japanese people, who have developed the sense of responsibility as have no other people on earth, know how to laugh. Exactly because they have so profound a sense of responsibility. So rich is the vein of laughter in the Japanese bosom that so many centuries of Confucian and Buddhist fasting could not exhaust it. Japanese storytellers still spread happiness from village to village in the long winter nights. And the low little wooden houses are shaken by laughter, as the deck is shaken by Japanese laughter today. On the horizon, the austere Mother, Japan, appeared, silent, and her children welcomed her, laughing. Everyone was selecting a joke from his memory and telling it, as if he wanted to find something on which to fasten the indomitable joy which burst out of his austere chest. And all together they let the laughs erupt, as if the joke were the reason.

On the horizon where the sea met the sky, Japan appeared more and more clearly, smiling and shining in the morning sun. And as the excited Japanese on the deck kept laughing, for a moment I got the impression that Japan, like an oriental Aphrodite, rose up from the laughter.

■ SAKURA AND CANNONS

■ We enter the scented gulf of Japan. One of the most beautiful seas in the world, the Mediterranean Sea of Japan opens up before us, laughing in the spring light. Narrow, shallow, cheerful, with indescribable charm. Nine hundred and forty small and large islands are spread from one end to the other. Fishing villages, small, low wooden houses that have been blackened by rain, longish boats like arrows, fishermen with pointed straw caps, white sandy shores, dark-green pine trees with their roots wet by the sea. A distant all-blue Greece—for a moment I was terrified that I had returned to my own country.

The ship glides quietly in the morning blue-green light. The sea gulls wake up hungry; a stork, with his feet hanging down, flies above us and for a moment his white, downy breast shines and I feel on my palm its softness and warmth.

Every moment the sight changes. Sometimes peaceful green islands, sometimes abrupt gray granites. Deep blue caves, and farther a Shinto shrine with its rising roof, with its red door, appears amid the flowering trees. And everywhere, extinguished volcanoes: terrible geological subversion must have taken place here. The land was torn, the waves entered, and now nine hundred and forty peaks remain above the flood. The lava was extinguished, the grass spread, the human couple came and rooted themselves in the meadows.

49

This sea that we pass today has been the blue cradle of the Japanese soul. Here were born and sunburned the slender sea bodies that conquered Japan painfully, inch by inch, and chased the wild Ainu to the northernmost shores. From here the daring sea fighters, half-merchants, half-pirates, started out and landed in the rich Chinese ports. And when they returned to their country, they carried in the holds of their ships and in their hearts the most precious Chinese wares—silks, arts, gods, ideas.

Our ship sails this Aegean Sea of Japan quietly, voluptuously, but the small boats that pass ride the waves as if in a storm. The sun is hanging high, the shores are sunk in light. The cabin boy, with his white gloves, delivers the bulletin of the radio news of the day. I take it with impatience, as if the earth were sick and I followed the centigrades of her fever every day in the bulletin.

TOKYO. THE METEOROLOGICAL STATION ANNOUNCES THAT THIS YEAR THE CHERRY TREES WILL BLOOM EARLIER, AT THE END OF MARCH, BECAUSE WE HAD EARLY WARM WEATHER.

A little farther down, the bulletin informs us:

WE ENTER THE DEFENSE ZONE. IT IS STRICTLY FORBIDDEN TO THE PASSENGERS TO TAKE PHOTOGRAPHS.

A romantic would be indignant seeing the exquisite sight of the blossoming cherry trees contaminated with cannon. A realist would curl his lips with a sneer. And he would wonder how the Japanese, the great realists, would condescend to take such interest and send a telegram about the flowers of the cherry trees. . . . I felt a great joy trying again to harmonize within me these terrible contrasts. I want to give a meaning to this manifestation. I turned to the Polish violinist, who was burning with anger, and I said to him, laughing:

"What happiness! We shall see the flowering cherry trees and at the same time feel a slight shiver of terror: behind the cherry blossoms are hidden the artillery, the retrenchments, the ammunition and the gasoline!"

But the Pole got up.

"Well, all this famous *sakura*, the blossoming cherry tree, is nothing but a mask? Useful to camouflage their cannon?"

"Didn't you know it? And isn't all life a camouflage of death? Woe to him who sees only the mask! Woe to him who sees only what's hidden behind the mask! The perfect glance is to see simultaneously, by one bolt of lightning, the sweetest mask and the abominable face behind it. And to harmonize within yourself, to create a new synthesis, unknown in nature, and to play this twin flute of life and death like a virtuoso."

The unfortunate Pole shook his blond head; he could not understand. And I, looking at the charming shores of the dangerous war zone, continued thinking and fighting to discern the difficult destiny of Japan, loaded with responsibility. It is no longer Zipangu, the mythical land with a lot of gold. Nor the country with the flowering cherry trees and the sensitive girls, who open the door to wash the teapot and have their hearts caught by the beauty of the snow-clad landscape: *Everything is covered with snow. Oh, where can I wash my teapot?*

The idyl has passed. The doors of Japan have opened, all the Western winds have rushed in and whirl about—factories, capitalism, proletariat, overpopulation, suspicion. . . . The machines have started working here and the hand that has turned them on cannot stop them. The horrible demons of our times have been let loose, superior and stronger than man who has created them. Japan has

also come to the ball and is going to dance, willy-nilly; it has not only joined the dance but is at the very front of it. The dance of the world may depend on the rhythm of her dance.

Because the center of the contemporary great agony is not found any longer in the Mediterranean. The Mediterranean Sea has become a local lake. The world has become wider, and whatever takes place in the Mediterranean is only the gossip of the neighborhood. The center has been transferred to the Pacific Ocean. Here the typhoon will break and will devour our civilization. Because here spin terrifying opposite interests from four different sides. Four huge countries stand, the one opposing the other: China, Soviet Russia, America and Japan. Here in the Pacific the great game, the future war, will be played. And alas for the vanquished and perhaps for the victors.

China, the chaos. The inexhaustible human spring, the yellow ants that ascend, full of mud, from the damp soil of the rivers, sink again and reascend. Thirty million were drowned in a river a few years ago and China did not feel it. In nine months, thirty or forty million came up again from the mud.

Soviet Russia brings a new idea to the world. And as with all new ideas, the discoverer wants to spread it all over the earth. She calls all men under her red flag, full of blood. The symbolic meaning of the hammer and sickle is double. The hammer breaks heads and constructs buildings; the sickle not only reaps ears of corn, but also cuts off heads. And the two missions, negative and positive, must be accomplished; otherwise the work will remain half finished and fruitless.

America, with her worship of machines, quantity, speed and record. Time has become money there, and the mind is at the service of matter. You feel as if the mind had been the master at the beginning, but it had ended as a

slave. What Europe has started, America has led to its ultimate consequence. This worship of the gigantic—that
is, of quantity—is dangerous because it has been one of
the most characteristic symptoms of decadence. Civilizations have always drowned in huge quantities and terrific
sizes: gigantic cities, colossal theaters and fairs, palatial
buildings. . . .

Japan, the fourth gorgon of the Pacific, the mysterious,
fatal country, struggles to mingle two great opposites and
create the supreme synthesis. She tries to merge her vigorous, self-controlled, oriental soul, like a terrible multi-
spiral spring, with the material equipment of the technical European civilization. Her old knights, the samurai,
wore on top of their kimonos heavy iron armor. Japan
struggles to remain as they were, tender and strong, sensitive and merciless.

Can she create such a synthesis? Or will the old Japanese
soul be lost, all the cherry trees wither, and this charming
country become a slave of the machine? A formidable
question. The future of Asia—that is, of the world—depends on the answer that time will give to this question.
Now, Japan is found in front of a dangerous, forked path.
One path: to follow Western civilization unrestrainedly,
to intensify the worship of machines, to negate her ancient soul. The other path: to preserve her soul, traditions, customs and to have Western civilization remain
only a realistic armor of her mystical body, a means for a
superior visualization of life which surpasses the materialistic perception of the world which is so synchronized
with its decadence. The service of the machine is obliga-
tory. We cannot reach the spirit if we do not complete
all the labors of matter.

The great contemporary feat which not only Japan but
the rest of mankind must complete, if it wishes to be
saved, is this: to give to its new body, which has become
gigantic from its material conquests, an analogous, gigan-

tic soul. Many have lost hope that Europe and America can complete this feat. Will Japan do it?

With this terrifying question, I stepped on the flowering land of the Queen of the Pacific.

■ KOBE

■ IN THE MORNING we entered Kobe. Light spring clouds covered the sky. The air was humid and it smelled of coal. Low wooden houses and, right alongside, towering skyscrapers with huge Japanese signs and banners. And everywhere, from the quay to the roots of the mountain, tall, smoking chimneys.

Two voices were arguing within me:

"My God, what ugliness! How the spring air has been contaminated by the smoke, and how far the leprosy of Western civilization has spread over the clean and smiling face of Japan, the geisha of nations! Not a blossomed branch will remain in the world where the sacred bird, the human heart, can rest and sing!"

"Stop!" cried the other voice, relentless, mocking. "Leave off your crying! Stop making yourself ridiculous fighting the unavoidable. Try to find the austere and straight beauty of the new reality. Make necessity your desire, if you want to remain free in this world of slavery! . . ."

It began to drizzle. The sky grew dark, and the ship soon filled with Japanese workers in their waterproof cloaks. They worked on quietly, silently and rapidly unloading the cargo, without a superfluous movement. Short, strong, sunburned men with bright, swift-darting eyes. "How quickly," I thought to myself, "these yellow coolies may one day empty Paris, London and New York!"

Hurriedly I leave the main American streets for out-of-the-way alleys. . . . I take a deep breath. . . . Laotian paper lanterns hang in every small shop here. An exotic torchlight procession. . . . In this multicolored light glow the smiling faces of men. Sidewalks are decked out with toys, fruits, kimonos, wooden sandals, pastries, boiled eggs, melon seeds, peanuts. . . . In a narrow, obscure alley, a tree in bloom. And behind it, a tiny, ancient wooden temple. Sticks of incense are burning in front of the temple, and on an upright old stone are inscribed these letters:

OH, HERE LIES FAITHFUL KUZUNOKI.

Now it is raining hard. I stop for a moment under the blossoming tree. A woman-beggar, twins wrapped in a blanket on her back—three human beings bound tightly to each other—stands at the door of the temple and reaches out her hand. In her other hand she holds a torn paper umbrella and shields her babies. I stretch out my hand and put a coin into her withered palm.

The woman smiles.

"America?" she asked.

"No. Girisha" ("Greece").

She opens wide her slanted small eyes and looks at me. Girisha? That was the first time she had ever heard that there was such a place in the world.

I look at her under the light of a red lantern hanging from the door of the small temple. I gaze at her wrinkled face, her decayed teeth. . . . If I only knew the Japanese word for "sister"! I could then help her with a good word. Buddha, her god, used to say: "Alms, in money, can nourish a man for seven years, but a good word can nourish him for seventy-seven years."

It was pouring. Rain in torrents was now falling on the red lantern, and the wet tombstone gleamed. The woman reached the umbrella toward my head, and I drew near her. The four of us, silent, motionless before the grave of the "faithful Kuzunoki," huddled under the torn paper shelter and waited for the rain to stop—happily breathing in the smell of the wet earth. . . .

I wake up at dawn. . . . I am impatient to see how a Japanese city comes out of its night's sleep. . . . Pure air after the rain. . . . The holy mountain, Maya San, glows like a dark rose, with its rich white villas in its bosom. . . .

The small shops have already opened. The Japanese go to bed early and get up early; they follow the rhythm of the sun. They spend a long time washing up, making a lot of noise. They drink a thick juice with a strong, repulsive smell. They eat all sorts of pickled vegetables and a large bowl of rice. The wife, kneeling, serves her husband. She brings him the tray with the various wooden bowls of food; she helps him to dress; she shines and ties his shoes. She opens the door for him to go out and silently does homage to him with a deep bow. Here in Japan the man accepts the worship of his woman without arrogance or harshness, and the woman worships her man without humiliation, like a priestess who has tamed her god, and sleeps with him.

The city is now awake. Wooden sandals clatter on the streets. Peasant girls pass by, across their shoulders a long, thick cane from which hang beautiful baskets filled with vegetables and fruits. The popular luncheonettes open— the cook, a turban on his head, stands waiting. The signs on the shops grow more visible, dragons wake up, the jumbled letters on the signs straighten out.

A small Buddhist temple has its paper lanterns still lit. A poor booth with no decorations—only a wooden statue of Buddha in the background, and at the entrance a trough into which the faithful throw their coins. I stop and look at Buddha, the beloved leader. He smiles quietly in the dimly lit place, his almond-like eyes looking down, his big ears listening to all the vain noise of the earth.

They listen to the coins as every now and then they fall into the trough, thrown there by coolies, merchants and women passing by. They also listen to the great silence which one day will cover the world like piles of ashes.

One of the faithful stops for a moment, claps his hands three times as if calling God to appear and listen to him. He throws a coin into the deep trough, and with his hands tied he prays. He prays for his business to go well. He begs Buddha to support and aid him. And Buddha, in his cool shadow, smiles slyly. I smile with him, as the soothsayers smiled in old Rome when they met each other in an out-of-the-way alley, and I continue my walk.

The sirens in the factories begin to blow. A large group of smiling working-girls in their colorful kimonos hurry past us. I turn for a moment and look at them. They start laughing, and I shout to them a cheerful:

"*Ohayo, kozai mas!*" ("Good morning to you!")

And a lot of fresh voices call back, "*Ohayo, kozai mas,*" to my greeting.

Chafing dishes are heated; makeshift cooking-stoves are set up on sidewalks; vegetable and fruit vendors display their stock of bananas, apples and Formosa pears. Porters with their bamboo sticks on their shoulders hurry past on their way to the harbor. Friends, meeting each other, start their greetings. Their palms spread on the knees, they bow deep slowly three times. And as they bow, they turn their head and ask about their friend's health, and express their joy at the meeting.

I believe there are no people in the world more polite than the Japanese. With them, all external forms of politeness have reached their supreme stylization. The famous smile of the Japanese may be a mask; however, this mask makes life more cheerful, and gives dignity and grace to human relations. It teaches you to discipline and restrain yourself, to keep all your pain to yourself and not to want to trouble others with your woes. And so, slowly, the mask becomes face, and what was simply form changes into substance.

A Japanese samurai, Katsu Kaïsu, has expressed this difficult ideal in a few verses:

> *Stand smiling before others;*
> *Stand austere before yourself.*
> *Stand brave in distress,*
> *Cheerful in everyday life.*
> *When they applaud you: stand indifferent;*
> *When they hiss you: immovable.*

The sun has already flooded the streets; the store windows shine. This is the time the geishas undress and go to sleep. Their night's work ended, their feet have grown weary with dancing, their fingers tired with playing the three-stringed samisen. Now they undress to rest. They untie their belt with the broad bow, the obi, which spans their back like a silken saddle. They take off their perfumed kimono, wash their face with orange-flower water, spread a quilt on the straw mat, and lie down to sleep. Very carefully, they rest their neck on a small, hard pillow, lest their *shimanta,* the high structure of their hairdo, be spoiled. For the geishas dress and do their hair according to the old, picturesque tradition; they don't follow, as do the *mogas* (modern girls), the European fashions, nor do they cut their hair or wear European dresses and hats.

"They follow the old tradition," say the *moga* gossips derisively, "so that their crooked legs and the bald top of their head will not show."

Perhaps so. But the geisha is one of the masks of Japan —probably one of its sweetest and most deceitful charms. The way she walks along the street, serious, smiling, with virgin childish eyes, you look at her and your soul cools off. Because you have grown tired of seeing the impudent white women with their provocative insolent eyes. . . .

Offices have opened. Nervous yellow hands are grasping telephones, cotton, sugar, iron, silk, chemical products, ships; all the great troubles of Kobe are waking up. Jammed streetcars, with their bells clanging, are crossing the streets. And the small, dainty, charming woman conductors, with their eternally curdled smile on their lips, are collecting the tickets, greeting passengers in a monotonous, metallic voice:

"*Arigato kozai mas! Arigato kozai mas!*"

Sidewalks overflow with men and women. Every woman carries a baby tightly wrapped on her back. Women, men, children carry infants on their back. Human kangaroos go about knocking their sandals against the stones. *Taka-taka! Taka-taka!* That is the great voice of the Japanese street.

I go back and forth. I perform my duty rambling about. I keep thinking of the Japanese humorist, Soseki Natsume, who wrote the famous satirical book: *I Am a Cat.* In it, a cat relates its daily impressions of people. Soseki is a rambler through life, a shrewd, refined Oriental, who maintains his inner unfeverish calm within the contemporary fever.

"Life," he says, "is full of joys. Commenting on the quality of the tea, watering the flowers in your garden, leisurely loitering before pictures or statues or telling or making up jokes—such are the joys of life. Why shouldn't these joys be the themes of literature? An individual from the middle class, for instance, in going out shopping, is sure that he'll waste time stopping before a police station to watch a boy turning over a mouse to a policeman, or to eavesdrop on the boastings of a braggart. If he wants to see and hear, he must not be in a hurry. Once he's in a hurry, he will see nothing, hear nothing—he will go straight to the market."

I enjoy rambling about in this way, and I keep in mind the words of the Japanese satirist. And I feel no remorse in this busy city of Kobe, because seeing and hearing while I ramble about the earth is my passion.

1. *Live calmly, performing your daily duty.*
2. *Always keep your heart pure, and act according to its dictates.*
3. *Respect your ancestors.*
4. *Make the Mikado's will yours and carry it out.*

These are the four great imperatives that govern the Japanese soul. The Japanese do not care about the awesome problems of metaphysics. Unlike the Hindus, they are not willing to lose their personality and vanish in the universe. Where the world comes from, where it is going —these are not questions that concern them. Wide intellectual horizons strike them as dim and sterile. They narrow their glance to take in the limited fullness of earth and sea, of the mounds of bones and ashes of their ancestors, of the threshing-floor of their country. For the Japanese, the supreme, the only creative duty of man is to work and function within the narrow circle of his race.

Japan—*that* is the universe of the Japanese individual. It has room for him to stay in it comfortably. His whole small body, nervously and invisibly vibrating like a spring ready to snap, and his whole soul, insatiable and restrained, finds in acting within the territory of his race all the potentialities for reaching his ultimate development. A Japanese has confidence in his heart. For, this heart is not individual, not his own, an ephemeral piece of pulsating flesh. His is the heart of all his race. In order to find the right path and regulate his actions, a Japanese has no need of metaphysical systems: he listens to the unmistakable voice of his heart—his race—and plans every one of his acts accordingly. This almost bodily certainty makes the actions of the Japanese simple, rapid, sure.

A Japanese feels that only when he acts does he live. The nightingale sings: "In the beginning there was the song!" A Japanese says: "In the beginning there was the act!" He believes that on this earth action is the only path to salvation. Whatever his occupation, a Japanese knows he can contribute with his energy to the prosperity and salvation of his race. He identifies as one and the same the interests of the individual and of the race.

The great Emperor Meiji, who brought the Renaissance to Japan two generations ago, used to write verses in his leisure hours. Every Japanese recites three of his verses like a prayer:

> *Wherever Fate has placed you,*
> *King or porter—*
> *Spend your life to its very end!*

Rising on tiptoe, a short Japanese industrialist, who had spent this entire afternoon showing me around in his factory, one that produces a powder to kill mosquitoes, spoke to me with fanaticism and pride, as if all Japan were glorified and growing greater as his factory expanded and prospered. The progress and fortunes of his business stood above his individual ambitions and economic interests. It was a close, sacred collaboration with his nation. Behind his ephemeral self that built factories and transformed matter, he made you feel as if all his race were watching and working. And this gave to the insatiable appetite of the industrialist the sanctity of a height beyond the individual need.

From the factory, the Japanese industrialist and I went to a restaurant for dinner. They brought us small napkins dampened in hot water, with which we wiped our dusty faces and hands. We drank lukewarm sake served in small cups. We ate. I remained silent. I was slightly tired. All factories are of interest to me up to a certain point; beyond that point they tire me and leave me indifferent. I like to see how man transforms matter and makes it serve him. The rest, what will interest the industrialist and the merchant, does not arouse any of my curiosities; the rest I consider a superfluous burden in my work, and I struggle to forget it as soon as I have learned it.

The shrewd Japanese acted as if he felt my inner discontent. Such finesse seemed impossible to me. Nevertheless, after some silence, when we reached the fruit course, he sighed and said:

"All these essentially do not satisfy my soul. I impatiently wait for the day to end, so that I may leave the office and return home. As soon as I get there, I take my bath; I put on my kimono, and go down barefoot to my garden. I weed, I water, I follow the progress of the flowers. I sit by the window and wait for the moon. My wife plays the samisen, and in a low voice sings for me my favorite old *haiku*:

> *Let's fall in love,*
> *Let's fall in love,*
> *Cherries of the mountain!*
> *I don't know anyone but you!*

He stopped for a little while, and I looked at this many-sided industrialist, admiring the sharpness of his mind and the mysterious, magic power of his soul. Did he consciously know that his sigh and these words were the best way to overpower me? After the brief silence, he smiled, filled the tiny cups with sake, and said:

"Today, our greatest poetess is Akiko. She has written a *haiku* which I like very much:

> In the house that mankind builds for many a
> thousand years,
> I also place a small golden nail!"

He laughed a strange laugh, half triumphant, half mocking, and added:

"I make a small change in her *haiku* and it becomes mine:

> In the house that mankind builds for many a
> thousand years,
> I light a small green candle, and I chase the
> mosquitoes away."

■ OSAKA

■ An old Japanese song tears my heart early in the morning as I look from the train at the thick marshes where the first heads of rice begin to appear:

In the rain and in the sun
In the muddy rice fields
Bent down, hunchbacked
The peasants work all day.
Master, think of their toil.

But the masters, the samurai and the daimio, until 1868 harvested the rice that the peasants sowed and thought only of war. They fastened branches of cherry blossoms on their bronze helmets and they started out for battle. After the renaissance of Japan, the fortunes of the proud warriors changed. They no longer taxed the peasants, they received only a small pension from the state. They tried to go into business, but since they were inexperienced and guileless, they went bankrupt. Then they threw themselves into politics, philology, journalism and teaching. From the feudal lords that they had been, they were now forced to change to liberals and socialists. Today, most of the Japanese leftists are sons and grandsons of the samurai. Nevertheless, the fate of the peasants, this everlasting, slow-moving mass on the earth, has not changed. They still toil in the rain and under the sun, bent over the muddy rice fields. And at night, as one of their pathetic songs says, "they dream that they still work."

The train is crowded. The Japanese are crazy about traveling. They go on pilgrimages to faraway temples or they run to see the cherry blossoms in spring or the chrysanthemums in fall, or the lotuses in August or the wisterias in May. They take with them only a little luggage. In the *ryokan*, the hotel where they stay, they will find whatever they need: pajamas, slippers, and even a toothbrush. And the teapot will always be at hand, full of green tea.

Many men and nearly all women still wear their national costume. When it is cold, they wrap themselves tight in their kimonos so the air will not penetrate to their bodies. This costume is very unsuitable for wintertime. The sleeves are broad and the air passes through them, the kimonos continuously open and expose the legs to cold. The women make desperate, charming attempts to cover their secret beauty or ugliness. But yesterday, in the evening breeze, I saw an ivory knee shine like an apple.

The Japanese race must certainly have had its origin in a very warm climate. It might have started out from the Malay islands in the south. The costume of the Japanese, their homes, their food cannot otherwise be explained. The Japanese homes are like cages: wooden, light, cool, and instead of walls they have reeds and folding screens. There are straw mats on the floor. You always walk barefoot at home. Air comes in everywhere. The small brazier tries in vain to tame the sharp Japanese winter cold. The traditional, customary food of the Japanese—rice, vegetables, fish—is suitable only for warmer climates. They seldom eat meat, butter and fat. Perhaps the reason the Japanese remain short is that they eat such food in such a climate. The younger generations who eat a lot of meat and butter and follow Anglo-Saxon customs have already changed physically. They are taller and more vigorous.

I started a conversation with a middle-aged, cheerful, freshly shaved, stout Japanese who sat next to me. He looked like a well-fed reveler who had spent his night sitting on soft pillows drinking tepid sake and watching the geishas of Kobe dancing. He would have escaped from the monotony of his home life to enjoy a free evening. "The sweetest woman," says a Japanese proverb, "is first the wife of your friend; then, the geisha; then, your maid; and finally, your wife."

I was wrong. He spoke a little English. He was a businessman. He lived in a villa in a suburb of Kobe and commuted to his office in Osaka. He spoke to me about his huge city with its two and a half million people and his face shone with pride.

"It is the Manchester, or, better, the Chicago of the Far East. Look at its chimneys, a forest. We send our cotton fabrics all over the world. We have 6,700 factories. We are the economic capital of Japan."

As he talked, his eyes sparkled. You felt that his thick, smooth body was inhabited by indomitable energy. In my life, I have often encountered fat people, full of energy and soul. You think their spirits are nourished by spreading their tentacles in the thick, abundant flesh.

The Japanese lit a big cigar and continued:

"We work. All day. Telephones, telegrams, statistics, invoices, exchanges. But in the evening, we enjoy ourselves. No other city in Japan has so many nightclubs, so many secret, gay restaurants, so many beautiful geishas. We have six thousand geishas in Osaka."

I enjoyed listening to that fat man talk. I looked admiringly at his short, plump hands, that knew so expertly how to earn money and caress the geishas.

"Are you a Buddhist?" I asked, just to tease him.

He laughed and looked at me slyly.

"Of course," he said. "Sometimes, when my business goes well, I go to a temple and put a few flowers at Buddha's feet. I have nothing to lose!"

"The world is an illusion of the five senses. Open your eyes, wake up, free yourself from the net of need."

"Yes, I know it," replied the reveling businessman, laughing. "That's what Buddha said and it certainly was right in his times, when his people lived in tropical forests. But if Buddha lived today and had his home in Osaka, I am sure he would be like me!"

I turned and looked at him as if I had seen him for the first time. Once, I had seen a wooden statue of Buddha, with a protruding huge belly, with laughter bursting out which spread from his mouth to his whole fleshy face; it extended through his neck, his three-fold belly and his naked legs to his swollen soles. . . . Yes, surely when this covetous businessman, who looked at me slyly, took his bath in the morning and, after it, sat naked, steaming, with crossed legs on the cool straw mat while his silent wife brought him green tea, he was exactly like gentle Buddha and looked at the futile world as at a soap bubble—tea, woman, business—which in a little while will burst and vanish in the air. . . .

May this fat businessman of Osaka be well and his business go well because, thanks to him, for a moment I saw and felt all the contrasts of the mysterious oriental soul.

A forest of chimneys, a multitude of canals cross like arteries the whole gigantic, smoky body of Osaka. One thousand three hundred and twenty bridges, innumerable barges loaded with sacks, boxes, iron, wood, noiselessly ply the black, sluggish waters. Yellow workers, coolies with dirty towels tightly wrapped around their shaved heads, whose sweat running on their naked bodies mingles with the coal.

Black Venice, without beauty and sweetness. It is in the highest fever of its life. The time has not come yet—it will certainly come after a few centuries—when the city will take on the patina of time long past; its port will be a little deserted, the ivy will climb its present skyscrapers, and pale tourists who feel beauty will come to enjoy it. Today, Osaka still lives wildly, insatiably and in a hurry, and it cannot tolerate loiterers. You see Osaka as you would see a living tiger in the jungle: you have neither the time nor the strength to admire it, however beautiful is its skin and however sveltely its body glides. Today, Osaka is a living beast and bites. Woe to him who wanders on its streets an idler and a poet.

You must have patience and prudence to wait until evening comes. Then Osaka, retracting its claws, sprawls above its canals and peacefully raises its head; tired from the day's hunting, it yawns and breathes in the cool breeze from the sea. At this time, when the tiger rests and digests, the varied lanterns glow, the electric and neon advertisements flow like waters at the theaters, the movies and the nightclubs. The closed doors open and freshly bathed bodies bow to welcome you.

The avenues of work are dark and deserted, and the narrow alleys of evening gaiety are lit by multicolored silk lanterns that beckon to you. The businessmen, the industrialists, the workers, the coolies wash, comb their hair, change clothes; the tense, greedy faces of daytime take on again their human expression. The tiger feels its satiated belly cooling above the canals—and, pacified, it half closes its eyes.

When the Laotian paper lanterns light and the women's wooden sandals sound on the streets and the spring breeze blows, Japan touches the root of the human entrails, and with difficulty you are able to hold back what the Byzantine ascetic called a "benign tear," when he wanted to give a definition of God.

The joy that I find far from my own country among such exotic, charming people moves me. I enter a bar. Three dainty geishas with their colorful, cheerful kimonos and their immobile, calm smiles sit under a yellow lantern that has a heartlike design. They smoke and wait. They wait for the man for whom they will lighten the hard work of the day with their laughter, their hands and their mouths. As soon as I enter, they rise as if they awaited me, they take me by the waist, we sit on pillows and the pantomime starts. I know only a few Japanese words: heart, cherry blossom, thank you, sun, moon, how much, no, yes and *gogiso sama*, which means "your food is delicious." How will I get along with such a poor vocabulary? Nevertheless, when I get up to leave, I find out that these words have been more than enough.

The geishas are good—*gogiso sama!*—and the fancy lanterns are also good; but when I woke up in the morning, a bitter drop sat on the lips of my soul. I felt as if I had taken the wrong path, as if I had betrayed my immediate duty. We live in a period when a sound man cannot and should not surrender to pure sweetness.

Behind the kimono and the lanterns, angry and desperate voices are heard. An endless army, deformed by its hopeless daily work, hungry and restless, looks at you with reproach. I recalled that the day before yesterday, a clever industrialist in Kobe proudly showed me his factories. When we entered his warehouses where a lot of women, young and old, work twelve to fourteen hours a day, I turned to him and asked:

"How much do they make a day?"

He pretended he did not hear my question and tried to change the subject, but I would not let him.

"How much does one of these women make a day?"

He lowered his voice, as if he were ashamed, and answered:

"Half a yen."

"How much?"

"Half a yen."

I shuddered. I recalled an official medical report on Japanese female workers, which was recently published:

"Eighty per cent of the workers in the fabric mills are women. They work fourteen to sixteen hours a day. Their health rapidly deteriorates. They lose weight from the first week. The night work particularly exhausts them. None can last longer than a year. Some die, some become sick and leave. Many thousands do not return to their homes. They go from factory to factory or they end up in the red-light districts. Most of them are sick, tubercular. . . ."

I look at Osaka in the morning light. It smokes and whistles like a man-eating dragon that has awakened and is hungry. A few centuries from now, cities such as Osaka will appear to our distant descendants like mythical monsters that devoured men.

The power of man to subjugate matter is wonderful, but this industrial conquest does not go along with the spiritual progress of man. It may be that the one is the enemy of the other. The only path that has remained for Japan, living among powerful enemies, to follow was that of industrialization. And as soon as she took the necessary road, all the rest came as direct, logical consequences: exploitation, injustice, disease, overgrowth of material power, atrophy of spiritual cultivation.

All day today I visited factories. My ears are filled with humming and buzzing, my eyes with machines and pale girls silently working. I filled my notebooks with figures. All day I was questioning, writing, again questioning. I know that the questions are of no use and that the figures are as flexible as dreams and an ingenious mind can arrange them in endless combinations and extract whatever conclusions he likes. If I were a Japanese working girl, I would write with thick black letters on the white comb in my hair an embittered *haiku*:

> *Yes, the figures say*
> *That I am happy*
> *But I get paler every day*
> *And today I began to cough . . . !*

"You said that a woman worker receives from half a yen to one yen a day. How could she live on such starvation wages?"

I sat in the office of a factory and drank tea with a brilliant engineer who had guided me through the inferno that prevailed in his factory. The engineer, without hurrying, lit his cigarette. He was calm, sure of predominance. He began to talk in a honeyed voice:

"You, as all Europeans, study the facts and come up with hasty conclusions. But if you want to judge us rightly, you must keep in mind the Japanese reality. An English worker makes two English pounds a week. With that money he can barely make ends meet. The life to which he is accustomed costs a lot. His clothes, shoes, house, furniture, food are all very expensive. Let's take the food and compare. The Englishman is used to eating meat, butter, milk and canned food; otherwise he cannot live. The Japanese is frugal in his diet, by nature and tradition. He eats vegetables, fish, rice and is satisfied. Life in Japan is incomparably cheaper than in Europe and America. Do you know what the buying power of a yen is? You live in a hotel, transient, and you don't shop for yourself, so you don't understand it. You can buy with one yen: one kilo of rice, one can of sardines, half a kilo of fish, three eggs, and five bananas! So an Englishman would die of starvation on the wages we give, while a Japanese lives and lives well.

"Then, do you know how simple our houses are?

Wooden or cane walls, a few straw mats, a mattress. Neither furniture nor superfluous decorations are needed. Holy bareness is in good taste. Our tastes are simple, our life inexpensive, our needs in a rich, productive climate very few. Thus, by paying small wages, we achieve two important results: we satisfy the simple needs of our workers and simultaneously we succeed in having our industrial products cost us very little.

"What are you thinking of?" the engineer asked me, as he saw that I remained silent.

"I am thinking of the danger. I see a great danger. If all countries close their markets to you, what would become of you?"

"It is very difficult to close all doors to us. We always hope that a big door, China, will remain open. That's enough. Half a billion customers. . . . But until this difficult moment comes we work as if it were never to come. Do you know about the two men who work and one says: 'I work as if I were immortal.' The other: 'I work as if I were to die at this moment.' We follow the system of the first man.

"Then, don't forget that the Japanese worker is crazy about machines. Anything in the nature of a machine attracts and fascinates him. It goads his self-respect not to be left behind, to surpass the white man. He works with faith. Is it individual self-respect? Patriotism? Fanaticism of the newly converted? You may accredit it to whatever you like, but he works with faith, twelve to fourteen hours a day without getting tired. . . ."

"And you, of course, benefit. . . ."

The engineer burst into laughter.

"What do you want us to do? To stop his enthusiasm? We benefit. We are industrialists and businessmen. We are not ascetics and philanthropists. Every social class has its laws, and woe to you if you trespass them, or if you change them for the laws of another class. If you give grass to a tiger, it will die; if you give meat to a sheep, it will die. . . ."

"But there are general human laws for all the classes. . . ."

"Naturally, and we observe them. We take care of our workers; we see to it that they sleep well, they wash and exercise themselves in order to be sound and strong. . . ."

"So that they can work better and produce more. . . ."

The thick-necked engineer laughed again.

"Naturally! We combine the ethical with the useful. Is there a more perfect combination?"

If I were a rich Japanese industrialist, I would write on a silk paper with red letters this *haiku:*

> *What is the supreme fruit of wisdom?*
> *To have the pie untouched*
> *And to feel that the dog is satisfied*
> *And licks your hands.*

When I came out of the factory and I breathed fresh air, I turned and said to my Japanese companion:

"Doesn't Osaka have any statue, any medieval castle or any flowering orchard to rest our eyes? My soul begins to go wild."

"Have the machines and the figures tired you?"

"That man's faith in machines and numbers has tired me. Yes, I know, the Americanization of the world is one of the saddest inescapable stages that industrial civilization will pass through before it vanishes. You are under that wheel."

"You're wrong. If you had a little patience and more love, you would see that 'robot' who spoke to us with the same joy and relief as you would see a statue, a castle or a flowering orchard. And this machine-like man, as the works of art you love, is a toilworn, tragic result of cease-less struggle."

"Yes, I know," I replied. "How tragic always is the story of man. But often I want to forget it, because otherwise how could I find enough strength to laugh? And if I didn't laugh, how could I bear the sight of life?"

Suddenly, as we talked thus, a grim castle on granite moles, surrounded by a river, appeared. Seldom have I seen a building expressing power and obstinacy with such austere magnificence. Seven floors gathered like springs, the roofs abruptly upturned as if they were af-fected by a great fire. Here there was neither the straight line of the balanced power of the Parthenon nor the peak of a Gothic church, raised and lost in the sky. Here was the upturned, billowing line, the will that leaps up to rush headlong, the power that has broken the balance, but has not yet spread out. It was the moment of ten-sion of the tiger that crouches ready to spring.

"This is the scabbard of a great soul!" I cried. "Who built it?"

"It is truly the scabbard of a great soul, of Hideyoshi, the great Napoleon of Japan."

"Of Hideyoshi?" I asked, blushing from shame. It was the first time I had heard his name.

"The greatest military figure in our history. He was short, dark, monstrously ugly, a *sarumen kanya*, as they called him, a crowned monkey. He was born in 1536, in a humble peasant home. His physical and intellectual vigor was unbelievable. He was fiercely voluptuous. He spent his nights in terrible orgies. And at the same time, he had a quick, composed mind, a military genius, vast ambitions. He wanted to conquer Korea and China and to establish an endless empire. 'I will make these three countries—China, Japan, and Korea—into one,' he said. 'I will make it as easily as I fold a mattress and take it under my arm!'

"He was also a great organizer. He regenerated the administration, the public economy, the agriculture, the commerce. He protected the Jesuits and the Europeans, who anchored at Japanese ports for the first time. Machines and guns and whatever good he found he bought from the 'white devils.'

"This formidable, many-sided man loved and was afraid of his mother, and was a most tender father. The report that a Korean mission sent, after an audience with Hideyoshi at his court, has been preserved: 'Hideyoshi is a short man with a very dark complexion, a very vile person. But his eyes throw fires that burn. He was sitting on three pillows, with his face turned to the south; he wore an impressive dark robe. Suddenly he withdrew behind a curtain and shortly reappeared in his daily clothes, holding an infant in his arms. He went back and forth in the room, and everyone kneeled and fell on the ground and bowed before him. At that moment the infant soiled itself. Hideyoshi nodded to an officer to take the child and have its clothes changed. He behaved as if he were all by himself in the room.'

"That is what the Koreans related about the hero. And farther down in the report they mention the answer he gave them. 'I pacified my country. I come from a poor family, but when my mother still had me in her womb, she dreamed that she would give birth to the sun. A soothsayer told her then: "Wherever the sun shines, this child will rule!" I shall gather a big army; I shall conquer China and the dew of my sword will fall on its four hundred provinces.'

"He had great ambitions, and he would have realized them had not death cut him down. All the dreams of Hideyoshi scattered. His beloved son, Hideshyori, was killed and a new family came to power. When you read the verses Hideyoshi wrote when dying, you shiver because he foresaw the tragedy and prophesied his fate:

I fall like dew
I evaporate like dew
And even the castle of Osaka
Is naught but a dream of a dream!"

◼ NARA

◼ GREAT SOULS can nourish our soul. They can broaden our mind and make room not only for the Greco-Roman provincial experiences and the narrow-minded fanaticism of the Hebrew Jehovah, but also for other distant universal lives. . . .

Today I travel from Osaka to the heart of old Japan, Nara, and I cannot get off my mind the great soul in the black-yellow, monkey-like body of Hideyoshi. His spirit, rich, full of contradictions, many-sided, is for me the supreme model of man: sensuality, worship for his mother, tenderness for his son, and at the same time unrestrained impetus in war, tireless activity in peace, and, finally, the grasping of the brush at the hour of his death to put in verses the fruit of all his life—*a dream of a dream!* The voracious conquest of life and simultaneously the consciousness that all is dream and dew. That, I think, is the highest peak a man can reach.

I look out of the window of my train, I let my mind flit like a butterfly above the spring fields, and I think of the heroes of the past. The time has come for mankind to have a new, wider renaissance. With the first renaissance, the mind became broader because it became acquainted with Greece and its divine forms of beauty. Later we became slightly acquainted with Egypt and India. The time has come to broaden the circle of our knowledge and our hearts to include China and Japan.

◼ ◼

Intellectual piracy, joy to the eyes, which, before they are covered with earth, wander around and plunder. I look around at my Japanese fellow passengers. A merry race, clean, freshly bathed bodies, fine faces carved in ivory. Slanted eyes of the snake. Simple nobleness, a race that has lived and has loved much and has had its natural politeness become a stylized tradition. I never tire of watching how they greet each other: they bow deeply, their faces take on the solemnity of a religious rite. They do not shout, they do not insult each other. I have not yet seen two Japanese quarrel.

I saw two bicycles collide on a bridge in Osaka and their riders somersault onto the stones. And I stopped and waited to see the fight. Both riders got up, shook the dust off their clothes, took off their hats, greeted each other without uttering a word, mounted their bicycles and rode away. At a stop, a peasant carrying a big bundle of clothes tried to get on a streetcar that was crowded. The conductor told him something quietly in a sad tone; the man with the bundle bowed and took his foot from the step of the streetcar. Japan overflows with people; their living together would be unbearable if they lacked politeness. The good word, the good behavior are like the cushions boats and tugs put on their sides in order to make their jostling as soft as possible.

We were approaching Nara, the sacred city, the first permanent capital of Japan, from 710 to 780 A.D. My heart beat fast, excited because I would see the famous Buddhist temples, the gigantic statue of Buddha and its unique park with its thousand deer. I knew—it always happened—that what I would see would be much above what I had imagined, and I leaned from the window in the hope of discerning from afar the first exotic pagodas, the wild cacti.

Quiet, sweet land, soft mountains flooded with subdued light. Fleecy, snow-white clouds passed in the sky and two long-legged storks flew away above the low black wooden houses. And suddenly the miracle: between these low houses, above the roofs blackened by rain, in the tender misty air, sprang up, full of beauty and richness, proud like a maiden, cheerful, a spire of rose light, the first blossoming cherry tree. The *sakura!*

And at once, as I saw it, there leaped to my memory a late afternoon when I stood opposite the gigantic, medieval cathedral, blossoming with saints, in Ulm, that distant city in the north. In the same way the cathedral rose above the poor houses, bright and rich above the roofs, reaching the sky. It seemed to me as if both the cherry tree and the cathedral transmuted all the surrounding poverty into unutterable richness and all the darkness of man and of air into light. Poor, little women, bent over the river, washed their clothes; their babies cried, and their men worked, humped, in the fields. No one of them saw the flowering cherry tree which stood above them, quiet and pleased, immobile, sanctifying the surrounding black area of the village because it performed the supreme duty that matter has—to bloom.

Wisteria is the emblem of innocent joy; chrysanthemum, of endurance and of immortality; lotus, of virtue, which rises immaculate above the mud. But the flower of the cherry tree is the emblem of the samurai because it is wedged on a strong branch and dies, falling to the ground before it withers—as the samurai dies before he is shamed. And for this reason, when he sets out to war, he fastens a branch of cherry blossoms on his helmet.

I wave my hand from the train window and bid farewell to *sakura*, which we leave behind. In the same way as I saw it, Gyoson, a Buddhist priest, must have seen it, one day, about nine hundred years ago, and spread his hand and entreated: *Let us love each other, cherry blossom! I know no one in the world except you!*

■ ■

Nara, the sacred heart, the Mecca of Japan. The old, rich, beautiful, noble city is today a large village. Her kings have left, her ships have burned, and she has become a widow. All her fingers fell; only the rings have been left. Only her gods remain, the eight million gods of Shinto, with Sun, the great ancestor of Japan, at the summit of them. The charming, calm, smiling Buddhas, who sit with crossed legs in the dark wooden temples and welcome the faithful with goodhearted irony, remain.

As I jumped out of the train, I stood surprised. Processions of men and women ascended the uphill road to Nara with banners and drums; other crowds arrived by train, by car, or by cart; others came on foot. I stood at a corner and rejoiced in the colors, the noise, the crowds going back and forth. Old men and young men, and women more than a hundred years of age come from the ends of Japan and, as the Christians in the Middle Ages, wander from pilgrimage to pilgrimage. They have yellow, orange and green banners, drums, and long flutes; they have leather or silk pouches in their belts and long pipes with microscopic bowls that have no room for more than two or three puffs of tobacco.

"Today is the Festival of Flowers," the station-master explained to me, with a deep bow.

The pilgrims have their heads wrapped in white towels on which flowers and letters are embroidered or stamped. They are the famous *hana mitenugu*, flower towels, which the Japanese wear in spring when they go to worship the blooming cherry trees. A pagan joy, a spring atmosphere, laughter and voices. A cuckoo sprang from a pine tree, whistled, and flew toward Nara. Also a pilgrim, he went to sit at the feet of Buddha.

At that moment, as I started out to follow its path, a company of *biku*, Buddhist monks, arrived on foot. They wear broadbrimmed straw hats and long yellow cassocks. They walk barefoot and everyone leans on a long staff that reaches above his shoulders and has a little bell at its top. Silent, gloomy, with their eyes on the ground, they follow the road to Nara. I wonder what these yellow monks seek under the blossoming cherry trees. Perchance they are self-satisfied to see how quickly the cherry blossoms drop off their petals. And thus they find a new picture of the vanity of life. One of them, Okono-Kumassi, sang nine hundred years ago:

> *Flowering cherry tree,*
> *How much you resemble life!*
> *At the moment I see you bloom,*
> *Your blossoms have already fallen off.*

A true but miserable view of life, only one side of the incomprehensible mystery; a religion that ignores that one ephemeral moment can, qualitatively, equal eternity. *Holding his mother's hand, the little blind boy comes to see the cherry blossoms,* says one song. So for one moment these monks with their long staffs, who went up looking down, appeared to me like an army of blind men.

I called a ricksha drawn by a slender, half-naked coolie.

"*Doo?*" ("Where?") asked this human horse, looking at me with his sweet, piercing eyes.

"*Ryokan,*" I replied with my little Japanese, "*sololi, sololi!*" ("very slowly").

I could satiate my desire to see this sight, the multicolored pilgrims who, all together, ascended, laughing, singing. A dark religion that the cheerful Japanese managed to fill with colors and flowers and the aroma of human flesh. Or ancient Greek flower festivals, which the Hebrew religion of pain blasted, still flourish here at the other end of the world.

They decorate their carts with flowers, they hang wreaths on the oxen; strong young men and beautiful

Japanese girls climb into carts and go to greet the geisha spring. They dance, sing, drink sake, forget their everyday worries. Life takes on its primitive, intoxicating essence, the water again becomes wine. Dionysus left Greece and settled on these distant shores. He is now wearing a kimono and holds cherry blossoms in his hands. The three great choruses—old men, men and youths—are restored, and thus the race, together with the trees, flourishes, and mortal life takes on an immortal meaning on this earth.

"*Irasshai mase! Irasshai mase!*" ("Welcome! Welcome!")

The owners, man and wife, and their two daughters and the plump maid came out of the *ryokan*. They bowed down to the earth and greeted me. I jumped from the ricksha, I bowed myself down to the earth three times and began to greet them. And afterward, with my face reddened from the bowing, I asked if they had a room.

"Great is the honor you do us! Our poor house never expected such glory! Your excellency is very courteous and we are grateful to you!"

Which simply means: "There is a room."

A small freshly washed yard, three flowerpots of blooming rhododendrons. And in a small pot in the middle of the yard, a marvel: a pigmy cherry tree, not higher than two spans, with a thick trunk like a man's arm. They have put it in the most honored position in the yard these days, as if it really were a great, sacred martyr and were feted. Around the yard are the rooms. I take off my shoes, I put on a pair of the many slippers that are placed in a row at the steps and I go up to the patio, covered with straw mats.

One of the greatest charms of Japan is the unimaginable cleanliness of the houses. Everything—the floors, the walls, the doors—shines. My room, with its straw mats, with the low, small table in the middle and a vase with three flowers in it, with pillows on the floor, and with a picture of a flowering tree on the wall, fills my heart to overflowing with happiness. A bare, pagan, cheerful cell, just as I like it.

I sit with crossed legs on the pillows; they open a wall, a simple folding screen, and I see down the street. They bring the teapot and a small porcelain cup and a few cleaned pistachios in a small saucer. I drink the tea, sip by sip; I chew the nuts; I am happy. The plump maid comes and brings me a violet kimono and a pair of crimson wooden sandals; she bows and says to me: *"Furo!"* ("Bath!").

The bath is ready—burning hot, as the Japanese are accustomed to take it. A big barrel, half pushed into the earth. I get in, I feel unsurpassed happiness. I put on the kimono, wear the wooden sandals, return to my room, drink more tea, and, from the open wall, watch the pilgrims as they go up the road beating the drums. I imagine the wooden, stone and bronze Buddhas would smile in the very old temples among the trees. I am not in a hurry to see them. I have overcome impatience, nervousness, haste. I enjoy every single second of these simple moments I spend. "Happiness," I think, "is a simple everyday miracle, like water, and we are not aware of it."

The largest park in Japan: 1,200 acres, century-old tall trees, pine trees, fir trees, peach trees, poplar trees, willow trees. Lakes with exotic fish, red with white wings; fish that play, spreading and gathering their veils like dancers. Doves, storks, swans. And, above all, a unique joy—more than one thousand deer that come and go, graceful, serious, like young princes.

Proud and without fear, they approach the passers-by and gaze at them with their long-lashed eyes. Every October they have their antlers cut from the root and a big celebration takes place. And even now, caressing their heads, you can see the roots of their horns covered with dry blood.

Pagodas, with their many upturned floors like wings ready to fly, rise among the trees. The *torii*, the sacred gates that look like the capital Greek Π, shine dark crimson among the green, glistening leaves. They are the sacred doors of Shinto, which means "The Path of God": he who wants to be saved must pass through these doors.

Shinto, the religion of ancestors, is the primitive religion of the Japanese. They worshiped the ancestors of the family; then the ancestors of the race; finally, the ancestors of the common father, the emperor. They believe that the dead live and govern the living. When parents die, they become spirits, *kami-sama,* and are in constant contact with their descendants. They share joy and sorrow with the living, they help and encourage or punish and revenge the living. All the air is full of the spirits of the dead. The spirits ride on the waves, the winds, the flames, and they work. All ancestors, good or wicked, worthy or unworthy, become gods. Good or bad gods with all the characteristics they had when alive. It is the duty of the living, if they want to be successful, to thank their good ancestor gods and try to placate the evil ones with prayers and sacrifices, with dances and songs.

Thus, all the Japanese—and particularly their emperors —are descendants of gods. For that reason, even today the Japanese people consider themselves superior to all other peoples on earth and their country as the country of gods. The greatest of all these gods is Sun, the goddess Amaterasu, the root of the imperial tree. Other great gods are the winds, the seas, the rivers, the fire, the mountains, and a multitude of famous warriors or kings. Eight million are the gods of Shinto. Every art has its patron god with the analogous tools of the profession. The blacksmiths, the carpenters, the masons, the fishers have their own gods; the apprenticeship of the son in the craft of his father is a religious act. A sacred ceremony used to take place in order to persuade the patron god to take the young apprentice under his protection.

Gods with a thousand faces, not only grim and angry, but also often cheerful, comical, with protruding bellies, holding a chaplet or a cup of tea or sake and bursting into laughter. As their faithful followers and the priests who worship them see them laugh, they burst out laughing, too. And the gods not only do not become angry but also rejoice that they make their children laugh. Thus the concept of deity is humanized: God becomes domestic and familiar, and the Japanese approach him as we approach a big, domesticated elephant.

Obedience, sacrifices and prayers: these are the three fundamental commands of Shinto. You must obey the emperor because he is descended from the greatest god, the Sun. You must offer sacrifices to your ancestor gods. First, the Japanese put at their graves and their altars real drinks, food and clothes; but later, pieces of wood wrapped with bands of paper, which symbolize the drinks, food and clothes. Finally, you must pray to your ancestors, after you wash your body with water and salt and purify your heart with exorcisms and fasting.

From all natural forces, from all trees and animals, from all men, living and dead, spread secret bonds which tie the whole of Japan into an inextricable unit. Even recently a Japanese politician expressed this old faith: "Whatever we have, we owe it to the spirits of our ancestors. We live only for them; they, only, make us live. There is no sacrifice, however great it may be, that we should not make for their sake!" When, in 1904, the Russo-Japanese war broke out, the generals issued this surprising proclamation to their soldiers: "Go not to uncertain death but to certain death for the sake of our ancestors. Their spirits are always with you; they protect and surround you!"

You can never know the Japanese soul unless you feel deeply the tremendous influence that this proud Shintoist concept of duty had and has on it. Only when you feel deeply this influence will you understand where this demonic source of power of every Japanese lies. You will understand why they defy death and why they all accept, with mystic exaltation, the act of dying for their country. Fatherland, Mikado, gods, ancestors and descendants are for the Japanese an inseparable, immortal power. Why should a man fear death when he believes that after he dies he mingles with all his race and becomes immortal?

I passed through the red doors of Shinto into the park and I shivered, thinking what vast power the white race would have if we had a great faith. Now we either smile idly and eruditely or spin fiercely in the hell of individuality, uprooted, without coherence, without hope. The Japanese believe in an illusion perhaps, but they reach great, fruitful, practical results; while we who do not believe in anything live miserably and die forever.

In this park my heart becomes wild. I go down to Nara. Some small shops sell the famous dolls of Nara, wonders of freshness and liveliness; others sell buttons, pipes, cigarette holders, small images of gods, walking sticks made of the horns of the deer in the park. Buddhist monks with slow steps go from door to door. They lean their hands on their staffs, nail their glance to the ground and begin muttering prayers. Every now and then they ring the little bells, insistently, monotonously, until the people in the house get sick and tired of them and open the door and throw a handful of rice in their bags.

I think of the refined, devout and sensuous civilization that flourished in this land twelve centuries ago. When all Europe was submerged in barbarism, here noblemen and kings ate rice in porcelain bowls, washed in golden basins, and raised the arrangement of flowers in gardens and in vases to an art. Their artisans carved exquisite statues, some of which are still extant; we look at them and our heart moves. . . .

Now the Japanese bluebird, the spirit, has left Nara. It went with different feathers, singing other tunes, and nested in the chimneys of Osaka and the skyscrapers of Tokyo. Only a few deserted nests have remained. I pass through the great temple where the largest bronze statue in the world, a Daibutsu or great Buddha, is found. He sits, cross-legged, on a lotus flower. He is fifty-three feet high, his nostrils have a diameter of three feet, and his big finger is four and a half feet long. To cast this colossus required 438 tons of copper, 8 tons of white wax, 870 pounds of gold and 4,885 pounds of mercury! It was cast in 752 A.D., when Nara was at the zenith of its glory. A plague had befallen the land and had reaped thousands of souls; the people were frightened and the fanatics cried that the epidemic came because the great goddess, Amaterasu, was angry that they had brought a new god, Buddha, to her country. The king was also terrified and ordered the casting of a huge statue; thus came into existence this gigantic figure, the Buddhified Amaterasu, a daring composition which took care of everything by blending the two religions into a Cyclopean, hermaphroditic body, full of sweetness and power.

I circulate like an ant for quite a while around the crossed feet of the monster. I gaze at his calm face, his smile, wide like a river, his broad chest with the two round mountain peaks. His Lilliputian worshipers come like waves, clap their hands three times, call Buddha. The gong sounds rhythmically. In a big caldron, at the threshold of the temple, they burn thickly smoking incense. The crafty priests, some like well-fed pigs, others like slender foxes, sit at the benches and sell bands of paper on which prayers and exorcisms are written; paper, tin and velvet amulets; minute Buddhas made of stone, antler and ivory. Soaked in sweat, they collect dimes. And Buddha stands above them; his head reaches the roof, he gazes at his priests and smiles. He looks at the crowds, who clasp their hands in mystical ecstasy, and smiles. He knows that everything is an illusion, a mirage of the senses; neither the people who worship exist, nor the god who is worshiped, nor the thick nor the thin priests who make a lot of money. The breeze blows and everything disappears.

I gaze at the statue and my mind does not let me depart. Its beauty holds me spellbound; its art is gross, hasty, clumsy. But this statue that mingled these two deities, the native and the foreign, so tightly into an inextricable synthesis has immeasurable importance. It imprints on bronze a fundamental alchemical ability of the Japanese soul to transmute whatever is foreign into something Japanese. The Japanese soul that thirsts for action and believes in the existence and value of the external world—what relation did it have to the Buddhist missionaries of the sixth century, who preached the vanity of every activity and the nonexistence of the visible world? "Empty your entrails of any desire!" Buddha cried out. "Intensify your desires, finish what we began!" the deified Japanese ancestors cried. "There is an immortal ternary reality: family, fatherland, Mikado!"

A terrible fight broke out and the native gods rushed to chase out the alien god who denied and destroyed. But the Japanese soul always has something feminine that longs for and accepts the foreign seed. Slowly the conception and the fertile assimilation in the Japanese womb started. They discarded what was not of use to them, they kept only what their soul could assimilate. They took a love for nature. All are one—plants, animals, men. All are deeply united with the roots of our heart. They even took the stoicism, the apathy before misfortune and death, the unwithering smile which always blossoms on their lips, even if their souls suffer. They even took from Buddhism their polite manners, their sweetness in social contacts, their sensitivity:

> O *withered leaf that fell on the earth, are you*
> *not cold?*
> O *withered leaf, I will take you in my bosom*
> *And until the sun appears again and melts the*
> *snows*
> O *withered leaf, I will warm you in my bosom!*

The sky was covered by clouds. I saw the bronze bosom of Buddha darken. All the faces of the pilgrims around me sank into dim light, and only the slanted eyes shone in the fleecy darkness full of electricity. The first raindrops fell and hit hard the thick leaves of a big rubber plant. I came out of the temple, I sat with crossed legs on a bench alongside the big caldron where they burned incense. Quiet, bitter sweetness, fragrance that ascends from the earth; long yellow lightning that flashes on and off, softly licking the tops of the trees. My eyes were half closed and I, almost unaware, felt the divine grace of Buddha descend on me and lick like a tongue my temples and my chest. The words of a great Oriental came to me quietly like a soft moss and wrapped my soul: "All men are happy as if they sat at a feast or as if they went up to a tower in spring. Only I am quiet, neither happy nor unhappy. I am like the child that has not smiled yet. All men have goods, more than they need. Only I am poor and I have nothing. All men are bright; only I am stupid. The waves drag me and I go and I have no place where I can lay my head. O Buddha, let me find shelter in your smile!"

■ THE GODDESS OF MERCY

■ NARA AWAKES, still wrapped in a diaphanous gauze of fog. The awakening of a city is good, as the awakening of a beloved woman. And I hasten to go down the street early to see its little morning secrets.

The plump Japanese woman of the *ryokan* pulls back the folding screen, the wall of my room, and brings me my breakfast on a black, wooden tray.

"*Ohayo gozaimas!* Good morning!"

We bow to each other and I begin to uncover the various wooden bowls: a yellow thick soup that stinks unbearably, slices of raw fish, a small cup with pickled cucumber and squash, and a large bowl of boiled rice. And the indispensable teapot with the green tea.

In order not to think of what I am eating and lose my appetite, I think of the wonders I saw yesterday afternoon in the famous museum of Nara: exquisite statues; paintings on silk fabric; divinely beautiful vessels, many of which came from distant places, from Tibet, Persia, Byzantium; chests with immeasurable riches; arms; costumes; sixty thousand precious stones. Imperial treasures that the widowed queen, Komno, donated to the nation in the eighth century. The manuscript of the royal donation is still preserved: "Forty-nine days have passed since the day of the death of my beloved master, but every day my passion grows and the pain makes my heart heavier. Supplicating the Earth or calling the Sky does not bring me any consolation. And I have decided to do good deeds to give joy to his respected spirit. And for this reason I give these treasures to Buddha so that the soul of the Emperor may rest in peace. May this donation help his redemption and may the chariot of his soul soon reach the world of the sacred Lotus. May my master enjoy there the heavenly music and be welcome to the bright paradise of Buddha!"

These words of love that a woman wrote twelve centuries ago enter and re-enter my mind, and thus I forget the Japanese food I am eating and go down the street satisfied. The park is deserted, only the deer raise their heads with their large, comprehensive eyes and look at me as I hastily pass by. I am in a hurry to reach the little train, to go to Horiuyi, a small village one hour away from Nara, where the oldest monastery of Buddha is. I crave to see the masterpiece of Japanese art, Kannon, the goddess of mercy, who is there in a nunnery.

In the yard of the nunnery, the flagstones are freshly washed, the flowerpots with red and yellow flowers stand in a row. Sweetness, quiet. I shorten my stride at the threshold as if I wanted the passing across this yard to last a long time, months and years. An orange cat with black spots sits on a balcony in the morning sun and licks herself with her little red tongue. It seems as if I hear light female voices chanting behind the garden.

I remember when I went with Sikelianos* to a nunnery on the island of Spétsai. Its yard was like this and the red flowers rose in the flowerpots and the sweetest of female voices sang hymns to another—always the same—god. And we both stopped at the threshold and our hearts trembled.

"What do they call these flowers?" we asked.

* Angellos Sikelianos (1884-1951), one of the leading poets of modern Greece, who wrote long poems and tragedies in verse, and whose best-known work is *Lyricos Vios*.

"Flames!" answered a nun.

I also remember that the yard of the nunnery of St. Clare in Assisi was like this. There were doves, and all the flowerpots had basil and the bell had a thin silver sound, purely feminine, which mingled with the heavy sound of the bell of St. Francis from the opposite monastery. As a man mingles with his wife. And now, at the end of the world, the same courtyard, the same female voice, the same stirring of the insatiable heart.

A door opened and a cheerful, plump little nun appeared. She looked at me smiling and didn't say a word.

"I want to see the goddess Kannon!" I said.

She placed a finger on her lips:

"Don't speak aloud. They are praying."

And she showed me the bench next to the orange cat where I was to sit and wait.

I sat and waited. At the corner of the yard, just across from me, a small cherry tree had blossomed. I listened to the buzz of the bees that harvested it. The soft female chants mingled with the bumbling bees, and, suddenly, Buddha sprung up in my imagination like a tall, blossomed cherry tree harvested by women.

Who knows how long I waited! The rhythm of the time changed, hours and seconds passed at the same speed. Suddenly, the little nun appeared again and nodded to me. The chanting had finished. The small chapel was empty. We came to the freshly scrubbed old wooden steps; I took off my shoes and socks and, as I ascended the steps, I felt a joy in my body, as if the soles of my feet mingled with the bare feet of the nuns, who for centuries were dragged across these burnished woods. . . .

A sparkling clean room, white small pillows on the floor, two large plates filled with flowers and fruit. In the background, a heavy white silken curtain.

"Where is Kannon?" I asked with impatience.

Smiling, the little nun ran barefoot. She raised both her hands and opened the curtain. Goddess Kannon appears shining in the fragrant darkness. She sits with her right foot across her left knee. With her left hand she touches her right foot, and with two fingers of her right hand she holds her firm, youthful chin: a charming, noble maiden with thick, voluptuous lips, and innocent, full-of-sweetness slanted eyes. You feel that she is not the merciful goddess who by acting cures pain. She does not go up to the unfortunate to console them. She is the goddess immovable, sitting on her throne, who cures the heart of man. The fact that she exists and you see her is sufficient to make you forget pain.

She only bends slightly as if she carefully listened with her huge Buddhist ear; as if she understood the pain of man from far away. And the daughter of Budda smiles because she knows that pain is also an illusion, an ephemeral dream that will vanish—you will wake up and it will have scattered. Then you will vanish and the whole world will vanish with you. The pain—God bless Buddha—will be defeated. That's why the little merciful one smiles with such calmness. That's why she does not move from her throne, nor extend her hand. She is certain of her victory. Which victory? Vanishing.

My mind had never created such a proud, immovable, sure goddess of mercy. Because my whole mind never wanted to be enveloped in the yellow garments of Buddhism. Only an utterly desperate man could imagine such a disdainful goddess of redemption. I admire and bless the miraculous hand that carved her. It is said that that was the work of King Sotoku, who was the Constantine the Great of Buddhism in Japan. He was a saint as well as a great lawmaker, warrior, poet and sculptor. His portrait is still preserved on a silk canvas: a sweet, proud, glowing face. This noble goddess truly resembles him.

Time stood still again above my head. I don't know how long I looked at this merciless goddess of mercy. I only remember that when I got up to leave, the little nun had fallen asleep on the ground, leaning on the arm of the goddess.

■ THE BIRTH OF

JAPANESE TRAGEDY

■ WHAT IS THE TEMPLE of the god Kasuga? A very old wooden altar at the end of the park in Nara with all the deer in it dedicated to him.

At the entrance there are large silk lanterns in the sacred colors of the temple, as high as the highest man; the colors are bright red, white and blue. The wooden floor has the clarity of water; on one side there are eight low red-lacquered tables, and on each one, a belt and a sistrum with large bells. On the other side are eight red-lacquered stools with a fan on top of each. At the background, four bookstands with old books, opened. On the ground, resting like a beast, the *koto*, a gigantic Japanese harp. And above, surrounding the wall, a broad silken band with paintings of female dancers.

After many wanderings I arrived at the park. I lost my way in the endless rows of stone lampposts higher than the tallest man. Heavy, impressive, carved on granite. You pass through them for hours and they don't end; they look like rows of exotic trees turned to marble. Ivy, moss and webs are woven around them, and the carvings of sacred inscriptions are lost in their midst.

When I first saw the temple, my heart leaped like a deer. But I was very thirsty; a spring ran outside under the trees and I dipped the wooden ladle. "Let's drink," I said. "Let's first think of the body!"

I drank, I cooled off, I sat on the threshold like a beggar and I leaned on the pole. I gazed insatiably at the musical instruments and the sistrums and the loosened belts of the girls with loose hair, who sat bent with heads between their knees, like bacchantes. I was happy. How long have I longed for this moment! I had reached the holy enclosure where the Japanese tragedy was born.

There is a profound religious tragedy in the world, which has its roots in the entrails of a deity, like the tragedy of the ancient Greeks. This tragedy was also born from dance and has as its leading character the god-hero. It is called no, which means performance, drama. It was born here at the end of the park of Nara, inside this old wooden temple of Kasuga, the holy dance. During the great festivals, the monks danced a comic dance here in front of an imaginary cave. It was the mythological cave where the goddess of Sun, Amaterasu, had been hidden when she was angry and did not want to appear again in the world. The gods gathered and begged her. Men cried, tormenting themselves in darkness while entreating her. But the angry goddess did not want to appear again and give light to the world. And then Uzume, a fat, gay goddess, jumped up and began to bounce and dance in a funny way. All the gods burst out laughing; Amaterasu also came out of the cave to see; she saw and laughed and forgot her ire and ascended again to the sky. The night ended, the world was full of light.

The monks of the Kasuga temple performed their comic dance at the festivals with music and pantomime. They wore wild or funny masks, bounced about, somersaulted, groaned, and impersonated drunk dancers. The music which they played was also comic; it was called *saru-gaku*, which means monkey music. Soon the dance and pantomime themes were enriched; local deities were represented and especially the miracles of Buddha or his past incarnations. Buddha soon became the central hero of the dance. The Japanese tragedy was created from these popular dances, monkey shrieks and pantomimes.

At the beginning, all the monks bounced and shouted together. Then little by little, the intoxication took on a kind of rhythm, the leaps and shouts turned to order and the characters were formed. Finally the words came and gave a noble and coherent structure to the action.

Now the god speaks and the others silently listen to the divine monologue. God with his hieratic mask dances alone; the persons of the chorus withdraw to the right side of the stage and, shyly and discreetly, they begin to comment about whatever they see and to reply to the words of God. The dialogue begins to form, the theatrical action is born, a new character enters the scene, the companion and servant of God, man. The play becomes perfect. Out of an incoherent natural force—out of leaps and groans and laughs—grows a well-regulated work, ritually dominated, with God as the protagonist.

The words came, God spoke, and men listened. But this divine monologue was monotonous and barren. Then man intervened, and so began the eternal fertile dialogue between God and man. The tragedy has been completed. The miracle has taken place.

The great dramatists came. They gave life and passion to the dialogue; they defined the position of the chorus and the instruments of music—the little drum, the big drum and the flute—and created the laws of tragedy. They sifted the tragic from the comic; comedy became pure; the mad words, *kyogen*, were invented. Tragedy was written in a lofty style and in an archaic language which was understood only by the well-educated; comedy was written in the language of the people, and its theme was taken from the satires and farces of everyday life.

Who wrote the comedies? We don't know. Common people who remained anonymous. But Japan has its Aeschylus and its Sophocles—Kan-Ami and his son Se-Ami, who lived in the fourteenth century. These two dramatists brought about a great revolution on the stage: musicians, poets, directors, dancers gave new, higher forms to music, to dramaturgy, to staging and to chorus in the Japanese theater. They have been the great rule-makers of the stage; they created a tradition which since then has regulated the no religious ceremony.

The stage must be twenty-seven feet wide and twenty-eight feet deep. It must be higher than the ground and its roof must be exactly like that of a Shinto temple; it is held up by four pillars at the corners. At the left, a covered corridor joins the stage with the backstage; the actors come and go through this corridor. They raise the heavy curtain which hangs in the background. A huge green pine tree is painted on the back drop; it symbolizes the period when the no theater did not have an indoor stage and the plays were performed outdoors under the pine trees of the temple. Of the one thousand tragedies that were written in the golden age of the no, 342 are still played today. Their subjects are the gods, the ghosts, the demons, or often human passions and lively adventures. Gradually, man acquired a very important position in the tragedy themes and replaced God. One of the characteristics of the progress was that the roles which were played by God were taken over and played by men.

The structure of the tragedy follows a definite rhythm: at the beginning appears Waki, who often is a monk or a councilor of some prince. He takes a few steps singing in order to imply that he is traveling. He reaches a point, stops and announces that he has reached the temple which was the destination of his journey. Then the protagonist comes, either as a priest, a peasant or a fisherman, and describes the scene and the holy tradition of the temple. And abruptly he disappears mysteriously. Was he the god or the ghost of a great warrior?

Waki stands dazzled by the supernatural appearances. Then peasants speaking a common idiom tell stories about the god or the hero who is worshiped in this temple. They withdraw, and Waki remains alone again and begins to sing. As soon as he finishes his song, the curtain at the background of the corridor is raised and the protagonist slowly, solemnly enters again, but in his real form now—god, demon, ghost. He wears a mask and begins to dance. With words and gestures, dancing, he reveals to us his soul and his intricate forlorn or heroic story.

All the movements in the no plays are simple, slow, full of religious grandeur. They leave a mood of depression. So that the audience will be uplifted again, a comedy is always played after the tragedy. The mad words bring back gaiety, the heart is strengthened and ready to attend the second tragedy. As in ancient Greece, at least three tragedies are played, and the total playing time can last an entire day and night. As the Christians attend the Passion of Christ through the night, as the ancient Greeks attended the passion of Dionysus, so the Buddhists now do the same with the passion of Buddha. Because Buddha, Christ and Dionysus are one—the eternal suffering man.

■ KYOTO

■ MY SERVICE TO Nara is finished. Now I am sitting at the *ryokan*, on a red pillow. My suitcases are ready; I am leaving shortly for Kyoto, the aristocratic old capital. I turn over in my mind whatever I saw and enjoyed in this tiny city. I think my soul has been enriched; I think my heart has been cleansed and uplifted because I saw a few works of supreme beauty and I sat in the holy park where the distant sister of our ancient Dionysiac intoxication, the Japanese tragedy, with downy, deerlike eyes was born, full of vertigo and divine essence.

I wonder what other joys wait for me in Kyoto, the widow royal city, where I will arrive tonight. Traveling is captivating hunting; you go out never guessing what bird will come along. Traveling is like wine: you drink and you can't imagine what visions will come to your mind. Surely while traveling you find all that you have within you. Without wanting to, from the innumerable impressions that overflow your eyes, you choose and select whatever corresponds more to the needs or curiosities of your soul. "Objective" truth exists only—and how insignificant it is!—in the photographic cameras and in the souls that see the world coldly, without emotion, that is, without a deep contact. Those who suffer and love communicate through a mystical intercourse with the landscape they see, the people they mingle with, and the incidents they select. Therefore, every perfect traveler always creates the country where he travels.

A Japanese folk song says it better than I:

On a little branch of a plum tree
On a little branch of a plum tree, the nightin-
    gale
Dreamed that it was night and snowing.
And on the mountains and the plains, indeed,
You saw nothing but snow that fell and fell
You saw nothing but snow. . . .
Another night the nightingale dreamed
That the branches of the plum tree where it sat
Blossomed.
And on the mountains and the plains, indeed,
You saw nothing but plum trees
You saw nothing but plum trees
That blossomed.
And the flowers fell and fell
The flowers of the plum tree fell on the
    ground. . . .

Sitting on a ricksha as on a throne, I look at the back, soaked in sweat, of the man who draws this little carriage as it moves rhythmically, left and right. I am ashamed that this man suffers so much, as he drags me with so many of my things—suitcases, books and a basket of fruit. I hear the broad soles of his feet splashing softly on the wet street. Most of these coolies die early of tuberculosis.

What is our duty, I ask myself, gazing persistently at his perspiring back. Only this: we should endeavor as much as we can to have only those who cannot offer anything better to mankind perform the duty of the coolies. The right and just hierarchy should be introduced, even if it is temporary, to replace the present unjust and inhuman one in which those who rightly ought to be coolies go on riding and commanding.

Justice does not mean that all should be masters or all servants. Justice means that he who is by nature a servant should perform the duties of a servant and he who is by nature a master should perform the duties of a master. I firmly believe in the inequality of men. And if today, in our time, an honest soul finds it his duty to hate the present organization of the world, it is not because there are masters and servants, but because some of the present-day masters have lost their old noble virtues and have become slaves of themselves.

At the station we encounter again the multitudes of pilgrims who come to greet the cherry blossoms. This poetic exaltation that captures the Japanese people every spring is an unbelievable truth in our industrial age. They stand before a blossomed tree for a long time and gaze at it silently, immovable. No one reaches out to cut a branch nor to smell a flower. Once, in the park of Nara, I raised myself on my toes in order to reach and smell a blossomed branch. Two Japanese who sat next to me looked at me surprised, in the way we would look at one who eats a flower.

The Japanese love the flowers not for their fragrance but for their perfect form, their delicate colors and their architectural structure in a vase or on the tree. For that reason, they raised into a great art the flower arrangements in vases, the *ikebana*, "the art of enlivening the flowers." If a Japanese really wants to be considered well educated, he must know how to arrange the flowers, how to place them in a room in springtime or fall, day or night, and how to place them when you want them to project a certain feeling—joy, loneliness and meditation, bitter nostalgia. . . .

The profound influence of Buddhist religion which sees everything in a state of brotherly love, in a sweetly colored atmosphere of vanity and sympathy. Rightly then, the Japanese tradition believes that this tender art of arranging flowers was brought to Japan by a Buddhist saint. One morning this saint saw some flowers piled up by the hurricane on the ground before the temple. He pitied them, bent down, and took them in his arms and kneeling for a long time, he arranged them in a bronze vase. He arranged them as if they were still hung on a tree. And when he finished, he placed the vase at the feet of Buddha. And Buddha moved his lips, so the tradition says, and smiled, pleased.

I will never forget the long, narrow streets of Kyoto in nighttime with their innumerable multicolored lanterns; the scented air whistled, laughed, and sometimes a gong from a Buddhist temple sounded sweetly, discreetly, and behind the green reed walls were heard the hard, nervous chords of a samisen with the sad song of a woman:

> *And at the night that the snow falls*
> *And at the night that all drink tea*
> *If you love me, come, I beg you. . . .*

Or another eternal Saphian craving of a woman:

> *All this long, long night,*
> *Long as the tail of a golden pheasant,*
> *Well, it is written for me to sleep alone.*

I had gone astray, without knowing it, in the alleys where the geishas live and saw smiling old women—old veterans who work now as doorwomen and welcome the men and help them take off their sandals and open for them the small inside door. . . . I stayed for a while at an open door. I bent down and looked in at the tiny yard. Blooming flowers in the pots, a fragrance of aromatic wood, two big paper lanterns underneath three broad wooden steps. . . . And on them shoes of all sorts placed in order. And another row of sandals and slippers hastily placed in a disorderly fashion. Certainly on this long night, long as the tail of a golden pheasant, the geishas—thank God—will not sleep alone.

I saunter until long after midnight, I feel too sorry to close my eyes. It seems to me that all this spring mirage is a nocturnal performance of a city in which Maras, the god of human delusion, is raised in the air for a moment. He will now blow, and everything—lanterns, temples, men, wooden sandals—will vanish. I go back and forth in order to see the architecture of the mirage while it is still there. This, then, is Heian-kyo, the "capital of peace," where the emperors of Nara took refuge in 794 in order to be saved from the powerful and greedy priests! In vain! The same refined and lascivious priests were the courtiers of the new palace in Kyoto. The same flowers of evil: Chinese fashions, shameless waste, piety and debauchery. The memorandum an honest courtier submitted to Emperor Daigo still exists: "The monks are inhuman, they do not care about religion, they have mistresses, they make counterfeit money, they steal and rob, they eat meat and violate all the orders." The noblemen spent their time composing verses, riddles, puzzles, arranging flowers, organizing holidays for the celebration of the cherry-blossom trees, the full moon, the water. . . . They covered the trees with flowers during the winter and with snow in the summer. They were crazy about dogs and cats, which were given official titles and many servants. When the king's favorite cat gave birth, the courtiers sent presents to it—silk ribbons or small mice on a golden tray.

As I pass through the streets of this city at night, I look at them as I would at a beloved person in the darkness. Every city has its sex, male or female. This one is all female. I recount its love adventures, its scandals, its lavishness and luxuries—and everything seems to me sacred and necessary. This city has performed its duty as a woman. It helped the people to make progress with its fatal feminine method: loving, wasting, raising luxury, perhaps, to its true height—the holy position of necessity.

I am glad that I have found, wandering the streets, the essence and the mission of this old, sinful city. This city gave for the final creation of the Japanese soul its feminine cell. I am glad that tomorrow morning when we both awaken and she will be uncovered before me in the sunlight, I will know why I should love her, forgiving all her sins, as a sinful woman who loves too much should also be forgiven.

May this lavishness, what we call luxury, excess, extravagance, be blessed! Civilization means to feel luxury as necessity, to surpass the animal by not being satisfied only with food, drink, sleep and woman. At the moment that the "wingless biped" craves for the unnecessary luxury, as he would for bread, he begins to become man. Whatever good this world has, whatever has been saved from the human masses, is luxury: a painting, a carved flower, a song, an idea beyond the average mind. Luxury is the greatest necessity of the superior man. The excess of his heart. That is the true heart.

I saunter the endless sumptuous palaces of this city that has been the capital for a thousand years. I stop at the "Blue and Cool Room," the steps of which have been so artfully placed that when the distant breeze of the Lake Biwa blows, the room is cooled. I enjoy the paintings— birds, flowers, waters, reeds; the statues; the inscriptions; and the royal drapes with the three sacred colors, red, white and black. On the walls there are wise sayings of Confucius: *The king is like the wind; the people are like the grass. The grass must bend when the wind passes.* The wind passed, the grass withered away—only the saying remained.

I passed through the deserted royal palaces that even the spiders do not inhabit. The kings died and only the sacred royal emblem, the chrysanthemum with sixteen petals, remains carved on ivory, on gold, on wood, or painted on the folding screens and fans. I pass through the gardens; I think that there is no more beautiful sight in the world than a Chinese or a Japanese garden, one of the highest peaks of wisdom and sensitivity that man has reached.

"I want you to design for me the most beautiful garden in the world!" the great Hideyoshi ordered the famous artist Kobori Ensu.

"I will," replied the artist, "but under three conditions: you should put no limit on the expenses; you should not press me—I shall finish it when I will; and you should never come to see it before it is completed—because you may think of a change and spoil my original plan."

Hideyoshi accepted the conditions, and thus the wonderful garden was made here between the River Katsura and the captivating hill of Nishiyama. Rocks, waters, bridges, trees, shrubs all are so wisely placed that your soul feels inexpressibly tranquil. As if you were one of the faithful and entered the temple of your god; as if you yourself were Buddha and entered nirvana, nothingness. Entering this garden, you do not recognize any more the joy of life or the fear of death. You can bend like Li-Tseu and pick a human skull and say: "Only I and this skull know truly that there is neither life nor death." Such a joy only death, the great gardener, can give us.

I wander around the museums, I look at the Japanese paintings, I insatiably admire the simplicity and the power, the inexpressible frugality of each line. That is the true art—bare, without vain adornments and gaudy colors. I look graspingly and warn myself: never forget these reeds that Kano Tanyu painted; remember well the refinement, the few gray-silver colors, the black, slight firm line—and the reed that bends immortally over the invisible water. . . .

Never forget this fire of Buntso Tani. We hear fire, we see flames, we burn. But we don't understand. Suddenly we see this very fire and immediately we feel deeply the essence of fire. We are terrified.

Farther on, in a portrait on the wall, a hermit in orange garments sits and gazes at Nothing. Still further, five monks dressed in red, sitting in a row at the terrace of the monastery, quietly and decisively look at the empty air, smiling. A wooden Kannon, the goddess of mercy, rises in a corner with a multitude of hands. And every hand has a different expression: it pushes, it holds, it caresses, it points out, it chases, it begs. . . . But her main hands are tightly joined into prayer. . . . Gardens, secrets of script, tea parties, arrangements of flowers—tender springs of joy that cannot rise from the bosom of white man. The yellow race is much more delicate than ours, and simultaneously, in a mysterious combination, more barbarous. Their traditions and history are sometimes full of fantastic sensitivity and of brutal cruelty.

In the Buddhist temple where I wandered today in Hono-zi, Nobunaga, one of the greatest warriors, statesmen and revelers ever born in Japan, was killed in 1582. A gigantic soul, highest in wisdom, first in drink and in war, and first in pleasure. He feared neither gods nor men. Tough, silent, he wanted to destroy theocracy, bring back peace and order to his country, save men from the gods. He dashed with his army to the richest and most sacred Buddhist monastery, Lieizan, opposite Kyoto. It was a beautiful city, a powerful religious center. "Go forth! Burn it!" shouted Nobunaga. The soldiers trembled and did not dare. "Burn it, the earth must be cleansed," again shouted the fearful leader. The monastery was reduced to ashes, thousands of monks and women and children were slain.

But one night when Nobunaga was feasting, he grabbed the head of his friend, Mitsushide, and derisively drummed his iron fan on his friend's forehead. Mitsu-shide accepted the insult smiling; but one night he took his friends and made for the temple of Hono-zi, where Nobunaga lived. The terrible tyrant appeared at the window and a torrent of arrows pierced him. He crawled inside, and as he felt the end of his life had come, he slew his wife and children and committed hara-kiri. He used to say, "Man dies once. Life is brief and the world is a dream; Let's die gloriously!"

The voices that sang were lost together with the throats, the harp- and flute-playing fingers rotted away along with the dancing feet. And only the paintings and statues, which fill the human heart with happiness, still remain in all these monasteries: a religious ecstasy, an immovable paradisian air, hermits with heads erect against the moonlight, spirits that pass over the earth like frost. And simultaneously, the most keen observations of life, a warm representation of the smallest detail, humor, joy, love of everyday life, colors—a golden rooster in a white landscape covered with snow; a samurai with a glittering armor and two big antennas on his helmet appears like a gigantic insect in a green glen. . . .

There is a deep mystery in these paintings—suggestive, penetrating, a light dream-atmosphere. They are never copies of nature, regardless of how faithful they look; they always project the object they represent. You feel that the painter loves the external form, but loves still more the mystic forces that gave birth to the form. He paints the invisible through the only means he has in his command: by faithfully representing the visible. "Render the spiritual life through the rhythm of things!" ordered an old Chinese saint.

The white man finds his supreme joy by pitting himself against the surrounding world as well as by imposing his ego and subjugating the natural forces to his task. The Oriental finds his supreme joy by plunging into his world and harmonizing his individual rhythm with that of the world. Today I enjoy this deep inner contrast between the two races while looking at the Japanese paintings. The main or central theme of Japanese painting is never the man whom we see painted; it is the air around him, the landscape, the mystic contact of his soul with the tree, the water, the cloud. The main theme is: brotherhood, identification, or, better, the return of man to his own world.

■ THE JAPANESE GARDENS

■ A GREAT DANCER lived in Japan two centuries ago. One time he ascended the steps of a monastery tower, famous for its view from the top; from there you could see an exquisite garden. When, however, he reached the highest step, a sense of uneasiness appeared on his face. He turned to his students who followed him and said:

"Strange! Something is missing here. A step. I beg one of you to go and call the abbot."

The abbot came. The dancer asked him whether a step was missing. "I have been the abbot for thirty years," replied the monk. "When I came to the monastery, the steps were the same. Nothing changed."

"A step is missing!" insisted the dancer. "I beg you, give an order to dig up the foundation of the stairs!"

The abbot ordered two workers to start digging. And indeed the step was found. It had been covered over by time.

"I was certain," said the dancer. "When I reached the highest step, I felt that something was missing for perfect harmony. One more step was necessary for perfect harmony between the height of the stairs and the view of the garden."

I stand at the little garden of the monastery Honganzi, in the center of Kyoto, and the finesse of that dancer disturbs and grieves my heart. If only one could develop such sensitivity as his touch! I look at the little garden: two rough rocks thrown as if by chance and at random, a small artery of running water, two low curved stone bridges, a few dry shrubs give you the impression of an endless desert.

"The great artist Simano-Ske-Asagiri designed it three hundred years ago," points out the fat, shaven monk, guardian of the garden. "Do you understand the meaning of this garden?"

"I understand," I replied, "as much as a thick-skinned Westerner can understand."

The monk laughed, pleased. He began to talk and I listened to him, enchanted:

"Our old artists," he said, "made a garden as we compose a song. A great, difficult, complicated work of art. At the beginning our great gardeners were Buddhist monks who had brought this art from China. Later, the art was passed to the great teachers of the tea ceremony, to the poets and painters, and finally to the specialist gardeners.

"Every garden must have its meaning and project an abstract concept: tranquillity, purity, wilderness, or pride and heroic grandeur. And this concept must correspond not only to the soul of the owner, but also to the soul of his family or his race. What is the value of the individual? It is something ephemeral, while the garden, as every work of art, must have elements of eternity.

"A monk imprinted on a tiny garden the omnipotence of God. How? By placing rocks with profound sensitivity, leaning them here and there, irregularly. This thought was suggested to him by a Buddhist tradition. Monk Daiti once ascended a hill and began to preach the teaching of Buddha, and the stones, as the tradition goes, were gradually covered by yellow moss and bent their peaks as if in worship.

"We have famous gardens made up only of rocks without a single tree or flower. Rocks and dried-out streams, and waterfalls without water, but sand. These rock gardens project grandeur, wilderness, inaccessible deity. And thus, the monk instead of withdrawing to the wilderness, comes to such a garden in the middle of the city and finds there all the desert that his soul needs for its meditation and salvation.

"Other gardens are adorned with trees, waters and greenery. Those gardens are not for the hermits but for people of the world who enjoy the sweetness of life. But the most famous of all the Japanese gardens are the *cha-niwa*, the tea gardens; they lead to a small room which is used for the tea ceremony. The sentiment they want to project is isolation, meditation, deliverance from the roaring of the world. Going to this sacred little house, you feel as if you were far away from the world, at a deserted shore, in an autumn twilight. In order to project the concept of loneliness, they cultivated in these gardens the moss on rocks and around trunks of trees.

"Our greatest artist of tea ceremonies was Rikyu, in the sixteenth century. He had also been a great artist of the garden. When he was still an apprentice, his teacher ordered him to sweep the garden well so that he could serve tea. Rikyu swept it very carefully and did not leave even a tiny piece of rubbish or dried leaf on the ground; he stood back to admire it, but suddenly he felt something missing. He went to a tree and shook it, and the autumn leaves fell to the ground. Rikyu left them. The teacher came and saw the lane covered with leaves and understood; deeply moved, he put his hand on the head of his student and said to him: 'I am no longer necessary; you are my superior.'"

The monk stopped and hastily went to place a stone that had been moved that day by the crowds of worshipers in its original position. "Did you see?" he asked me, "how unbecoming this stone looked placed that way? It blocked the other two stones in front of it and diminished the view."

"Yes . . ." I murmured, and my heart was sad because I had not understood anything.

The art of the gardener in the Far East is a wonder, indeed a wonder of love and patience. The day before yesterday I had seen a pine tree in the yard of a monastery. The trunk stood erect, but all the branches bent down toward one side of the trunk. And all the foliage looked like the dense, curled, green tail of a peacock.

"How has this pine tree become like that?" I asked with admiration.

"With patience and love," a monk replied to me. "Every morning when its branches were still soft and flexible, we caressed and pressed and bent them to take on the design we wanted."

And today when I listened to the monk talk to me about the gardens, I thought that there was another art of gardening there, equally admirable, a continuation of the original: the making of your tiny heart into a vast garden and giving it the meaning which best becomes you: joy, loneliness, austerity, sensuality, tranquillity, whatever your substance may be.

I said it to the monk, and he shook his head.

"What you say is more difficult. Let's begin from the outside gardens. They come first; the garden of the heart comes afterward. And then comes the most difficult, the most mystical, the supreme garden which is neither trees nor stones nor ideas."

"Only air?"

"Not even air."

"And what is this garden called?"

"Buddha."

■ CHA-NO-YU

■ IF I WERE TO form my heart in the shape of a garden, I would make it like the rock garden of the monastery Ruan-zi, in Kyoto. Not even a single green tree, not even a flower. The trees and flowers exist outside the high fence. The entire garden is a sandy desert and upon it are scattered small and large rocks, about ten of them. So-Ami, who designed it in the sixteenth century, wanted to represent with this garden a tiger that fled holding its babies in her teeth. And indeed, you feel as if the rocks, as they are placed, are overtaken by panic and run frightened, and the idea of the tiger is impressed upon your mind. Only, instead of a tiger in the imagined garden of my heart, I would place there godliness.

That's what I was thinking this morning when I came down to the little garden of my hotel and I saw the gardener caressing and bending the branches of a small plum tree to take the idyllic and impressive shape of a weeping willow. I stood there for a long time and admired the slender, dexterous fingers of the old gardener that tamed nature with such sweetness. In this humble area of his mission, this old man followed the same laws as the great hermits who accomplished the same difficult victory by subjugating the natural forces to the scheme that their mind had decided upon.

The sun was already high when I started to go to *cha-no-yu* for the tea ceremony to which I had been invited. And as I went, the long legendary history of the tea came to my mind. From very old times, the Chinese used tea as a medicine. They credited it with miraculous properties—to relax the nerves, to strengthen the sight, to calm the soul, to fortify the will. In their long wakefulness, the Buddhist hermits drank tea so as not to faint from exhaustion. The tea helped their sacred ascension, and thus they gradually came to consider it a sacred herb and drank it according to a definite religious ritual.

One day tea arrived at the Japanese shores from China, together with Buddhism. It was considered a sacred aristocratic drink. A few friends gathered in silence gazing at flowers or at a beautiful painting, drinking tea sip by sip, and feeling their body and soul in utter calm. During difficult and wild periods it was a great relief. Behind an isolated garden, in a small room, a few, at most five, friends sitting and drinking the mysterious drink (as it still was) and talking about God and art, forgetting the wars. In this way the first sacred atmosphere which gave birth to *cha-no-yu* was created. Then the great teachers came who defined the rules of the ceremony: how the room should be in winter, in summer, in the morning, at twilight; how the garden should look; how the guests and the host should behave; how the tea should be boiled and served; what conversation ought to take place and what subjects should never infect this sacred contact. . . .

All this old art pleasantly came to mind while I, passing through the workers' section of Nishizin, stepped onto the threshold of the distant house where the famous tea ceremony would take place. The path in the garden that led to the entrance of the tea pavilion, the *sukiya*, was not more than twenty feet long. However, the garden was put together with such art, the rocks, the little trees and the stone lanterns were placed so impressively that immediately the feeling of absolute loneliness was born within you.

At the end of the path, crystal-clear water ran from a little fountain; we bent, as one should, and washed our hands and mouth. We took off our shoes and, barefoot, we climbed the three steps and entered into the sacred, simple room which was covered with yellow straw mats. A bare room without furniture. Only a vase of cherry blossoms on a low tiny table and a fire at the corner where the teapot boiled. Often they put small pieces of iron into the teapot so that a melody might come out when the water boiled, and so that the guests might hear and remember "the far-off waterfall, the distant sea that breaks against the rocks, the rain on the reeds, the pine trees that rustle in the wind. . . ."

On the wall, hung from a long silk band, the picture of the greatest teacher of *cha-no-yu*, Rikyu. "Tell me the secrets of your art!" a ruler asked him once.

"In winter," Rikyu replied, "you should arrange the room to appear warm, and in summer, cool. You should boil the water properly in order to capture the taste of tea."

"But these things are commonly known," the ruler said contemptuously.

"When you find a man," said Rikyu, "who not only knows but knows how to apply these things, then I will go to sit at his feet and become his disciple."

I was looking at the great teacher and thinking of his words when a door opened noiselessly and a geisha dressed in a precious black kimono entered and bowed, bending to the ground. Behind her appeared her assistant, younger than she, who also bowed silently in her black kimono with a golden bow on the back. Both sat down. The first, before the boiling teapot, began to wipe the teaspoons and small cups with a silken cloth. Alongside, and a little behind her, sat her assistant. Deep silence; you heard nothing but the water that boiled cheerfully, dancing.

The door opened noiselessly again, and little girls, eight or ten years old, entered with short, dragging strides; they were dressed in gay red kimonos with black bows, and their little faces were heavily powdered like masks. Each one held a clay saucer which contained egglike pastry made of rice and honey; he who ate it would not be sick for a year. They stood before each guest, bowed to the ground and left the saucer before him.

The tea was now ready. The first geisha served it in round porcelain bowls, and her assistant took the bowls and placed one before each of us. We took them in our two palms and began to sip the tea. Thick, green, very bitter. We drank it, and the old geisha, the hostess, began again slowly to clean and wipe the tea tools, the spoons and the pot. She rose. She bowed deeply, behind her bowed her assistant, and with slow steps both disappeared behind the door. The ceremony was over.

I went out in the garden. All this silence and slow rhythm of *cha-no-yu* had projected in my blood the rhythm of calm. Unexpectedly, I recalled the noontime I had arrived on the island of Mýkonos and seen the windmills on the surrounding hills moving slowly in the light. I remember then how my heart was caught in that light; so strongly had this moribund movement forced my blood to take on its rhythm for that moment. In this same way, now, my heart was caught. I walked along the path quickly. I came out to the living streets, I saw the coolies with their carriages, running; the factories whistled, noontime. The workers stopped their work in the noisy Nishizin Quarter, where the large famous silk factories are. I walked quickly, as if I wanted to escape from a nightmare. All these tea ceremonies in our time seemed to me like the hashish that we take to blur our eyes to the horror rising inside us, so that we will not see around us the coolies nor these pale working girls of Nishizin.

■ KAMAKURA

■ My DEPARTURE FROM Kyoto was heartbreaking. At this railroad station, too, I left a drop of my blood.

Dawn, the earth smiles, the small-blossomed peach trees shine in an old farm. Leaning against my train window I see the bony, tortured body of Japan. Mountains made of lava, extinguished volcanoes—some still smoking, ravines opened by earthquakes, hot springs, all the tragic history of Japan is written with stones, boiling water and flames. And if the atmosphere is so clear, Japan pays dearly for this purity. It is created by violent atmospheric currents which sometimes break into terrible typhoons, uprooting cities and villages.

But when the earth and the air calm down, the Japanese rise, rebuild their houses and temples; the air has been cleared, the earth puts on again its fresh mask full of flowers, and the Japanese soul rejoices as if awakened from a bad dream. And, as if the soul is in a hurry to enjoy itself before the nightmare engulfs it again, it carves on wood and on stone the joyful gods, picks up the plume and writes small migratory songs of seventeen syllables, the *haiku*, and of thirty-one syllables, the *tanka*; it takes the brush and paints the beauty of the world becomingly, as light as frost.

> *The color of the flower withered away*
> *At the moment I admired, in vain,*
> *The passing of myself through the world!*

So the great Japanese poetess Okono-Kumassi sang a thousand years ago. But this concept of the ephemeral is transubstantiated in the brave soul of the Japanese; and instead of becoming fatalism and despair, it becomes craving for joy, for work, for creation before the earthquake, the hurricane and death.

For that reason the Japanese selected as their supreme symbols the rising sun, a flower (the chrysanthemum) and a fish (the carp). The sun symbolizes the three great virtues: knowledge, kindness and bravery. The chrysanthemum endures and blooms in the snow. And the carp rushes up against the current of the river and defeats the force that pushes it down. . . .

The Japanese are a temperate, vigorous, brave race. I bend through the window and look at the peasants dipped in mud up to their knees, preparing their farms for the sowing of rice. The work is heavy, the land is little: only 12 per cent of Japan is tillable and there is not enough to nurture its children. The peasant boys leave their farms and crowd the cities, working in factories. Today Japan is going through the critical hour that England passed in the middle of the nineteenth century. What did England do to feed her population then? She became industrialized. If she had remained agricultural, she would have overflowed, and the British would have fallen into the sea; England was industrialized and thus she was able to feed a population three times larger than she had room for. Japan has begun to do the same. The villages will now be deserted, the factories will be increased, the patriarchal life will come to an end. . . .

Now we pass by the charming Lake Biwa: the earth sank one night and it was filled with these beautiful blue waters that so cheerfully shine today in the sunlight. Fishermen get on the train, they hold the arrow-like fisher-baskets containing the bait. They are going to lean them against the banks of the lake. Sunburned bodies, kind faces, jolly people. The fisherman was, until recent years, the other pillar that held up Japan. The fisherman and the peasant. Fish and rice. Now another has entered in the middle with an unsmiling face and pushes them to the side: the laborer.

When the savages are hungry, they scatter in the forests, they begin the exorcisms and beg the animals with tasty meat—the deer, the buffaloes, the gazelles—to have pity on them and come and fall in their nets and feed the human race that is in danger. Surely, the fishermen, too, feel this same contact with the fish! Because, the day before yesterday in Kyoto a procession took place to honor "the spirit of the fish." The fishermen gathered, raised the banners of their work-nets, rods, baskets, waved big, colorful fish made of cloth, and all together went to the temple to thank the God-Fish that deigns to get into their nets and feed the Japanese.

■ BUSHIDO

■ I SIT AT A RESTAURANT on the main street of Kamakura. The door is open and at the entrance hang broad orange cloth bands with black exotic letters. It is still drizzling. It is twilight and you see the people passing lightly in the thin net of rain.

The ceremony of eating begins: the green tea; a wooden pail of boiled rice instead of bread; you fill your bowl with a wooden ladle once, twice or three times. "Three bowls of rice is the right portion for a man and two for a woman," the Japanese say. They bring the famous *tempura* with a thick sauce; they also bring the *nabe*, a small frying pan, on fire, and we begin by ourselves to prepare the national Japanese dish, the *sukiyaki*, a sort of shish-kebab like the Caucasian *saslik* and the Greek *suvlaki*. We put butter on the pan, then thin slices of meat, onions, celery, slices of tender bamboo, mushrooms, to-matoes, and we begin to scramble them with a wooden stick. In a small bowl we beat an egg. Bending above the pan we follow the broiling. As soon as a piece of meat is broiled, we dip it into the egg and eat it. Then we take the porcelain bottle with the lukewarm sake and fill our small cups with it. . . .

I eat, I feed my body which I tired, despite its will, wandering here and there. I feed and water my "brother donkey" with sympathy. Now we come from the stone where, they say, the fiery reformer of Buddhism, Nisiren, stood in the thirteenth century and preached the austere

"Truth of Lotus." The beautiful, impudent ladies were mad about this wild Japanese Savonarola and ran with a masochist's pleasure to listen to him castigate them—until one day the ruler was frightened by his revolutionary sermons and ordered his head cut off. Three times the executioner raised a sword and three times the thunderbolt smashed it.

That's what I was saying to my body in front of the stone of Nisiren to make it forget the fatigue and hunger. But the body refused. It did not believe. It wants to see, to hear, to touch in order to believe. I often say to it that because of this unfaithfulness, it will never go to the kingdom of heaven, it will remain in the domain of earth and will be eaten up by the worms.

When I came out of the restaurant, the drizzle had stopped, the paper lanterns had been lit, a light smell of bitter almond had spread in the air. I took the street with the lit cherry trees that leads to the temple of Hashiman, the god of war. I was about to leave for Tokyo and I had to bid farewell to the true patron of Kamakura.

In the blue darkness, surrounded by old pine trees, the temple of war rose threateningly. Irreverent, upturned rooftops, wildly patterned beams, heavy doors with dragons, all deserted—this temple truly was the heart of the old bellicose city. In the dark it appeared like a giant samurai who lies in ambush under the trees with his heavy helmet and bronze antennas, his two swords and his silk fan.

It is the spirit of Yoritomo, which still sits here, on the steps, amid the very trees he planted as he figured in his mind the awesome batallion of samurai that would save his country. This rough, grim ruler was one of the highest examples of the samurai: he lived a simple Spartan life and believed fanatically in Shinto, Buddhism and the emperor. "Make your life simple," he ordered the feudal lords, "in order to be ready for the sacrifice; our emperor is the son of God, and our country is made of the bones and spirits of our ancestors."

And so the wandering medieval knights of Japan, the samurai, started out from this temple of the god of war and created great works with their valor, austerity and justice. Simultaneously ascetics and warriors, they believed that only through strict life and self-denial could one be saved. "Look deeply within you and you will find Buddha!" Discipline your body and soul, exercise your will, set as the supreme good not life but honor and duty. The world is worthy of nothing as compared to the soul of a man!

They despise the pleasures and the easy life of Kyoto and the finesse of the court. They live away from the imperial ceremonies and the life of the courtiers. In the mountains, in abrupt ravines, on the frontier their towers and castles rise as guardians of the borders. Civil wars break out that last for centuries, and the poor peasants, inexperienced in war, have no other refuge but their feudal lord. The population is divided into two classes: the nobles who own the land, and the slaves who have no property and work on the farms and in the shops of the lords. The nobles have only one occupation, war; the common people are considered unworthy of using arms —their supreme virtues are obedience and love of work.

I wander around the temple in the dark, I touch the steps where Shizuka danced in front of Yoritomo and gave a mournful, hoarse cry. Blood, love, cruelty and a firm, relentless task creating a new type of man who will not be afraid of death. The old Japanese virtue, firmness of heart, *fudoshin*, should return: standing immovable and indifferent in the most horrible trials and tribulations, calm in battle, "as the old man sits in the council or the monk in his cell." Keeping your body ready to die. Because, of what use is the body other than when the time comes, it could be thrown away by the soul that wants no part of its infectiousness?

Always be ready! That is the great commandment of the samurai. When you go out of your house, you should go as if you were never to return. Thus, the commandments of the samurai were gradually codified, and the *Bushido*, the guide of knighthood, was created. Strict commandments, a Japanese hierarchy of values:

1. Honor and duty above all.

2. Blind obedience to the emperor.

3. Boldness, disdain of death; be ready to die at any moment.

4. Relentless discipline of soul and body.

5. Polite and kind behavior to friends.

6. Ruthless vengeance for the enemy.

7. Generosity (frugality is one of the forms of cowardice).

With these fiery commandments, pure, hot-headed Don Quixotes, the samurai, flooded Japanese history. With the same commandments, they fought, elevating *Bushido* to a new religion. The contemporary Japanese tried to mold the new generation of entirely modernized knights who would flood the world history.

Don Quixote was ridiculous because he had a high tragic ideal and fought to realize it through comic means. He went out with a wooden spear and the visor hat of the barber to face the new arms of his times: the guns and the cannons. The Japanese have immense ambitions, but the means they use to realize them are entirely modernized. And the method they advance is all patience, silence and willfulness.

I will never forget the report of an Englishman about the Japanese troops in Manchuria the year before last: "They often walked fifty miles a day through mountains without roads in very cold weather. The soldiers camped in the mountains without tents and without fire. They put straw inside their clothes so that they would not freeze. They ate only rice and sometimes fish or meat. Sometimes when they did not have rice they ate frozen bread. They drank neither tea nor coffee; only water. And all this happened while they were trailed by two hundred thousand Chinese. They fought like demons. Only the army of Genghis Khan could fight like them."

I wonder what is the historical mission of the new Don Quixote of Asia?

▪ TOKYO

▪ SKYSCRAPERS, ENGLISH PARKS, double small wooden houses with charming little gardens, small aquariums with the golden fish, Parisian fashions and silken kimonos, fabrics with imprints of old impudent photographs of female and male movie stars, samisen playing their swan song and, next to them, barbaric radios and jazz. Red, yellow, and blue paper lanterns, and advertisements that look like waterfalls of electric light, dainty geishas heavily powdered, boy-like *mogas* (modern girls) with their rackets in their hands, walking in strides. Ginza, the infernal American heart of Tokyo, the dark alleys with the smiling little women at the threshold chewing melon seeds. . . .

In vain the old Japanese soul fights to save whatever it can—lanterns, kimono, samisen—but the American earthquake tears them down and raises up to the surprised Japanese sky its terrible conventionality. A day will come, and it will not be far off, when the old Japanese soul will put on her most expensive kimono, and put up the highest, most elaborate tower of her hair. She will put on powder and make-up, and one night when the radios begin to scream and the modern girls begin to drink their cocktails, she will sit on the sidewalk of Ginza and commit hara-kiri. And they will find written on her fan a sad *haiku*:

If you open my heart,
You will find the three strings of the samisen
Broken. . . .

I went with Yoshiro, a modern girl who studied in America and now works in a tourist office. It was evening, all the lights of Ginza had been lit, thousands of people, men, women, took their daily *ginbura*, their walk, in Ginza.

A gay, erotic atmosphere: the willows shine in rows on the sidewalks; the women well dressed, powdered, and made up; the yellow dandies, the *mobos* (modern boys) in their American suits; the *mogas* in their tight skirts and with their impudent glances; and here and there the arousing fragrance of a geisha who passes by still fighting valiantly in her traditional fragrant kimono.

I go with Yoshiro, a tall, determined, manlike girl, and I tell her the *haiku* which the last Japanese woman in kimono will write when she commits hara-kiri one fine evening. The modern girl laughs and looks at me ironically:

"Do you feel sorry for her? Let her commit hara-kiri so that we may escape! Let her commit hara-kiri as the bow and arrow broke into a thousand pieces when it saw the musket, as the plume feather did when it saw the pen. Pffft! Antiques! Let them go and stand at the Ethnological Museum, in its show windows, with a lot of moth balls!"

She remained silent for a moment; but she was boiling inside with anger and did not try to hold it back.

"That's enough!" she cried angrily. "It's time to stop putting on this circus and have the tourists come and loiter here. If you could know my anger and shame when old American ladies come to my office and ask me to suggest exotic sights to them: geishas and *sukiyaki* and tea ceremonies and if they could attend a Japanese wedding or funeral, as if we were monkeys!"

I tried to calm her down, but the modern girl had flared up.

"You don't know what we girls have suffered for so many years! We were hungry, but we ate little, because that was what we should do. We spoke with half a mouth, we laughed with a slow low laughter when a stranger was in front of us. Our face must be longish like a melon, our mouth like a thimble, and our knees were crooked because when we were infants they tied and distorted our feet. We never took part in sports, and we ate rice and seldom meat and thus our bodies became emaciated and deformed. And we did not marry the man we loved but the one our parents liked, and we had to worship him and call him master and put on and take off his shoes and we knew that he had mistresses but those were the traditional customs and we had to obey the 'spirits of our ancestors'! But, tell me, isn't it better to obey the 'spirits of the descendants'?"

I looked at my companion with joy. I did not have in front of me the quiet, smiling, childish eyes of a Japanese woman; the eyes of Yoshiro shone as if the first revolutionary flames burned in them. Of course, they had lost their mysterious oriental charm, but are the eyes of the Japanese women made for the tourists? This girl is a vehement transitional type who will certainly sweep away all the kimonos and the crooked knees and the oriental exotic charm. I had before me the future Japanese woman, and I felt that what this girl said was more valuable than all the erudite sociological books that have been written about Japan. And whatever she does, her wishes are of incalculable importance.

"Are you interested in politics?" I asked her.

"Very much. I read Japanese and foreign newspapers

every day. My country has a great mission, and the times we are going through are difficult. And I feel the need to see every day what my country does and which way it goes. Our responsibility is great."

"What responsibility?"

"To free Asia. All the Asians—Chinese, Siamese, Hindus. To lead them, to open a path."

"Are you dreaming of a new Genghis Khan?"

"Not of Genghis Khan. But of a new, modern, more international Meiji. Our old Emperor Meiji liberated Japan in 1868; the new one will liberate Asia."

"And if Europe and America do not want that? And if it is not to their interest to liberate Asia? Then? War?"

The girl stopped for a moment, as if she were the entire Japan and had to make a decision. She carefully weighed within her the pros and cons. Her eyebrows had come together and waved, moving up and down like scales. Finally she lifted her head and said quietly:

"War."

I shuddered. I spoke to many Japanese officials and non-officials but I never gave so much importance to an answer as I did to that of this modern girl. I felt deeply within me that the future spoke through her mouth. Suddenly she stopped before a bar.

"Don't ask me any more questions!" she said almost imperatively. "Let's have an appetizer," she suggested, as if she had suddenly regretted all she said, as if she had betrayed the secrets of her country to a foreigner.

We entered the bar. Modern girls with crossed legs drank, talked with young men, laughed. The radio screamed. Someone put an old record on the phonograph and a light old Japanese song began.

"What does it say?" I asked my companion.

"The same, the same," the girl replied, laughing. "Love, goddamn it, is always the same."

Her eyes suddenly became wild.

"I wanted to be a man!" she said. "Only the man can become completely free. The woman, regardless of what she says, cannot. Regardless of how modern our mind is, our heart always fights with very old arms."

Tokyo passes in front of me like a moving picture. An endless city. Millions of people, the third largest city in the world (after London and New York).

Asakusa, the popular noisy section around the old temple of Kannon. I pass through it slowly, trying to impress on my mind all the cheerful, festive figures who go to worship the goddess. Wooden steps, rubbed and polished by thousands of feet. At the entrance there are two large red lanterns. Broad deep trough where the faithful throw their dimes bribing the goddess of mercy. Two big wooden beasts at the entrance of the temple laugh, looking at the crowds. And underneath one of the beasts, an old blind man sells amulets to ward off the evil eye; he takes a sheet of white paper, then he smears with ink the palm of a little child and presses it on this paper, promulgating with a melodiously sad voice the miraculous imprints of the child's palms.

The temple is dimly lit by big paper lanterns. In the faint light you discern many men and women sitting with crossed legs on straw mats, groaning. A big drum beats rhythmically, heavily. Dum! dum! dum! and the people stick their foreheads to the ground and groan their magic phrase which will open paradise for them: *Namumyo horengekyo. Namumyo horengekyo!*

"What's the meaning of this?" I asked the sly monk who guided me.

He was lame, slender, cockeyed, with golden teeth, and his breath smelled of sake.

It means: "Glory to the Lotus of Truth!"

"That is the signal. When you knock on the door of

paradise and the awesome voice is heard from inside saying 'Who is it?' you will say the signal, *Namumyo horengekyo*, and the door will open."

"Are you sure?"

The shrewd monk looked at me sideways with his
cockeyed small eyes, smiled and said:

"Positively!"

This unfaithful creature smiled derisively and looked to
me, so that both our smirks would be united in faithless-
ness and irreverence. But I looked at the people piled up
in the temple with their ecstatic, radiant, almost redeemed
faces. And I turned around in my mind, through my
teeth, the exquisite words of a sage whom I don't recall:
"If you think you have found redemption, you have found
it; if you don't think you have found it, you have not!"

I buy aromatic candles, amulets and red paper fish
that bring happiness, and I leave in a hurry for the holy
house of General Nogi. I like this great silent man, and I
am in a hurry to see the house where he lived and the
room where he and his wife committed hara-kiri one
evening in 1912. Endurance, Japanese steel that bends,
makes a circle, but doesn't break. I look at the bare little
room where Nogi and his wife committed hara-kiri at the
moment the coffin of the great Emperor Meiji was to be
taken away. On the straw mat full of blood they found a
few verses:

> *My great master*
> *Goes to mingle with the gods.*
> *And I, with a burning and longing heart,*
> *Follow him to the heavens.*

Nogi followed his master in his death and together with
him became one of the fathers of his race. The Japanese
women have him in mind when they embrace their hus-

bands in bed and crave that the son they will give birth to will be like General Nogi. The heroes, I think, in a strong race are the real fathers. The spirits of the heroes, in a strong race, enter the houses at night and sleep with the women. The other fathers, the living, prepare the body; the dead heroes plant the soul. But the race must be strong for the ancestors to have such power.

And I recalled, alas, our race over there in Greece and its dead ancestors. . . .

In the heart of Tokyo there is the palace of the Mikado, surrounded by a river, behind high walls, invisible, full of mystery, unapproachable. Here the emperor is a sacred person, a true taboo, and none can raise his eyes to face him. He is not a mortal man, he is an abstract concept, a symbol, full of substance and power, a true *Tensi*, son of heavens, or *Tenno*, heavenly king. The red imperial line continues unbroken from 660 B.C. up to the present Mikado, Hirohito, the 124th.

A few years ago, Ito, a famous Japanese prime-minister, wrote these unbelievable words: "The throne was founded at the moment the sky separated from earth. Our emperor is the son of heavens. He is divine, he is sacred. All have the duty to worship him; he is inviolable." And the hero of Port Arthur, Takeo Hiroshe, wrote in verses during the Russo-Japanese War:

> *Our duty to the emperor is*
> *As endless as the dome of sky.*
> *Our duty to our country is*
> *Immeasurable as the depth of the sea.*
> *Time has come to pay our duty!"*

The simple, powerful catechism of the soldier is very characteristic: "Who is your leader?" the officer asks. "The emperor." "What is your military duty?" "To obey and sacrifice myself." "What is the great bravery?" "Never to look at the enemy, but to move forward." "What is the small bravery?" "To get angry easily and to resort to violent action." "When a man dies, what remains of him?" "His Glory!"

As long as faith lives in the soul of the Japanese, it will be fertile and it will give birth to great works; when hesitation and criticism begin, faith will be reduced to superstition and it will become sterile and humiliating, and the Japanese soul, if it is still strong, will get hold of another faith in order to be saved and give birth again.

As in science where an "hypothesis," even if it is wrong, causes the discovery of true natural laws, so a "wrong" religious or political doctrine may give birth to a great civilization. Certainly every doctrine, fortunately, is not eternal, nor is every scientific hypothesis. But the time comes when both become "false" because the human mind grows and it does not fit into its old boundaries. Then science finds a new hypothesis equally wrong but broader and more fertile and baptizes it "truth." And new discoveries begin, until they, too, end and other hypotheses take their place. And the arduous march uphill begins again. I wonder what the new doctrine of Japan will be.

"In order to understand in which direction the new Japan walks," an enlightened Japanese told me, "you must remember how our country was before it opened its doors to the Western civilization in 1854. Our emperors had been closed for centuries in the palace of Kyoto as in a monastery: all the power was in the hands of the great shogun, in his castle in Yedo, as Tokyo was called then.

"The country was divided into three hundred feuds, and the feudal lords, the daimio, were bankrupt and feeble. They had been weakened by the indolent, prodigal and sensual life of the court in Kyoto, and the greediness and suspicion of the great shogun. The famous samurai had become braggart bullies roistering through the taverns and geisha houses; people continued to die, exhausted from hunger, civil wars, earthquakes and fires. Here is what an official report of 1783 about the famine said: 'The famine is so terrible that out of five hundred families in the village only thirty have remained; all the others have died. A dog is sold for as much as eight hundred yen, a mouse for as much as fifty yen. Corpses are eaten, and some have despatched the dying and salted their flesh to preserve it as a last resort against starvation.'

"Surely we would have a social revolution, had the 'Black Ships' of Admiral Perry not appeared in the Japanese waters on a day in 1853. Japan was upset. The people were divided into two camps. But what could they do? Resist? The 'Black Ships' had cannons, they sailed against the wind without sails. The 'White Demons' were stronger; we opened the doors to them. Whatever has taken place since then has been an irresistible logical necessity. We got involved and had to go on and on. There was no going back. Because the others were so far ahead, we had to reach them. If we did not reach them, we would be lost."

The Japanese remained silent, thinking.

"No one discusses things with necessity," he said, ending his silence as if he answered his own inner contradictions. "He accepts necessity and tries, as much as he can, to change it to freedom. That's the supreme mission of a man and of a nation. To change geographic, economic and historic necessities into freedom. It was not a question of whether or not Japan should accept Western civilization; it was a necessity. The problem for us is only one: Will Japan be able to assimilate the Western civilization, as it did Hindu Buddhism and Chinese art, and give it a Japanese appearance? Many hope so, many are afraid, no one knows!"

He smiled. He shrugged his thin shoulders.

"All this is petty arguing," he finally said with contempt. "Action is what counts! Look at the Englishmen; as soon as they understand the danger of thinking, they hang a leather punchbag and begin to punch it; or they take thick sticks and hit a wooden ball; or they take a big ball and kick it. So they have escaped from thought and conquered the world!"

■ THE JAPANESE THEATER

■ A HOLY GIRL DANCER of a Shinto temple, O-Kuni—blessed be her name!—one day around 1600 left the temple, went out on the streets, stopped at a popular square in Kyoto and began to dance, ringing a bell and singing religious songs. She no longer wanted to dance in the darkness of the temple for God and the priest. O-Kuni began to dance and sing in the streets and bazaars for the vendors, the fishermen and the craftsmen.

The people rejoiced. Other female dancers also came, with their bells, their fans and their lovers—the lover of O-Kuni, Nagoya Santsaburo, was famous for his good looks—and began to improvise dances from square to square, first religious then popular, comic dances. They called these dancing games *kabuki*, which means "I am losing my balance, I make follies," or, according to a Chinese ideogram, "song-dance."

The people were taken in by this new cheerful entertainment and O-Kuni with her boy friend and a few other female dancers decided to form a permanent theatrical troupe and establish a stage. They erected their primitive stage in the dried-up bed of the Kamo River, which passes through Kyoto, and began to give their first performances —dances, songs, pantomimes, farces—with the accompaniment of drums and flutes.

The success was amazing. The large cities of Yedo and Osaka begged the troup to come so that the workers, the merchants and the craftsmen of these cities might also enjoy the *kabuki*. The tours began. Other dancers came and joined them; new theaters were established; a fresh air of joy spread each evening after work in the market places. But, as was natural, love came along with the beautiful girl dancers. The scandals started, and after the performances the dry bed of Kamo echoed with laughter and erotic cries and the honest, prudent citizens passed the bridges horrified; until one day in 1629 a terrible decree was issued which prohibited women appearing on the stage, for reasons of public morality.

A new period began. Schools opened where men could study the female roles, where they could learn to dress, walk and move like women. Some *onnagata*, men who played women, became famous for being "more women than the women." And in their private lives they spoke and behaved like women in order not to lose the tone of their voice and their womanly behavior. The acting began to acquire rules. From improvisation and game, half erotic and half comic, it started to become art. The *kabuki* became a living organization that became hungry and grabbed and digested nourishment wherever it found it. It took the fast stiff motions from the famous *Bunraku* doll theater of Osaka; it took the grandeur and opulent garments from the hieratic no spectacle; it even took many no plays, adapting them in a more popular, faster rhythm. It even took the samisen, the three-string lute that had come in 1633 from southern islands.

The child of O-Kuni kept growing, became wild, set aside the overbearing no; it conquered the cities. No had been reduced to a dummy in hieratic inertia, and no new breath blew on it to revive it; it was dying, together with the nobility, of grandeur and dignity. The *kabuki*, the urchin of the street, was fed on the jokes, the farces, the worries and the life of the people; it was a sin for a nobleman to go to these popular shows; however, at night, shadows from the aristocratic palaces edged their way through the dark streets and took refuge in the *kabuki* to see and hear this new wonder.

Here, also, the actors proved to be brave; in the midst of insults and contempt, in poverty and misery, they created a culture. The actors of *kabuki* were considered the dregs of society—something between a beggar, a pimp and a bum. *Kawaramono*, dregs of the river. In the census they used a special number for them as they did for the animals. In 1868 the great reformer Meiji agreed to attend a performance of the *kabuki*; since that day the position of the actor has been elevated and purified; he has become equal to the other members of society.

In Japan the profession of the actor had been and still is hereditary; the sons succeed their fathers and create theatrical dynasties. Thus today we have the dynasty of the great actor Kikugoro—Kikugoro Onoye the Sixth and Tatsuro Ishiwara the Seventh. When an actor has no sons, he adopts the son of some other actor or his best disciple. He who wants to become an actor must study the art from early childhood. I've seen eight-year-old children playing with unbelievable discipline and grace. The difficulties are so great, the tone of voice must become so flexible and the gestures are so stylized, according to tradition, that no one can begin to study to be an actor after he has passed twenty.

The *kabuki* is thriving today. I sit at a corner in the orchestra of the theater and I wait for the curtain to rise and my heart rejoices as I recall all these adventures of the theater: the struggle, the humiliations, and the victory of the heroic child of O-Kuni. I recall the temple of the sacred dance *Kasoga* in Nara, where the no theater was born, surrounded by hieratic stone lanterns and high dark trees. In Kyoto I often went down to the dried-up river to the cradle of the urchin *kabuki*. Poor women washed their clothes in green water, beating them against their washboards, giggling; hobos hung their rags to dry;

charming little donkeys grazed on the fields; the air smelled of soapsuds, dung and grass. And I joyfully went back and forth as if I wanted to find the spot where the rebel O-Kuni stepped with her bare feet when she began to dance, because nothing in life gives me greater joy than the small beginning of a great power.

I will never forget the sources of the Rhone in the Swiss Alps. A blue vein of water as narrow as silk ribbon edges under the green glaciers, advances hesitantly, and does not know where it will go and what will become of it. It moves on slowly, it grows, it joins with other ribbons of water; it makes a decision, it digs its path, it is not afraid any longer, it does not hesitate, it knows. It becomes broader and deeper, it waters villages, it turns mills, it floods melon fields, it passes through cities, splitting them, and it runs—it already knows where—toward the sea. I likewise admired the River Cyrus which springs bubblingly from a blue lake high in Armenia. In the same way great civilizations originate from a simple talk or from everyday needs. Surely our dancer O-Kuni had gotten angry with some priest on that day. They might have reproached her because she found a lover—and she, the little geisha of God, irritated, took her little bell and her fan and went down to the dry river to dance. She knew nothing about the future and the culture she created at that moment, and cared less. She lived only for the moment that anger had flushed her yellow powdered nostrils.

The soul of man is a wonder, a spring that leaps up from the mud of flesh not knowing where it goes and what it wants and why it has the incomprehensible urge to ascend. . . .

A mute person, dressed in black with shaven head, sits on the forestage, at the right side of the proscenium and holds two wooden rattles. He waits, immovable. We all wait with him. Now he will knock the two rattles he is holding and the curtain will open. It's three o'clock in the afternoon. That's the time that the performance begins in the famous theater, *Kabuki-za*; seven plays will be performed until eleven o'clock. On the yellow curtain high black swords are painted in rows; nothing else. The spectators in the orchestra sit on velvet seats; in the balcony some sit with crossed legs on pillows. The huge room, with a capacity of fifteen hundred people, is full; the entire month of April is dedicated to the memory of the great actor Kikugoro Onoye the Fifth. The thirty-third anniversary of his death is being celebrated, and for his sake all the great actors of *kabuki* perform plays that he liked. The program says: "Fortunate is he who happens to be in Tokyo this April!"

The mute person raises his hands: tak! tak! tak! And the yellow curtain with the black swords slowly opens. Gardens with rocks, a castle, and in the back a deep ravine and a river, with cherry-blossom trees on the precipice. At the right of the stage, three men dressed in black sit on a balcony and play the samisen. It is the chorus that will follow the drama, commenting on the landscape, welcoming the new personages and accompanying the heroes with the samisen when they rejoice or lament or dance. A narrow aisle from the left of the stage passes through the orchestra and ends at the back of the room; it is the *hana-michi*, the blossomed street by which the actors come or leave if they want to show the grandeur of tragedy.

The stage is deserted, the samisen play nervously; suddenly the chorus begins to cry with horror, "Oh! Oh! Oh!" and a terrible samurai comes out of the castle.

The weight and opulence of his costume are indescribable. A loose, dark-green kimono, with large white figures like starfish, like octopuses. A bronze helmet with two long antennae, which quiver and glisten like those of an insect. His eyebrows are slanted upwards, his mouth is thickly painted and a red smear at the right end of his lower lip distorts his mouth and gives it an expression of contempt.

He slowly descends the steps. He fills the stage, he moves slowly, heavily as if he cannot easily co-ordinate his awesome power, as if he were an entire army with vanguard, main body and tail and when he wanted to change position moved only a section; and his servants, crawling, kneeling, come running from everywhere and arrange his kimono, adjust its folds, bring him a sword. They mobilize the whole of him. I have never seen power made so visible.

This is the terrible ruler, Tsuna, who has fought with the demon, Imparaki, has defeated him and cut his arm off and now keeps it under guard in his tower. He knows that some day the demon will come and wrestle with him in order to retrieve his arm, and Tsuna waits for him, always ready. An old aunt of his comes and begs him to show her the demon's arm; the ruler orders his men to bring it. But the aunt is none other than the demon, transformed. The role is played by Kikugoro Onoye the Sixth. I cannot describe the motion of the demon, creeping, graceful and relentlessly restrained, a spring that trembles and presses to break out; but he checks himself and advances very slowly with abrupt steps that vibrate almost imperceptibly into giddy runs. And when, like lightning, he snatches his arm and begins a wild fight with the samurai, like a dizzy dance, elusive, violent, with swords and fans, you feel as if two rampant leopards are fighting and making love—then you understand that here power and grace have reached the highest peak. The peak of the leopard. There is no higher.

The drama lasts about an hour. Again the mute raps his two sticks and again the narrow curtain falls. Intermission. I go back and forth through the corridors. I explore this large theater, an entire neighborhood: the halls are full of small shops where they sell cards, toys, fans,

candy, kimonos, sandals and umbrellas. There are six restaurants, Japanese, European, Chinese. There is a clinic,
and a room with toys and nurses where they take care of
infants while their parents attend the performance. I
look at this strange backstage, but my eyes are still full of
the flight of the two great actors; I think it is one of the
spectacles that will be uprooted only with the roots of
memory.

Before the new drama begins, a unique intermezzo is
presented. The curtain rises. The stage is entirely draped
with crimson velvet. Dressed in black, two hundred actors of *kabuki* who are descendants, relatives, and suc-
cessors of the great actor Kikugoro Onoye the Fifth are
prone on the floor, as if they are worshiping. The entire
dynasty and its court. They remain for some time motionless. Then the son of the great actor rises on his
knees and begins to speak. He talks about his father,
about faith in art, about the desire to preserve their tradition and not to let their art decay. He speaks and again
bows his forehead to the floor as the curtain gently begins to fall.

The other dramas were full of supernatural creatures,
demons and exorcists, or represented simple human stories: two lovers committing suicide, a mother sacrificing
herself to save her child, a son avenging his dishonored
father. They have moderate literary value, but here you
feel that the Japanese theater was not created for the dramatists but for two great aims: to give joy to the eyes and
to exhibit the art of the actor. The art and the grace of
the staging and of the costumes are superb; the actor is
the master of the stage and is worthy of it. Intoxication
and discipline; freedom and stylization; impulse and wisdom. Such art and grace will amaze you if you follow
closely just one single detail—for example, the fan. In the
hands of the Japanese actor, the fan becomes a living
thing, an entity with a thousand faces, charming, chal-

lenging, threatening; a bird that opens and closes its wings and is lost, lightning that flashes its light on and off —red, green, blue, like a spirit. When suddenly, with an abrupt motion, the samurai opens his red fan over his head at the most critical moment of the fight, you feel as if, all at once, a terrible red bird sits on his brow and his head jets flames—and his adversary retreats, horrified.

This is a new world, full of mystery and inexpressible charm. The Japanese actor, even more than the paintings, the statues and the exotic temples, makes you feel that you have truly left the provincial point of view, that beyond the domain of the white race there is a world more profound and more dangerous because it has more grace and power. A deeper meaning.

■ JAPANESE ART

■ KANO TANYU, a great painter, lived three centuries ago. He who has seen just one of his paintings —a reed bending in the breeze, a stork looking at its image reflected on the waters—can feel the simple secret of art. With frugal means, without colors, with shades of only white and black, he reaches the most difficult peak of perfection. Rembrandt looks intoxicated when confronted with this sober artist.

One day the abbot of a Buddhist monastery commissioned the painting of a folding screen. Everyone waited impatiently for the great painter to finish his work so that they might enjoy it. Finally Kano Tanyu informed the abbot that the screen was finished. The abbot, dressed in his finest habit, came down; the painter uncovered the screen, the abbot bent over and looked: an old man with long beard stood under the trees, gazing outward. Behind him two youths stood respectfully. The abbot immediately guessed that the old man was Li Po, the great Chinese poet, who had always before been painted with a wineglass hung on his back and a waterfall running in front of him as the poet stood and admired it. In this painting by Kano the wineglass was there—but where was the waterfall?

"Is it not Li Po?" the abbot asked, surprised.

"Yes, it is Li Po."

"But then, where is the waterfall?"

The painter, silent, went and opened the opposite

145

door. The garden of the monastery appeared and, among the rocks, a small clear waterfall flowed. The abbot understood, smiled, nodded and thanked the painter with a deep bow.

Nothing illustrates so vividly as this little story the understanding the Japanese have of art. Art, for the Japanese, mingles inseparably with nature, which continues it and completes it. The work of God and the work of man are completed by being organically complemented. The painting, the statue, the temple do not stand suspended in the air; they are found in secret, deep relation with the rivers, the rocks and the atmosphere. And these in their turn are found in mystic contact with ancestors. And thus, a line of a painter, a roof of a temple, a gesture or a cry of an actor expresses the whole of Japan.

For this reason, here more than anywhere else, in order to know the complete meaning of a work of art, you must see it amid the trees and waters and the hills where it was born. As long as I stay here and go from temple to temple, this simple truth unwinds clearly in my mind. You see a sacred crimson door among the trees; you understand that you have reached a Shinto temple. You pass the door of God, you enter a long row of very old, moss-covered trees. Tranquillity spreads like moss in your bosom; you advance, you pass through a series of stone lanterns, you enter the garden of the temple; the old worm-eaten shrine shines through the trees; you bare your feet, you mount the shining steps. There is a low bronze caldron overflowing with crystal-clear water. As the clouds roll by above they are reflected on the water. A light breeze blows and the water ripples. All the natural forces here act freely without human intervention and intellectual limitation. It is as if you really were at the cool heart of the earth, full of clouds, leaves and air.

I never would have believed that with such simple means the human mind could enter the highest mysteries. Here you find yourself facing divine nakedness. Naked woman, naked water, naked divinity—all are one. Your heart overflows like the caldron of shining water at the threshold of the temple. Loves, ideas, joys, fears pass over it and flow above it, as clouds and leaves. Your entrails become fresh and cool like the green heart of the open banana leaf.

Sometimes in the Shinto temples, before you reach the last altar, huge wild figures carved on thick trunks of trees rise in small chapels. These dragons represent natural forces—fire, earthquake, flood. But you are not afraid of them. You know that they also are the spirits of your ancestors, your own forces, and you can exorcise them. You know that they are preparatory stages on your path to deliverance. You will surpass them and reach impersonal, supreme emotion in the depths of the sacred place.

Certainly a faithful Japanese feels this emotion more deeply than I. And this emotion regulates his whole life. I shall return to my country, which is full of narrow logic and smart small businessmen; but the Japanese will stay here. He will come again and again to the temple. Gradually he will transmute his viscera forever, and when he sees a man on the street, he will greet him differently; when he starts to carve wood or stone, he will blow his breath into them differently, and when in the evening after a hard day's work, he sits in the tiny garden that every Japanese house has, he will face his wife and children and the falling darkness of night differently.

So, going from temple to temple, I begin to understand Japan. I know now that the smallest movement of a Japanese is perfectly harmonized with the glistening surface of the Shinto water that reflects the world. I understand now that the Japanese paint this way because they love flowers and children so much; I begin to guess the meaning of the smile around the Japanese lips, which until now has seemed inscrutable to me. I understand now why the Japanese women walk undulatingly and what constitutes the charm that makes you forget their ugly mouths and crooked knees. And I know why in the humblest things they make—a wooden box, a knife, a small cup, a fan, a doll, a wooden sandal—there is some deep spell, love and understanding, beauty and simplicity. And their dances, their theaters, their tea ceremony, their gardens, their houses have taken on their real meaning now that I have bowed over the Shinto water of the temple and I have seen my face together with the face of Japan.

Once, years ago, I had leaned over a well together with a woman. Our two faces, the one attached to the other, moved for a moment on the dark, glistening, trembling waters. And suddenly I felt that I loved that woman.

It seems to me that I truly begin to love Japan.

■ THE JAPANESE WOMAN—

YOSHIWARA AND

TAMANOI*

■ "HE WHO DOES NOT have children," a Japanese told me one day, "does not know the *oh!* of things." And once on the Holy Mountain, passing through the wild snow-clad mountains, I stood before the cell of a hermit —a cave with two icons, a jug of water and a stool, and the old hermit sat outside and shivered. I stopped and exchanged a few words with him.

"The life you lead, my old man, is hard," I said. "You torture yourself."

"I torture myself," he replied. "But these pains are nothing, my child. The real ordeal is something quite different."

"What?"

"To have a child and lose it. That's the real *oh!* There is no other *oh!*"

Today, however, I became acquainted with another *oh!* in the narrow, crooked, crowded streets of Tokyo. An *oh!* darker and heavier and harder because it shames man. Powdered and painted heads, terrible masks that appear through little windows of doors and call out. . . . For days I had wanted to see these frightful neighborhoods in Yoshiwara and Tamanoi, but I had always postponed it because these sights provoke shame and horror

---

* Prostitution was made illegal in Japan in 1958, and the activities in Yoshiwara and Tamanoi were abolished.

that I cannot overcome. Physical and spiritual sickness and degradation of man fill my heart with indignation, not for the unfortunate who suffer, but for the human nature that can fall so low; for the flesh and soul of man that cannot withstand temptation.

But tonight I tied my heart up in a knot, I got into a taxi and said to the driver, in a low voice, because I was ashamed:

"Yoshiwara!"

As we passed through the central noisy streets, it began to drizzle; multicolored umbrellas were opened, the streets glistened. . . . The houses became lower and lower, the pedestrians fewer and the neighborhoods darker. Suddenly the Laotian paper lanterns increased, the taxi stopped.

"Yoshiwara!" the driver said to me and showed me an endless street, flooded with lights. I got out.

In the middle of the entrance to the street, there was a big triumphal arch, the famous Kuruwa, which has been so much sung by bohemian poets and wealthy revelers. For centuries Yoshiwara has been the gay kingdom of convenient love, and through this arch for centuries the samurai, the artists, and the people have passed in cheerful processions. Above the arch were written the proud words: "Listen to my voice, you who are away! Come near, take a look! Pass through the Kuruwa and you suddenly will see Paradise open before you!" Thus Hell speaks always. But let us pass through this often-crossed threshold of popular, purchasable love and let us see.

A clean street with bars, barber shops, drugstores, fruit stores. . . . Honest, middle-class citizens walk, holding bags of sweets. Quiet, as if they were going home, without hastening their steps in shame. The Japanese have not passed through the Christian anathema of flesh, and the handy pleasure is not a sin for them.

I am encouraged by this and I move on with them. . . .

On the right and the left of the street, rows of small wooden houses with curtains on the doors. Outside each threshold, behind the railings, sits a Japanese in a kimono, the "caller," who invites the passers-by. Next to him, in a well-lit window display, long like a bier, are pictures of the women of the house, and the caller cries: "Come! Look at the pictures and choose! Come, we have the most beautiful girls of Yoshiwara! Step in! One yen! One yen! One yen!"

A group of young and old men approach, look at the display carefully. I approach with them. In the background of the narrow showcase are about ten pictures of girls, whose faces are so heavily powdered that they all look alike. Their elaborate architectural coiffures, their small innocent eyes, their tight scarlet mouths—dead masks, unbearable bitterness. . . . The long bier is lit with a low green light, and as I bend over the crystal to gaze at the female bodies in a row on the cotton, suddenly it seems to me that I see drowned women staring at me under deep green waters. . . .

I move on. The next display is lighted with violet; the curtain of the door moves and a woman in a powder mask shows her head and smiles at me. At once, another appears, exactly like the first; then a third, again the same. It seems that they are deliberately made up so heavily in order to level out every individual characteristic, to be made into masks, and to have behind the masks only the female sex, as if the Orientals do not want to come in contact with a definite person, but want to enjoy an impersonal, animal-like and simultaneously religious, primitive pleasure.

I walk for hours, I look at the women. The horror that captures you here in Yoshiwara is humanly bearable. Here everything—houses, women, voices—have an air of freedom from care and of gaiety; the big horror is in the other neighborhood of pleasure, in Tamanoi. Narrow alleys, with not enough room for two men, dark, an insoluble thick smell of soap suds, carbolic acid and human stench. Thousands of crumbling shanties, a narrow window at every little door. A woman's head of indescribable tragedy appears at every pane. There is just enough room for it. The face is made up with a trowel. She smiles at every passer-by. Her smile has been crystallized, wedged between her dried powder and her thick lipstick. She does not move, does not change, stands immobile all night. . . . Sometimes the mouth moves with difficulty as it whispers a sweet, tender word, then closes again. . . .

Men pass by, an endless procession. They look at every woman carefully in order to select. Sometimes they say a word, usually a number—fifty sen, thirty sen, twenty sen (cents)—and again remain silent and go on to another door to find the item they like at a better price. . . . A drunken father drags his little son, about eight years old, by the hand. The boy wears short European trousers and a downy, broad-brimmed hat, like that of a Catholic priest. His father stops from door to door and shows him the woman, who smiles at him and calls him. But the child is afraid, and begins to cry and refuses to go on. But his father bursts out laughing and drags him to another door. . . .

I walk hastily. I cannot bear this horror. I buy two apples, as if I want to have them accompany and encourage me. I force my eyes to look at and not be afraid of the terrible heads that appear in the square windows. Like *karkan*, the Chinese torture: a pierced, very heavy plank through which they pass the head of the condemned. So these women look as if they hold on their necks the entire door, the shanty, the whole of Tamanoi, all Tokyo, all mankind. I feel ashamed, as if we men had left them to assume the heaviest responsibilities. As if these women were fighting in the most terrible position on the battlefield, and we men hid.

And suddenly I overcome the disgust. I approach a window and stop. I gaze at the mask that appears. There is so much powder on her face that as she smiles at me the crust cracks like a peeling, painted wall. But she has two human eyes. Once, in a distant northern city, I had seen a monkey behind bars, leaning her cheek on her palm, looking at me with inexpressible grief. From time to time she coughed. You felt that she complained because we had closed her in this cage, unjustly, illegally. . . . Why? Why? her sad human eyes kept asking.

I throw back my head to chase away this sad memory and I see again the woman's head in front of me, smiling at me. I struggle to make myself smile. The woman is encouraged; she says a word. I do not understand it. But the tone is so smooth, so entreating that I feel that the wall between us has fallen down. And, indeed, the little door has opened, and without being fully aware of it, I find myself sitting with crossed legs on a poor mat. Bare walls with a few pictures of sailors, a mattress spread on a straw mat. In the old times, these women bore these mattresses on their backs as they walked the streets. . . .

It is cold. The woman kneels, silent, and pushes in front of me a small brazier filled with burning charcoal.

■ THE GEISHAS

■ WHEN DANTE CAME out of the Inferno, he walked the streets, stooping, pale, with his eyes wildly staring, as if he had seen frightful, hopeless scenes. It seems that I walked the streets of Tokyo in the same way the day after Tamanoi, because a friend of mine who has lived in Japan for years grabbed me suddenly by the shoulder and shouted at me, laughing.

"What kind of face is that? You remind me of the unsmiling Florentine with your long face like a shoe last!"

I told him of my tour last evening in the "sad city." My friend frowned. He has been in Japan for twenty years. He speaks excellent Japanese and loves this country as much as his own.

"You must not leave Japan with this bitter memory," he told me. "Come with me tonight; you will see other women, full of innocence, like naked gazelles. You will see what our ancestors loved so much; the women at whose feet shrewd old Socrates himself sat as a disciple and learned the meaning of love, beauty and exaltation. You will see the fine hetaerae dressed in fragrant silk kimonos and you will sit at their feet and, if you are a good student, you, also, will learn the meaning of love, beauty and exaltation."

"I am sick and tired of masks!" I said, irritated.

"What masks?"

"The faces of the Japanese. All of them, men and women, smile like masks. And you don't know what is

behind that mask. I long to see a true face, with warm
flesh, laughing, getting angry, insulting me. I don't want
to see any more masks!"

"But there is no mask!" my friend said, laughing.
"Or, if you prefer, there is no face. And if you take off
this mask, you will find another exactly the same—up to
the end. Like the Japanese toys in which you find a doll
inside a doll and another inside the other doll and so
on to the end! There is no face! That's the face of Japan.
But let's leave the philosophies aside; it's getting dark.
Come!"

Two big cheerful paper lanterns hang from a low roof.
The door is open. We enter. A freshly washed small yard.
Tiny old pine trees in flowerpots, a stone basin full of
water with yellow flowers floating on it. In the portico,
five or six smiling girls appear. They kneel in a row; they
bow. Then they rise and their cheerful voices start:

"*Irasshai mase! Irasshai mase!* Welcome!"

They take off our shoes, they put on soft leather slippers and show us the way. We climb upstairs. The polished wood shines and it smells of cypress. Small rooms
like cells, closed by folding screens. In every cell covered
with light straw mats there is a low, small lacquered table,
soft pillows, a brazier. A *kakemono*, a picture hanging on
the wall. And in a small vase a few flowers.

We sit down on the floor with crossed legs. They offer
us tea and pastries made of rice. Then sake and pine nuts.
A little girl enters and bows and her little nose touches
the straw mat:

"The bath is ready!" she says.

We enter the bath for only two minutes, just to re-
fresh our bodies, then we put on the *yukata*, a light
kimono like a pajama, and we sit down again on the
straw mat with crossed legs.

Joy, purity, sweetness! As I drink the lukewarm sake I

think how simple life is, just like this cell; what an innocent and sacred contact love is, just like the water the thirsty drink, bare without any sentimentality. I feel the air of the ancient Greek understanding of love here—giving joy to the woman and receiving joy from her is not a mortal sin.

The geishas surround us, they gaze at us and laugh. Their eyes are clear, pure, without impudence and overt display, as if we went to a friendly home where they loved us and had a party for us. A mature geisha, who does not dance any more, and only plays the samisen, rises. My friend caresses the little geishas around him and explains to me that up to their fifteenth year, a geisha is a student, a *maiko;* she learns how to dress, to put on make-up, to dance, to speak, to be liked by men. Then when she reaches her sixteenth year, she is a perfect geisha and performs her duties; she goes where they invite her, she dances, plays the samisen, entertains men, gets paid, and returns to her mama—her matron, who bought or rented her from her parents and now feeds her, brings her up, dresses her and collects her receipts.

The mature geisha sits in the corner, puts her samisen on her knees, takes from her bosom a big triangular ivory pick and begins to tune the three strings. The youngest geisha, a tyro, jumps up to dance. She stands in the middle of the floor, kneels and bows before each of us silently. A small charming girl wearing a green kimono embroidered with cherry blossoms. The dance begins. A quiet, simple pantomime that presents her waiting for her beloved; she pretends to take a love letter from her bosom, read it and put it again in her heart. She waits, then suddenly starts, exclaiming joyfully as she sees her beloved appear.

The dance ends, the girl salaams again, touches her forehead on the straw mat, bows before each of us and comes to sit down near us, smiling. But the samisen continues to play, and now the mature geisha begins to sing, continuing the theme of the dance: *Tatsue hi no naka mizu no soko—mirai madema misto yato!* ("And we shall pass through flames and seas, united, man and woman, even beyond death!")

The cheeks of a third geisha burn. She is about twenty years old. She leaps to dance her favorite dance. She dances faster and more impatiently. The beloved has come and has left. Now she dances, cheerful and satisfied. As she remembers her experience with him she rejoices. Her kimono is black with big gold lotuses; sometimes in the fury of the swirl it opens and her pink inside gown shows. When her dance is finished, she also bows and comes to sit near us, breathing heavily. We play, laugh, chat. I request my friend to ask the older geisha, who played the samisen, what the greatest joy of her life was. But she remains silent. We ask her again.

"I don't remember any joys," she answers. "I remember only sorrows. When I was seven years old, my father sold me because he had many debts. And as soon as I was bought, I began to study dance, samisen, songs, in order to be liked by men. Hard, very hard work."

I ask the little one, who looks like a furry cat, leaning on a copper brazier.

"What is your greatest desire?"

She blushes and bends over the fire. We beg her to tell us but she does not answer. And then the oldest laughs softly, an embittered laugh, and says:

"To get married! What else? To find a man to take her away from here! That's what we all want!"

The atmosphere becomes heavy; I repent a thousand times for asking silly, hopeless questions that have upset them. The old geisha leans her samisen again on her knees and begins the song: "I have been a geisha here for many years, and I wait for my beloved. And today at dawn I dreamed that he came; I woke up and I cried and cried and I still cry. . . ."

The other two geishas jump up and begin to dance. An erotic, quiet chase without any impudent gesture. Perhaps the man and the woman are together and play. They play innocently and cheerfully like two little goats in the grass.

They bring another small bottle of sake and oysters. The small room with its yellow straw mats shines quietly, mystically, like a temple full of little red lanterns, like a temple at the period of its long night rites. There is a smell of sake, of oysters and of powder that melts in human perspiration. And when we wake up at dawn, the two girls kneel and touch the straw mat with their foreheads and bid us farewell; we feel as if we had come out of a garden full of flowers and had retained in our hands and hair a very sweet and bitter aroma of blossoming almond trees.

■ FAREWELL TO JAPAN

■ This mission is completed; our wanderings on the distant Queen of the Pacific with her thirty-eight hundred islands have come to an end. We have seen, we have heard, we have rejoiced, we have grieved; the entire cycle has closed. What still remains? To say good-by.

I bring to mind what I have seen. *Ills:* the pale girls in the factories, the workers' ghettos in Osaka and Tokyo, the shuddering Tamanoi with the masks that appear at the doors. *Joys:* Nara, Kyoto, statues and paintings, exquisite gardens, the tragedies of no, the performances of *kabuki,* dances that will delight my eyes until the earth swallows them up, cherry blossoms, the geishas who danced one night. . . .

I think there is no country in the world that reminds me more than Japan of what ancient Greece might have been in its most shining moments. As in ancient Greece, so in old Japan and here in whatever of it still lives, even the smallest thing that comes from the hands of man and is used in his everyday life is a work of art, made with love and grace. Everything comes out of agile, dexterous hands, which crave beauty, simplicity and grace—what the Japanese call in one word: *shibui* ("tastefully bare").

Beauty in everyday life. And many other similarities: both peoples had given to their religion a cheerful aspect and had placed God and man in goodhearted contact. They both had the same simplicity and grace in dress, food and abode. They had similar celebrations devoted to the worship of nature, the *anthesteria* and the *sakura*; and also from the same root (the dance) they produced the same sacred fruit, the tragedy. Both peoples had tried to give to physical exercises an intellectual aim. The Japanese worship exercise with the bow. Why? This is how a Japanese instructor of gymnastics justified it to me: (1) the bow presupposes thought. You accustom yourself to thinking before you speed the arrow, and this habit is necessary in your everyday life, if you want to acquire great moral power; (2) the bow intensifies discipline. It accustoms you to remaining cool-headed, and this has incalculable value in the life of man; (3) the bow teaches you to make every movement gracefully.

The ancient Greeks received the first elements of their civilization from the Orient and from Egypt, but they succeeded in transforming them and in freeing the sacred silhouette of man from monstrous gods by giving human nobility to the monsters of mythology, theology and fear. In exactly the same way, the Japanese took their religion from India and the first elements of their civilization from China and Korea, but they, also, succeeded in humanizing the physical and the monstrous and in creating an original civilization—religion, art, action—adapted to the stature of man.

This is one of the faces of Japan—the face of beauty. But it has another face, austere, hard, determined. And this countenance reminds us of the face of Soviet Russia. The same worship of the machine, the same awareness of danger surrounding them, the same determination to reach and surpass the West. The same gigantic jumps in industry and likewise a secret ideological goal beyond industry. The same faith in Messianic world mission. And the two peoples are in the same first stage in the execution of that mission: the conquest of Asia.

A slender Japanese teacher, with the teeth of a boar, told me:

"I accept that our national history, as we teach it, is a little staged; it does not report verified events, it does not have a scientific aim. Its aim is moral: to give to youth models of bravery and sacrifice for our country and our race. We have no need of erudite historians and critics; we have need of brave souls ready for sacrifice. We must, we must create such souls, otherwise we are lost. Because, don't forget, the Japanese soul rotates around these two poles: (a) it feels a great danger from without; (b) it feels a great mission from within.

"Danger: We feel that we are surrounded by terrible enemies. We must become powerful. Army, navy, air force, agriculture, industry, commerce, all must reach their highest point of development and strength. But as we become more powerful, so the danger grows, because our strength forces our enemies to intensify their efforts and ally themselves against us.

"Mission: We feel that we have the responsibility to awaken and liberate Asia. We don't forget what a great prophet of China, Sun Yat-sen, said in a speech in 1924 in Kobe: 'Asia has twelve hundred million people; Europe has only four hundred million. If all the Asians unite, we shall be able to see freedom.' We don't forget these words; our responsibility is great because we are the head of Asia."

The yellow little teacher spoke and his neck stretched like that of a plucked rooster and his voice became hoarse. And like him, 233,862 Japanese teachers will cry when they gather the young generation around them and shout: "Don't be pygmies any longer and don't let them deride you! Take physical exercises! Grow tall! Eat meat! Become strong! Sharpen your wits, your body, your heart! Look at the machines, the airplanes, the steamships, the cannon, the factories! Be alert! If we don't become better than the white people, we are lost! Look at the earth! Resurrect your ancestors! Follow their commands: silence, discipline, determination! Asia belongs to us! The world belongs to us! *Panjai Nippon!* Long live Japan!"

That is what the Japanese hoarse rooster cries, and opposite him the Russian, too, swells his chest and cries. And between them Asia calls its innumerable chicks.

The old Japan of beauty—with its kimonos, its lanterns, its fans—disappears, vanishes. The new Japan of force, with its factories and cannons, wakes up and grows wild. And the rising sun in its flag surprisingly resembles a burning-hot cannon ball. Will Japan ever be able to create a synthesis out of its two fundamental components, beauty and power?

Let us hear the voice of a young Japanese prophet, Hanni Ito. I like this young man because he dares say "I" and mean all his race. I like the purity and youthfulness and prophetic audacity of his gospel, the "New Orientalism." Whatever he says is precious because it enlightens the present-day critical, still chaotic moment of the Japanese rush upward:

"What is the New Orientalism? We believe in the Rise of the East. Western civilization is rotten and inane, as the waves of capitalism that have swept qualitative virtue from the earth have clearly shown us. Oriental civilization is deeper than the Pacific Ocean; it is still in the springtime of its youth. The long-awaited day when the East will flower has come. The new international way of life will bloom on the Chinese continent; the flower of friendship between the Japanese seaman and the Chinese peasant must blossom. The two big brothers of the East must get up and walk hand in hand.

"Let's raise our material civilization in the East, so that we may make our workers enjoy their labor. Let's use capitalism only as long as we need it to make our life happy. How dreadful are the countries which pile up mountains of food while thousands of souls die of starvation! Let's chase away poverty and misery from this world! As the spirit is found within the flesh, so happiness is found within materialism. Arts, religions and songs can be born out of it. But the chaos that is called 'our times' cannot make materialism flower. We must intensify our production to its utmost limit and share the goods of our production with everyone. That's the hope of New Orientalism!"

"Listen, O Japanese! Japan can become the savior of China as China can also save Japan. It is not correct to say that China is of interest to us not as a people, but only as a customer. The Chinese are a great people, very ancient, yet also truly new and their soil is virgin. China is not Marxist nor Fascist, nor imperialist, nor colonial. It is virgin. Its fate is united with that of Japan. If in a world war, Japan is defeated by the white people, all the Orient will darken, because no nation in the West knows the meaning of justice and love. If, however, Japan wins, then China also will be liberated, and British India and French Indo-China as well; the whole East will be liberated from the materialistic white civilization. Save China from the arrogant, capitalistic West! Save Japan! Unite the continental soul with the spirit of the islands! Create a new Orient. A wide red sun is the flag of New Orientalism; under this flag we shall fight for the happiness of the Orient and of mankind!"

These words of the young yellow prophet go back and forth in my memory like flames as from the fast-moving train I watch Japan go by. Like a harpy I discern the stunted Japanese peasants bending over their rice fields, sunk in the mud up to their knees. The cherry blossoms have already withered. Other trees begin to blossom now, the wheel of life turns on, the first wisterias hang like violet grapes and fill the air with their fragrance.

In the train I look and bid farewell silently and motionlessly to the pale, smiling Japanese women, loaded with their infants wrapped on their backs. I look at them as at great warriors. How different the Japanese woman is from posters or from romantic, superficial legends. A delicate doll with an elaborate coiffure and with high wooden sandals, who knows how to smile, to bow, to put on and take off her kimono. But when you come here you soon feel that behind this powdered mask lives and struggles a person full of will power, patience and bravery. And brave love. *We are*, says the woman in a Japanese folk song, *you and I are the two pieces of a pine leaf that dry out and drop without separating!* Her external sweetness does not originate from her weakness but from her disciplined will power, which can face any misfortune without wavering. Regardless of how poor and unfortunate she is, she never complains. And she freely accepts her fate, as the good warrior accepts his position in the battle.

■ FUJI

■ THE TRAIN, GROANING, spurns the mountains
and the plains; Japan passes by. A limpid sky, the clouds
scattered away. The mountains and the shores laugh
lightly in a transparent atmosphere. The face of no other
country resembles that of Greece so much as the face of
Japan. Lacy shores, blond sandy beaches, fishing villages,
boats like arrows with square dark sails. I open my eyes,
I open my mind, I fight to keep in my memory the lines,
the colors, the faces, the joys, the griefs, the anxieties
that I have lived through in this country, all the airy play
that vanishes. . . . I struggle to condense all the Japanese panorama into a unified image, into a rich and simple thought. I wonder what will filter and remain in my
mind ten, twenty years from now. A lot of riches, a multitude of diverse elements that cannot be made into a
unit.

And suddenly the solution! The outline that I sought,
the simple line that has room for all, the salvation. In the
train coach all men and women suddenly get up, full of
emotion. Windows are opened, mothers lift their children high; they extend their hands toward the right—out
there—and joyfully cry: "Fuji! Fujisan!" I leap up. I have
been in Japan for many weeks and I have not yet seen the
holy mountain. The sky has been covered, it has rained,
the sacred mountain has been hidden behind dense,
fleecy clouds. And now, let me turn to the right myself,

let me shake my head a little, my eyes will be filled with happiness.

I remain motionless for a few seconds. I do not know which is the greatest happiness: standing at the threshold of joy and saying, "If I want, I'll get in; if I don't, I won't. I am free!" Or, without losing a moment, passing the threshold and entering. I think the trembling on the threshold is the supreme happiness. For a few seconds I bridle my craving to turn and look. I guess that this is the ultimate, the true, unmasked face of Japan, and that this will give me the answer to all my questions.

I turn. Sky-high, pure white, snow-clad from the foot to the summit, disciplined in the simplest curves, full of grace and power, airy, tranquil and silent, the holy mountain of Japan is silhouetted on the sapphire sky.

One day, as I looked at Mount Hymettus from his study, Ion Dragoumis,* a brilliant man full of contradictory forces and lofty anxieties, turned and said to me, tightening with bitterness his thick, sensual lips:

"If I had seen this mountain every day with pure eyes, my life would have been different!"

The Japanese see Fuji with pure eyes. Surely, looking at it, their souls take in its silhouette, austere, restrained, full of grace. This mountain is the true ancestor god, who created in his own image the Japanese. Legends, gods, fairy tales, phantoms, all the play of the Japanese imagination, were also created in his own image.

All the children of Japan have drawn Fuji in their school copybooks innumerable times, and from doing so they have learned to draw firm, simple lines that combine power and grace. Fuji subjugated the Japanese hands into its rhythm, and in the smallest thing, carved in wood, stone or ivory, you will discern the nobility of Fuji's form, the decisive flow without vain unnecessary

---

* A nationalist Greek leader and writer, who greatly influenced Kazantzakis in the early part of his career.

curves. The heart of Japan is not, as the Japanese song says, the cherry blossom; the heart of Japan is Fuji: an indomitable fire, covered, in a disciplined way, with untrodden snows.

When General Araki sent his mother, who was dying, a small piece of paper on which he had drawn Fuji to tell her that he could not come to see her because his military duty detained him, surely his dying mother would immediately have understood the meaning of his painting. Because Fuji is, in the inner language of the Japanese, the holy ideogram which means duty.

I look at the holy mountain and my heart fills with response. Unquestionably when every Japanese gazes at Fuji—and he always does—his heart fills with a better and deeper response. A country that has such a mountain as the supreme regulator of its life is certainly a great country, which unites power and grace—silent, determined, dangerous.

HIDEYOSHI

■ HIDEYOSHI*

(*Returning victorious from China*)

God has dawned, the light stirs in the forest,
Bathed, pale in the great night-rain,
The lean-boned female country shines.
The ancestors leap out of the net
Of her entrails, put on their best
And make way to welcome Hideyoshi.
The flowering cherry tree's tempestuous flurry
Breaks sweetly out upon her rich kimono,
Her crimson clogs revealed in haste
Come loose, all light her ankle shines,
Descends along the blue
And on her ivory comb a golden,
Newly carved *haiku* cries to the sun:
"A thousand good welcomes, my love,
With all the fires and coolness of May."
But he, erect on the bowsprit, with the crust
Of war still in his hair, indifferent,
Surrenders to the wings of the gust,
Short, deformed with jutting ugly mug;
This hunchback plucked away
At the clipped-off wings of Victory, the Siren;
The castles, the silks of all China,
The gardens, her waters and watermelon fields,
All in his hands—and he dying of starvation.
Children, wines, women—all outbursts

---

* Translated from the Greek by John Chioles.

Of burning thirst upon his hopeless bosom;
In his mind he used to scare away the caravans
Of his imagination, and the sacred fairy tales
Of virtue and of honor, and now, laughing,
Undresses on his lap, the truth.
On the whitewashed sky's journey and return,
The stars went off and on with ease
In his haughty mind's madness
And in his apelike heavy embrace,
While he played the open-close game
With his blue silk fan in the night.
He thirsts and hungers and in the rich meadow
Of loneliness, within the passion of his mind,
He wanders alone; so in the darkness
Of his sacred curling silence he stands speech-
    less;
And full of joy, he harvests from the earth
Freedom's blossomed thorn.
Within the deep armpit of death
He built a nest and there laid down
With confidence all his eggs.
The warder of the soul was crushed
And without bridles, without rules
The lawmaker lives and reigns.
Standing on the prow he feels on one shoulder
The jumping spirit of joy, and on the other,
The terror look from a fat crow.
And from the land a great clamor was heard,
Cheers, welcomes, flutes,
The garrulous echoes on the seas,
The doves set fast sail in the light,
The yellow ant-swarm of earth
Waves the banners done in silk;
The whole country growing taller
To reach her short-spruced son,
His clan grow wings in their kidneys,

All flesh turns to soul in haste
And in the exalted heads the soul turns fire,
Setting the froth of the sea in flames.
And he, tired and sick, rushes upon
The beloved shore and palms
A lump of earth, crushing it to dust.
Silent, he looks at the ant-swarm on the quay
And the far-off mountains and the blossomed
Trees and the sky's empty dome—
And Victory at once and hopeless became
A smoke-trail wing and vanished.
The redeemed brains turn on a smile
Surpassing glories, honors and passions,
And rejoice in the lucid tranquillity
Of dream's barren oblivion.
"Begin!" The moving eyebrows give
A slow signal to start the revelry,
His glance, shining like a ruby,
Heavy, nails itself on the dances
And, starving, grazes like a bull
On hands and feet of youths and maidens.
His brains, the voracious tentacles of octopus,
Slow and silent suck the flesh,
And all the breasts crackle like pomegranates.
Upon the precipice of Nothing burst those fiery
Fruitful orchards, the hearts, and the smell
Of Death is jasmine and the bosoms
Uplift the sweetest bastion of man;
Bitter, happy, shameful, heart-rending, the
        beds—
Over all that stinking-skunk woman is master.
Night fell, the lanterns are lit,
The dandies and dancers and madams slip out
To the festive halls of the palace;
Deep frigates sail along the harbor
And slave girls are loaded with food,

Gold for Hideyoshi, gifts from kings.
But he leaps up, heavy, with brimstone
Fumes from armpits and from nostrils;
With red lacquer he paints his wounds,
And ragged, barefoot, on the steps
He stands like a mask gazing down
At the slow climb of the bowed, kowtowing,
Rich and golden-saddled royalty.
The ancestral cry is dragged through his en-
      trails,
Like a naked, rusty, starving army band
That licks its lips and drools and raises
Thousands of thick necks, phalli, and cries out:
"Eat and embrace for us, too, Grandson!"
The whole thick dark race tingles
His arms, his loins, his throat
And the fickle mind is stunned with fear.
A thousand-year-old hunger tightens
His guts, and from the army of his dead
The temples of Hideyoshi tremble.
Pitiless, awake the stars keep watch,
And holy Fuji rises in his brain,
The soul charges on, scares away, claps its hands,
And pushes the ancestors back to Hades with
      wrath,
Raising its rags into a flag.
He no longer wants to eat, nor drink, he is set
      free—
And happy!—from every hope and ideal;
He no longer wants his good deeds
To set a trap for God, now he leaves
His new soul erect to scatter in the wind.
The earth howls at the far end of his brain—
Sacred, tall drunkenness flogged him—
He lets out a cry and storms into the wild
Lit courtyards of the palace and forces out
In haste with lashes of the whip whole clusters

Of women, violin players and kings.
He blows, and the stained revelry
Of the earth goes out—dances, gods, wines, candles—
And she disperses like frost, the daughter
Of our imagination and our mind, she who moans
The great architectonic of the wind.
Pure light has been set free from anguish,
Hideyoshi crosses to his chambers
With sparkles flying off his black footstep
And reaches at last the sacred leaves of the heart,
The immaculate leaves of loneliness, and enters.
A deep garden within unconquerable walls,
Without water, without a single tree, only the spider
Who weaves time and the rocks that rise
One after the other on the battle line.
The water lines are steaming like ammunition men,
And in the way they lean frightened upon their other,
So does a tiger jump silently from ridge
To ridge holding one of her cubs
Wound up like a ball in her teeth.
The brains from joy are frisked
And he on guard caught the tiger in surprise:
"Yoo-hoo, Good fortune with your dung-heap bitches,
There is no food here nor drink; I stand
Guard and drive far away your race!
Cry of loneliness, my companion,
No eagle-like offspring nor vultures for you, so long,
O barren eagle nest on the cliff, my heart!"

PART II:

CHINA-1935

■ CHINA,

THE TURTLE OF NATIONS

■ My friend Liang-Ke, in his blue silk robe, his round mandarin cap, his black satin slippers, stood next to me on the prow of the ship. We gazed together at the sandy shores of China which we were approaching.

Rainy morning, gray sky and sea, hungry sea gulls flying over our heads. Far away in the subdued light of a spring day after rain, the farms gleamed full of emeralds. "China, China . . ." I was humming in my mind, and my heart was beating.

Chinese junks with broad raised green and red sterns, with dragons carved on the prows, and yellow little men going callously up and down the ropes. A fishing boat with a queer coldness passed scratchingly close to the ship. Two Chinese men were standing up pouring sea water on the taut sail, while another one knelt, holding the steering gear tightly. For a moment their white teeth shone, and then they disappeared again in the waves. I had just time enough to see the dragon of the prow—black with orange lines, the jaws open and the forked tongue flaming out of it. And his goggling red eyes staring at the muddy waters and threatening the evil spirits of the storm.

My friend Liang-Ke rubs an amber bead in his thin fingers and his slanted eyes laugh. On the ship I have often seen him dip his hand in water and slowly caress his amber. "Thus," he says, "the skin of our fingers can preserve its sensitivity. And you know how useful this is in life: love, statues, fruits, precious woods, silk fabrics, all need a sensitive skin. Even ideas!"

179

Now his voice comes again, sweet, low, with a slight shade of irony:

"When you reach the heavenly kingdom which, they say, is made of mud brought down by the rivers, and of the ashes—the hair, brains, flesh—of our ancestors, what do you expect to understand?"

"I am not coming to understand," I answered, annoyed a little by the teasing and tired tone of the voice of the refined old Chinese. "I am coming to saturate my five senses. I am not a sociologist—thank God!—or a philosopher or a tourist."

"What are you, then?"

"My forefathers, the ancient Greeks, said that the soul is the simultaneous exercise of all the senses. I am such a soul—an ephemeral animal with five tentacles caressing the world. I perform this duty as best I can; and thus I am not afraid either of irony or of disappointment. China for me is a new meadow where my five senses can graze."

The sensitive Chinese smelled his lump of amber and smiled:

"Have you noticed," he asked me, changing the subject, "how amber smells when you rub it? And my fingers feel as though they were giving off sparks. . . ."

We remained silent. The sun had risen a little and the shores of China could be seen clearly; the first little houses began to appear, mud on mud. Beyond, you could imagine the entire body of China. The endless muddy plains of Kwangsi, Honan, Szechwan and the vast "Chinese Plain" which is a thousand kilometers long and five hundred kilometers wide and feeds over two hundred and fifty million people.

The mountains go up in steps, the level of China rises as you move westward until it culminates in the mysterious Tibet and the eternally snow-clad Himalayas. And between the mountains flow the great rivers, the Yellow, the

Blue and Yangtze. And up north, a dragon thirty-three hundred kilometers long and from eight to ten meters high guards the borders. The Chinese Wall, the only man-made structure visible from the moon. . . .

And on this vast yellow threshing floor, over half a billion bodies move like ants: coolies, mandarins, merchants, fishermen, peasants. Some with pigtails, others with shaven heads. The northerners, tall, stout, with wild Mongolian blood; the southerners, sickly, thin, impudent, and agile like monkeys.

Empire, democracy, communism, chaos. Generals are sold and bought; they move from camp to camp dragging the hungry, ragged masses behind them like multicolored tails. Whoever offers most—Japanese yen, English pounds, American dollars, Russian rubles. There is no country, no race, no language, no religion. A mixture of races. And every Chinese has in his yellow bosom a multitude of souls. Barbarism and refined decadence, senile infantilism and primitive crudity, atheism and mysterious complex religious preoccupations, unbearable filth and, next to it, jasmine and roses. . . . Lips afroth with rabies. Then suddenly an old mandarin passes by, his face shining with refinement, and you feel that this Chinese has passed by all the crying and the laughter and his lips have caught the breath of life, the smile, the supreme flower of wisdom. . . .

The most ingenious worm on earth, the silkworm, is the true symbol of China: nothing but belly and mouth, it crawls over the mulberry leaves, eats, defecates and eats again—a lowly, filthy tube with two holes. And suddenly all the fodder becomes silk, the miserable worm is wrapped up in the wealth of its ingenuity and it sprouts, in the course of time, two white fluffy wings. No other culture has so much poetry and sensitivity as the Chinese. Man has never redeemed his spirit from mud so completely as the Chinese. By what method? By the sunset, following the rhythm of things, as an old Chinese wise man has said; or as the silkworm would say, by eating as many mulberry leaves and filling his stomach as full as he can.

And thus everything here is sanctified. Because everything emanates from the spirit, passes through the most greasy and indescribable substance and returns again to spirit. The soil is impregnated with the rotten bodies of the ancestors. The air is thick like water because it is full of mystic powers, good and evil, higher than man. The power of Tao, the primeval divine substance, is everywhere and sanctifies everything. Once the great sage Chuang-tze was asked: "But where is what you call Tao?"

"There is nothing in which it is not found."

"Tell me exactly where it is."

"For example, it is found in this ant."

"Is it found even lower than that?"

"Yes, it is in this grass."

"And even lower?"

"Yes, in this stone."

"Even lower?"

"Yes, in man's excrement."

We entered deep into the Gulf of Po Hai; we anchored in Tientsin, the port of Peking. Low houses surrounded by river mud and cow manure; women in black trousers, with huge hips, sit on the soil and give the breast to their babies while others jump like magpies with their deformed feet. Crowds of children in rags or stark naked, with swollen bellies, wail in the mud. Men sit indifferent before their threshold performing their physiological functions with a serene expression on their faces. A stink like that of spoiled fish or rotten eggs spreads from the ground and bathes you; the air has something thick and indescribable about it.

"How is your sense of smell getting along?" asked my friend Liang-Ke, laughing.

"It's enjoying itself, it rejoices," I replied. "The Tao is everywhere."

My friend remained silent for a moment. His yellow face became serious. You could feel the ancient culture of his race in his refined features, in the lively movement of his eye, in the cut of his lips, in his high, unwrinkled forehead. His diaphanous flesh was full silk like that of the silkworm at its highest stage of development. After a brief silence he opened his thin lips and said with barely perceptible malice:

"Don't think it will be so easy for your five senses to browse in China and endure the filth and stench and the horrible spectacle of nakedness, hunger, sickness. Standing injustice. Try to see the white men sucking the blood of China and remain indifferent and smiling. It's not so easy. It takes terrific endurance. I remember . . ."

He paused as if he hesitated to speak. He threw a quick piercing glance at me, thought for a moment, and then suddenly made his decision.

"I remember when I was young and I had just returned from Paris. I had completed my studies; I was bringing new ideas to my country. My father, an old mandarin, smiled but said nothing. One day he received an invitation: black, thick letters on a precious red paper. He called me and said: 'Go. You have come from Paris with new ideas. This dinner will do you a lot of good.'

"I went. It was summer. The dinner was given in the garden of a big aristocratic house. The guests were noble mandarins, most of them old gentlemen with small eyes, sensual lips and expert hands. The dinner was given in honor of a dignitary unknown to me, a rich old man dressed in silk and wearing a large ruby on the top of his black cap. They put him in the seat of honor, opposite the door, on a high throne. Facing him, in a humble position, the host sat on a stool. They served the most rare and intricate dishes, the most refreshing drinks; at every moment we bowed and drank toasts to the health of the old man who sat on the throne in the middle, all smiles, dignity and sweetness. At the end of the dinner, the host rose, bowed three times and proposed a toast. For years, he said, he had looked at the sky and longed for this moment. What a great honor for him to have such a nobleman step into his poor home. What a joy for him tonight to open his eyes and see him.

"The old man thanked his host, praised the dishes, the garden, the host, the guests. We stayed a little longer, chatted about flowers, women, the moon. Then we got up. The dinner was over. The doors were opened. It was already midnight. We stood in two rows bending to the earth to greet the old man as he passed between us. His rich silk litter came and waited before the door. The old man had passed through the garden, reached the gate and was putting out his foot to step across the threshold.

"At that moment, one of our company leaped up, drew his sword and like lightning cut off the head of the old man. For a moment the headless body stood tottering and then rolled noiselessly as far as the middle of the street. The attendants bowed and then drew the curtains of the litter as if their master were inside. The host bowed deeply and closed the door."

My friend Liang-Ke looked at me, smiling, and paused.

"Why did they kill him? Why?" I cried, shivering.

"The old man had decided to die," my friend responded quietly. "He wanted to protest with his death against the decadence of our country, against the young people who returned from abroad bringing new white gods. He had arranged it with his best friend, the host. And everything took place in order, according to tradition. I saw you shiver. Hold fast. You've reached China."

◼ PEKING

◼ COULD PEKING BE the most beautiful city I have ever seen in the world? Perhaps I merely glanced at it for the first time at a felicitous moment.

It was twilight, and from afar on the vast dusty plain the smoky walls of the three cities of Peking, the one after the other—the Chinese, the Tartar and the Imperial—suddenly shone. Cyclopean walls, thirty-three kilometers in circumference, fourteen meters high, twenty meters wide at the bottom and sixteen at the top. Half-demolished towers, castle gates three floors high, with roofs raised toward the edges, with bull heads on each corner to chase the evil spirits from the holy city with their bronze horns.

Once upon a time, silk yellow flags with green dragons waved on these walls and golden bells joyfully rang on the towers. Today, grass waves at the summit of the ruins and swarms of impatient hungry crows hover as if they were flying around a carcass. China is all grass, ruins and crows; the stones are broken and dislocated, the grass dominates the statues, the ivy ascends and tightly enfolds the towers.

But this was a spring evening, long rows of acacias around the walls had blossomed, the fragrance of the flowers struggled to overcome the stench of China's dead bodies. Multicolored living crowds moved with us, buzzing under the vaulted castle gates. Fat, slanty-eyed Tibetans, hairy Manchurians, gigantic, mysterious Mongolians, slim monkey-like Chinese with long pigtails on the backs of their heads, men and women of the desert with their slender feet, their sacked dry bodies and their infuriated huge eyes. Along with us also entered the good little donkeys of the Orient, full of dust and patience, and the two-humped camels with their wide paws, and herds of pigs, and Tartar women with their high cork heels and the paper flowers on their hair, and Chinese women with their atrophied, deformed feet, and Buddhist monks in strange frocks. . . .

The blossomed acacias remained behind us. And the sharply pungent, thick smell of China rose to stifle us once more: a stench of warm urine, of rancid castor oil and of sour human sweat. Clouds of dust are raised by the soles of our feet; the streets, the temples and the houses decay, the dead rise like mounds of soil from the earth, the rotten flesh of China enters your throat and goes into your lungs. When we passed the castle gate and everyone, men and animals, followed his own way, another exotic vision filled my ears, my eyes and my nostrils: Peking. Endless broad streets like dried-up river beds; and from everywhere, narrow, winding brooks, the alleys; low leper-eaten houses, cool workshops where they beat iron and bronze, refined lacy carvings on the doors, thousands of men and women in blue clothing, and against the golden-green twilight sky a grass-covered pagoda rises like a huge cactus.

The Chinese banners bedeck the air, longish red and black signs, upon which are interwoven thick characters with a mysterious spell—as if their alphabet were the dark jungle where the old snakes of wisdom mingle erotically and wrestle with fury. Red acacias climb the walls. Their light fragrant clusters hang over stinking housewomen sitting in heaps, like swept up piles of dirt, in their small yards and delousing their babies. Two coolies bent over a barrel full of swamp water dip their huge wooden ladles and water the street. The dust settles on the ground while the stench rises up. Men and women pass by and breathe comfortably the evening Chinese scent, and only a delicate Westernized Chinese girl grabs her handkerchief and muffles her small, sensitive nose.

On a cool square a multitude sits cross-legged. In the center, a girl, slender, with disheveled hair, holds the large scissors which she opens and closes continually while she sings and dances slowly. A harsh voice, a hyena howl, an incomprehensible harmony. An old woman sprawled on the ground, stooping, bald, plays a strange elongated lute. Nearby, an old man with glasses and sparse gray beard and two or three thick hairs on his upper lip is sitting on a stone reading a religious book. As he fans himself, his body from the waist up moves rhythmically with his monotonous voice in a lamenting lullaby. And all around, women listen to him, gaping, with bleary eyes plagued by flies. Sweltering heat. And across at the butcher shop the butcher hangs his jacket over a loin of beef.

Two-wheeled carriages drawn by the coolies who run, panting. The sidewalks are covered with goods—old eggs preserved in lime, innumerable pickled vegetables, sour fruit. And next to them, the fairy-tale shops that sell silk lanterns, ivory fans, precious green gems and transparent porcelains with light drawings. And other darker shops that sell all the oriental love secrets: ointments for raising the eyelashes, herbs for rediscovering youth, secret potions to attract men, women and boys.

The multicolored lanterns are lighted in the streets, the market places have closed, the full moon rises in the sky, the Chinese—men, women and children—have eaten their rice and come out for their walks. They chew the seeds of the watermelon, spitting, coughing, walking one behind the other, like ants. A young couple walks by in the middle of the street, holding on to each other's braided hair; this is the tenderest form of Chinese love expression—it is like the scorpions who, when preparing to mate, hold on to each other's tails for hours.

In an open-air cook-house, the customers have finished their meal—the stench hangs still on the whole square—and now they are seated in a circle around a storyteller. He is a half-naked young man with shaven head. His gaze is like a flame. He is unfolding a fairy tale. He gesticulates, changes his voice, now like a woman, now like a boy, and then the whole sound of his voice becomes heavy and tired like that of an old man. He plays all the characters of the tale. He somersaults, worships, weeps, and then—probably the nobleman speaking—his voice becomes wild, laughing sarcastically. His audience hangs on every word. From emotion the ecstatic multitude breaks out in sweat; the stench then becomes unbearable, and I walk away.

A long buzzing, the yellow crowds walk about the lantern-lit streets chewing watermelon and honeydew seeds and peanuts. A rustling similar to the silkworm feeding on leaves. I couldn't hold back—it was by now midnight—I, too, was taken in by the chewing mass and I approached a cross-eyed Chinese with a long braid who sold peanuts. He knew some English and began to chat with me:

"Where are you from?"

"From Greece."

The cockeyed Chinaman bursts into laughter.

"Why do you laugh?" I ask, peeved.

"Because you down there cut each other's throats," he says.

Never in my life did I feel such shame for my race. For a moment I felt as if I would grab the laughing Chinaman by the braid. But I held back. I felt he was right.

■ THE FORBIDDEN CITY

■ WANG AN-SHIH sang about a thousand years ago in China:

> *Midnight.*
> *Everybody in the house is sleeping,*
> *Even the hourglass has stopped.*
> *But I cannot sleep,*
> *Because the trembling spring flowers,*
> *Whose shadow the moon throws against the*
> *   wall,*
> *Are more beautiful than what a man can bear.*

In the same way I, too, cannot sleep on this spring night. Not because the flowers in the moonlight are unbearably beautiful, but because my eyes have seen the wonder to-day: absolute beauty ascending from the ground, blossoming, shining in the sun for a moment, immortal, and falling again to the ground.

As the fakir's eye forces the seed to sprout, to flower, to bear fruit and to rot away, so today on the snow-white marble threshing floor I saw the beginning and the end of an unexpected human victory. And I still hold the vision within my eyelids and I do not want to sleep and lose it: the acacias had blossomed, Peking buzzed like a bee-hive full of yellow bees, the castle gate of the Forbidden City was wide open, and in vain the two bull heads with gilded wild horns tried to chase away the evil spirits and not let them step into the sacred space. A few years ago, as soon as the imperial court had been dissolved like morning dew, the locks had broken, and the evil spirits, the "white demons," had gone back and forth freely in the deserted palaces and the imperial courts.

The little carriage, the ricksha, stopped at the entrance and I stepped down. Vast, mythical, this wonder extended in front of me: wide marble steps, short, fat, laughing bronze lions with heavy bells on their chests like court jesters, all-gold fairy-tale palaces whose kings have become grass, moving lightly on the rooftops. High gates falling apart and marked with three old established words in golden cheerful letters: TAI—CHU—MEN ("Large happy gate"). Gigantic bronze incense burners like caldrons. They are now deserted, without burning coal, without fragrant smoke. In one of these burners I saw a yellow wasp with black stripes weaving the empty cells of her hive. Bronze long-legged storks with high necks, wild marble turtles; and next to the winged imperial dragon was the mythical bird with the long wings, the phoenix, the *feng*, the bird that symbolized the empress. Inside the bronze bird they used to put scents and when the emperor passed by they set them on fire.

The famous gardens have been deserted. The jasmines, the roses, the red acacias, the chrysanthemuns are no longer there. Wind herbs and wild lettuce wave on the gates of the palaces, on the "large happy gates."

The palace where once the harem of the emperor buzzed now shines, surrounded by high, blood-red walls. Hieroglyphic letters appear on the walls like skeletons, like human ribs, like lacerated hands and feet. The rooms are deserted, the walls are peeling and crumbling, the roofs crack, and the yellow, green and blue varnished tiles are breaking loose in fragments. Many large halls have become museums where precious remains of the great treasures are piled up—paintings on silk, earrings, bronze bracelets, fans and small ladies' pillows of porcelain. And on the porcelain are painted weeping women under willow trees. On the shelves are vases with exquisite forms, like breasts, like loins, like necks of women. Tarnished silver mirrors, mortars for cosmetics, green necklaces, a multitude of candles that on a tragic night were extinguished forever.

I pass slowly and let my eyes feast for a long time on the paintings that have remained. Most of them are on silk, others are on wood or fine paper. Beauty, voluptuousness, tenderness. Rivers with slender reeds. Small boats with rambling, wandering women. Tiny full-red flowers at the ends of branches, setting the trees on fire. But this is no fire—only spring. Farther, on a silk fabric, are painted lightly like a dream, like frost, the rocks, the clouds, small villages, short, plump women sitting cross-legged on the grass. A girl holds a basket of flowers and places them at the feet of Buddha and looks at him, begging with tight lips. Why should she speak? He hears her unspoken cries.

A hermit smiles under the wild rocks. Golden pheasants stand like queens and gaze at the endless snow-covered landscape. A light, spiritual intoxication takes hold of you; the mind is elevated, it no longer cries like a peasant, it looks far away to a light, wavy frost, where all the beloved earthly designs are silhouetted, illumined for a moment, and then fade away.

I pass through the grass where once upon a time the famous garden of the harem bloomed, and I discern at the side, amid the thorns, a marble pavilion: this is the bath of the beautiful princess Chsian-Fee. With a dome and low-vaulted doors, it is deserted, without water, full of cobwebs. I wander from palace to palace like a ghost. I caress with my hand the two eternal symbols which are carved everywhere, on the sides of every stairway, high on the tops of every door: the Cloud and the Fire, the symbols of passion and vanity. A flame created all these wonders;

it was put out, it became smoke and passed into cloud. Only a soul that remembers and loves can come here and force the cloud to return in its primeval form. "I declare war against time," cries the soul, and turns back the wheel of time, and everything is resurrected.

When I ascend to the Temple of Heaven, where the emperors once a year offered sacrifice to the ancestors, I feel that man is truly sacred, mysterious, a wheel full of magic powers that creates matter in the image of his heart. And at the four corners of the horizon, four high marble doors; and at the top of each door, two wings; on one wing is carved the cloud and on the other the flame. You ascend the broad steps and reach the second marble terrace, a little narrower, again with four winged doors. And again you climb up farther and you reach the third, the highest terrace. All around as far as the eye can see, an endless plain, the desert that surrounds Peking. And your head feels that it is elevated in the sky; and you feel that the wings that leap from the four doors—the clouds and the flames—have lifted you to the blue space where the spirits dwell. And the emperor had only to stretch his hand in order to touch his ancestors. Here, on this high marble platform, he could feel that he truly was the Son of Heaven. And simultaneously he could feel his tremendous responsibility to men.

Throughout the day, wandering like a ghost in these deserted palaces, I reiterate in my mind the tragic fate that weighed on this unapproachable idol, full of responsibility. His person was so sacred that he could not come in contact with his people. He lived isolated, a holy prisoner in his court, and his every act was regulated according to the strictest protocol: in the spring, he lived in the eastern palace, wearing green clothes and eating wheat bread and lamb. In summer, he lived in the southern palace, wearing white clothes and eating dog meat. In winter, he went to the northern palace and wore black clothes and ate pork. The houses were the same color as the emperor's clothes. When he went to offer sacrifice or hunt or wage a war, his carriages were also painted the same color. Thus, imprisoned by inviolable laws, the emperor was a religious puppet who was dressed, washed, scented and transferred from temple to temple. No one was allowed to look in his eyes. One had to bend to look at him and not glance above his neck or below his waist. And when one wanted to talk to him, one had to put before one's mouth a tablet of precious green stone, lest the breath reach him and infect him.

His responsibilities were superhuman. He was the intermediary between his people and heaven, and all the success and failure of his nation was attributed to him. If the emperor was good, the rice grew, the cows were productive, the rivers did not flood, and no plague fell on the people. A Chinese religious song says:

> The thought of the emperor is omnipotent.
> When he thinks of the horses, they become
>   vigorous.
> The thought of the emperor is wild.
> When he thinks of the horses, they rush to
>   battle.

The emperor was the center of the mystic forces. His strength sat coiled within him, he unleashed it on his country and brought good crops, health, peace. Every year he alone marked the course of the first stream in the Temple of Earth. And he was the first to taste the early fruit. If the earth stopped producing, he was blamed because he no longer had the power to intercede with the heavens and bring happiness.

The supreme virtues were five: justice, generosity, nobleness, prudence, and loyalty to duty. When these virtues wavered, it meant that the emperor faltered. He was the big central wheel and all the secondary wheels followed his rhythm.

I gather wild flowers and camomiles that sprout on the marble steps. I hear my steps echoing in the deserted rooms of the palace and a superhuman joy buds in my mind. I remember the spring on the island of Crete in the plain of Messara; it is an awesome spectacle: early in the morning, before the sun rises over the plain, sometimes you see high on the dimly lit horizon huge shadows, like an army hastily marching in straight lines. The sun comes out and the armies disappear. The Cretans call these men who are created and disappear with the dew *drosoulites* ("dewlets"). Like them, the Chinese kings passed from the earth and vanished.

■ CHINESE SYMPOSIUM

■ PAINTING, SCULPTURE, poetry, social nobility, refined voluptuousness, love of water, flower and woman are characteristics of the Chinese civilization. But nowhere do you feel so tangibly the finesse of this ancient people as in their kitchen. The Chinese cuisine has been famous since antiquity and still is for the wise, elaborate, often suspicious changes that are performed on fish, meat, eggs and vegetables. As in artistic creation, the original sentiment is transubstantiated in the mind of the creator and comes out as a work of art, so the culinary ingredients change appearance and substance as they pass through the expertly wise yellow hands of the Chinese cook.

A friend of mine in Japan told me: "When you go to China and you are invited to dinner, either don't eat anything—that's the most prudent gesture—or, if you eat, never ask what was in that most delicious dish you ate."

As I've always heard, the Chinese eat amazing things: dogs, cats, rotten eggs, cakes of worms and centipedes, and sauces of boiled cocoons. . . . Imagine my terror when the old mandarin, Vei-Ha, to whom I had a letter of recommendation from a mutual friend, invited me to dine one evening.

"There are three kinds of Chinese restaurants," he told me, smoking through his long amber cigarette holder, "the *conanr-je*, the *lo* and the *tang*. The first is for the common people, the *lo* is more opulent, and the *tang* is

195

for official dinners, receptions, weddings and parties. We shall eat in a *lo*. But again, among them, some are famous for their pork meat, others for their sea food, especially for their crabs. And we have others which are famous for their precious sauces. Others are famous for their location: on the water, or in the garden, or high on a terrace. . . . What do you prefer?"

And because I remained silent, he added with refined Chinese politeness, "So that you will not be bored eating with an old mandarin, I shall invite a Sister of the Cottage famous for her beauty. . . ."

"A Sister of the Cottage?" I asked, wondering.

"That's the way we refer to our geishas here in Peking. In Foochow they call them 'White Figures,' in Canton, 'Pearls.' She will sing a little for us, she will say a few nice words and will leave."

"Thanks to you," I said pleased, "I will spend a perfect Chinese evening."

"Not 'perfect,'" he replied, smiling. "In order to be perfect, a Chinese evening needs something else."

"What?"

"We shall see," he responded with an enigmatic smile. "You Europeans are annoyed by some of our customs. But we shall drink 'wine of snakes,' and perhaps . . ."

"Wine of snakes?"

"You know we have various magic wines—of snakes, of monkeys, of chickens. We pour blood of these animals in the barrels and the wine acquires magic power. He who drinks wine of snakes gets courage and strange curiosities. You will see."

As if I had already drunk wine of snakes, I arrived, before sunset, full of curiosity, at the restaurant on a high terrace. I was the first to arrive, and waited. They brought me tea and jasmine and a saucer of watermelon seeds. I sipped the fragrant tea and looked down, all around the sprawling Peking. All the houses are, according to Chinese custom, one story, and built among trees that grow over them; this made the vast city look green like grass. Only the pagodas and the walls of the Forbidden City with their yellow, green and violet tiles stood out. And far out there, the desert.

The sun set, the evening star shone cheerfully in the deep blue sky. The air was cool, a rhododendron in a pot at the corner of the terrace had blossomed from the root up. Tranquillity. Quiet, simple joy. I think of the words of Confucius: "Now I understand why happiness occurs so seldom in this world: the idealists place it too high and the materialists too low, while it really exists next to us, no higher than we are. It is not the daughter of heaven or of earth, but the daughter of man."

But now the old mandarin appeared on the terrace, freshly bathed, fat, closely shaven like a Buddhist monk. Behind him, the guests, in black and blue robes, with skullcaps, smiling, good-humored. And behind them the headwaiter of the restaurant, fat and flabby, like a eunuch.

The tea with the jasmine and the porcelain saucers with the watermelon seeds came.

"The watermelon seeds," said the philosopher, "play an important role in the life of the Chinese. They teach him to be patient, to make the same motions for a long time and thus calm his nerves. That's why our peasants, when they have a good harvest, give away the watermelons on the condition that they will get back the seeds. Without the watermelon seeds, who knows how many more revolutions we would have had, and the history of China would certainly have been different."

The mandarin clapped his hands and the dinner began. We wiped our ivory sticks with thin paper tissues, as is customary, and large plates began to come one after the other. With the chopsticks, we filled our small porcelain bowls in front of us. In Japan they bring each person his own tray with all his food on it; here they bring large serving dishes from which each one serves himself.

I ate without asking what each dish was. Sometimes they said to me: "That's turtle soup; and the small pieces of meat inside the soup are the feet of the turtle. Those are the tender fins of shark. That's lacquer-polished hen. These are mushrooms which we should dip in the pepper." Then came the famous "rotten" eggs. They preserve them in lime, and in time the yolk and the white change and become a greenish, glistening, gelatin-like mass.

"Forgive me," the old mandarin said, "these eggs are only fifteen years old. The best are those which are twenty-five years old, but they are not easy to find. Aren't you eating them?"

"No," I said laughing, "they are too fresh."

"Then let's drink of the wine of snakes to get courage."

We filled our small cups with old rice wine.

"Let's make a toast to Greece!" said the old mandarin, raising his cup. "Confucius and Socrates were two masks that covered the same face of human logic."

The wine was strong, without aroma, and stripped the throat.

"Let's drink two more cups," I said, "the human logic is in danger!"

"So much the better!" said the poet. "Wine will give its place to music which is the supreme logic. And you know how much Confucius loved wine, women and music. Exactly as your Socrates."

I recalled the *Alcibiade* of the great vagabond poet François Villon, who took Alcibiades as a woman, and I smiled.

The mandarin clapped his hands again and the fat headwaiter came running.

"An invitation!" he said. "I want the boy to take it immediately."

They brought him a rose printed sheet of paper on which he wrote a name and signed it.

"I invited," he told us, "the Flower of Twilight, our famous geisha. She is no longer young, but you will like her. She has all the wisdom and all the graces of maturity."

A new plate came, the dessert.

"They are lotuses," said the philosopher. "Eat them to forget your country!"

We drank wine again, the boundaries of things began to blur. And then, noiselessly as a ghost, a woman, painted, with slender eyebrows like erect swords, long green earrings, a much-caressed and kissed face, appeared at the end of the terrace. You felt her face had been melted by much contact with hands and lips, and it reminded me of the marbles of Porziuncoa (the small chapel of Saint Francis down in the plain of Assisi) which have been worn down by the many kisses that the Franciscan pilgrims bestowed on them.

"The Flower of Twilight," said the old mandarin and bowed.

The famous, much-kissed woman sat down, opened her fan, and smiled. Her eyes, long and slanted, moved slowly, and gazed at each of us for a long time. At long last she opened her mouth and began to sing with a soft voice a melody of the desert. I imagined it was a song that the camel drivers sing when they pass through the terrible Gobi Desert. Monotonous, insistent, desperate. In India, when the sun sets, such is the prayer they sing in the Buddhist monasteries, the famous "melody of the tiger."

The song ended; the hoarse, tired voiced stopped; her slender hands were raised, embracing her cup of tea. "I am pleased to meet you," she said. "I will not sing any more tonight. I am slightly tired."

She reached in her hair and gave to each of us a jasmine warm from the heat of her body, and at the moment we made a toast to her health she disappeared. Only the fragrance of the jasmine was left with us.

"The Flower of Twilight begins to wither away," said the diplomat after a brief silence. "Autumn has fallen."

"That's a terrible moment for a woman," said the philosopher. "It's time for her last lover, death, to come."

The old mandarin nodded at the headwaiter again; he wrote a name once more on a rose sheet of paper and, turning to us, he said:

"A shadow has fallen on our table. With your permission I have invited a *shan-kon*."

All the slanted Chinese eyes glistened, and the poet, who sat next to me, explained:

"*Shan-kon* means a beautiful boy. I don't know what the ancient Greeks called it. Women always leave some bitter taste in our mouth, and then come the tender, good-hearted boys who sing or dance for us and we forget this bitter taste. Drink some more wine of snakes to gain courage."

The Chinese got up and made room for the *shan-kon* to dance. I filled my cup with wine and waited.

A ringing of bracelets was heard on the stairs. We all turned to see. And there at the top step appeared a slender boy, dressed in heavy, golden, embroidered silks. His little face was thickly powdered, his eyes were painted to the end of his eyebrows, and his thin mouth smiled like Buddha. The old mandarin, moved, applauded.

"Now," he said looking at me slyly, "now is the 'perfect' Chinese evening!"

■ THE YELLOW CIRCE

■ ONE HUNDRED AND THIRTY-FIVE Chinese ideograms are written with the root "woman." Of these, only fourteen express relatively good meanings; thirty-five of them have the most shameful and base meanings of the language, and the remaining eighty-six meanings are without any special connotation. The root "woman" combined with the root "shield" means rogue, unethical, traitor. If it is repeated three times it means adultery, intrigue, shamelessness.

The Chinese consider the woman a dark, mysterious, man-devouring force. "As soon as she is twelve years old," they say, "woman is as dangerous as the salt of the smuggler."

Today, passing through a narrow street, I saw a woman with loose hair howling on the roof of a house.

"What happened to her?" I asked.

"Nothing; she is cursing the street!" they told me.

I stopped for a while and stood there looking at her. She gesticulated, became harsh, and finally her exhausted voice gave out. Her blood flushed, her lips foamed, it was hot. She had to fan herself. That's the kind of mania that comes over Chinese women. They are quiet and obedient, they work, wash, delouse, cook. In the boats they hold the oars and row. In the fields they dig and plant and reap. But suddenly they are caught by a mania like rabies. For years the anger is suppressed in their heart, but suddenly it overflows. Then they go up to the roofs and curse the streets. Empress Lu, in 190 B.C., was a quiet, good little woman. Suddenly one day she was overtaken by this madness. She cut off the hands and feet of Tse, the king's mistress. Then she put out her eyes, cut off her ears, poured burning lead down her throat and threw her into a sewer. And finally, as she had not yet overcome her anger, she went up to the roof of the palace and began cursing at the street.

The Chinese call the beautiful women "devourers of the city," "destroyers of the world" and "evil nymphs."

> *In the north, there is a woman*
> *You see her and lose your kingdom*
> *You see her again, and the world vanishes!*

What are the Chinese standards for a beautiful woman? A delicate nose; long and thin eyebrows—like the outline of distant mountains; small and limpid eyes—like water in autumn. The most favorite characteristic in a Chinese woman is a dimple on the cheek which they call "the dimple of wine," and red on the cheeks which they call "the flower of intoxication." But what drives the Chinese mad is a woman's feet; from the foot emanates the deepest source of their pleasure. The Christian missionaries in China do not ask their yellow followers the usual question: "Have you fallen into temptation?"; they ask them: "Have you seen the foot of a woman?"

The fiercest erotic craving of the Chinese is centered in the foot of a woman. And the smaller the foot, the greater their ecstasy. Maybe that's why many centuries ago the women, out of a desire to please the men, began to wrap their feet tightly in childhood so that they would prevent them from growing. Gradually, after many years and much pain, the four toes turn down, the sole rises, the bone is deformed, the whole foot becomes atrophied; then they put on tiny silk shoes. This long preparation is very painful. The little Chinese girl aches and cries; she remains immovable, her face becomes pale, her eyes are vacant. "Every little foot," says a Chinese proverb, "costs a barrel of tears." But what's the pain as compared to beauty? The foot becomes tiny, the calf slender, the thighs and loins swell and the whole body rises trembling, unsteady, ready to fall. Thus the woman reaches the supreme ideal of Chinese beauty; with her tiny feet she can now capture a man.

When I first saw these deformed feet, I felt the undeniable repugnance that the deformed human body always brings out. And as women walked with open hands, tottering a little, bending forward, you thought that they would fall at any moment. I felt a discontent and turned my eyes away. But slowly their exotic dark charm began to grow on me. Not only did my glance stop at their deformed feet but also at their uncertain childish walking. As the Chinese woman walks slightly staggering, with open arms, she projects all her motion, clumsiness, hesitation and grace. What primarily appeals to the strong man in a woman is her weakness, her uncertainty, her trembling and even the deviate pleasure he gets from a small irregularity or deformation of her body; all these are achieved by the Chinese with unsurpassed wisdom by so unnaturally deforming the feet of women.

And thus, without idyllic sentimentalities or pretended motherly tenderness, the most dangerous and charming type of courtesan was created in China, full of hardness and intoxicating poison, the true priestess of the frosted moon. Here pleasure is not what the naïve erotic manuals of the white race relate—bodily joy, the two sexes complementing each other, happiness. Here, pleasure is the primitive relentless struggle, the indomitable hatred between the two sexes, the two tremendous inimical forces which create and destroy the world: the man who wants to lift his head upward and the woman who enraptures him, whistles and throws him down again to the ground.

Walking in the streets of Peking, of Nanking, of Hang-chow and of Shanghai, I often started, as one does when one suddenly faces a glistening snake rising up with its forked tongue sticking out. A Chinese woman had passed by, tightly wrapped in her black silk sheath which opened and closed at the sides, and her body glowed through the slit, relentless as a sword; her eyes gleamed at the sun or the moon, cold and invincible, slanted and deceitful, and as attractive as the eyes of a snake.

Circe certainly would have been Chinese. All the white sirens appear so naïve and safe, novices, illiterate in the art of love; they are clumsy and superficial and confuse pleasure with happiness or sport or gold. Here, pleasure breaks the boundaries of the individual, surpasses the hu-man cry, reaches at the root of the earth—at the animal, at the plant, at death.

Never in my life will I forget the Flower Boat at the bank of a river that I entered at twilight in a Chinese city. Flower Boats are the floating brothels adorned with flow-ers and creeping plants, where the Circes of the yellow Aphrodite live upon the waters. Mattresses, straw mats and pillows are on the floor, and on top of them sprawl silent and immovable yellow Sirens. Their painted lips shine in the dim light like open wounds; all their eyebrows are shaven, and two painted swordlike lines leap up from their slanting eyes like the antennae of an insect. And the heavily powdered faces resemble each other as much as if they were one face; here the ephemeral individual masks are smashed, the women lose their names; all the faces, in the same cosmetics, are consumed into a mysterious, eternal synthesis. You truly feel as if you are entering into an an-cient temple inside a cave near the river, where the dark, many-breasted goddess of the human species is worshiped.

Suffocating smell of hashish, light blue smoke; now the eyes accustom themselves to the dim light, and you discern in the background among the white masks a few slender sunken-cheeked Chinese smoking. The waters of the river rise and fall like breathing and the boat shakes. The beads, the earrings and the bracelets of the female idols also shake and sparkle in the dark. All this moving water, the thick river, full of rotten fruit, harmonizes with the mission of the woman.

It had already begun to get dark; the multicolored lanterns on the deck were lit and all sorts of flags were hung on the ropes. The boats were shining, gay, festive, and the first fireworks leaped up whistling in the darkened sky. A woman began to sing slowly, shrieking as if meowing, without any sweetness in her voice to touch your soul. The lament of an animal, the call of a jackal in the moonlight, the wailing of a bitch—the primitive voice of a woman before she has learned from her husband to utter sounds and shape them into words. And your guts which are much older than your mind and heart are torn and cry like a dog or a jackal. That's the simple, very old secret of Circe: to return man back to the animal. That's the eternal secret of woman. And of all the women, the Chinese are able to give to man its sincerest form, naked from any sentimentality and sweetness.

The Japanese geishas bend over the man, at the erotic moment, as if he were sick and they wanted to cure him, or as if he were a crying child and they were opening their bosom to nurture him. The Chinese woman bends over the man as if he were a mortal enemy caught in war; and she knows there is no pity.

When I came out of the Flower Boat, I took the road along the bank of the river. As I walked, I thought of an old Chinese song:

From the mouth of the viper in the cool reeds
From the sharp sting of the wild wasp—the
harm they can do to you is slight.
But incurable poison is the body of a woman.

I was thinking that the body of a woman is not poison. It is only the subordinate instrument of the great universal power to push us downward that no one can resist, for resisting it would be a sacrilege.

■ CHINESE SUPERSTITIONS

■ THIS MORNING IT rained hard and the streets were deserted. The Chinese are afraid of the rain in a mysterious way; it is often mentioned in their history that a battle stopped because it began to rain, or that they would have slain many more if it had not started raining. The Chinese believe that when it is raining, Heaven and Earth mingle; the male element of the world, the *Yang*, and the female, the *Yin*, are mating and it is sacrilegious for anyone to go out and come between the couple.

The everyday life of a Chinese is real martyrdom because he feels that he is surrounded and spied upon by terrible invisible forces. If a rooster cries on his roof, his house will burn. If a dog with a white tail enters his house, one of his relatives will die. At the table they all eat from the same plate, because if they change dishes the hostess will die. On certain holidays, they worship and address the fox, the weasel, the snake, the porcupine and call them "your excellence," because these animals are considered to have a mystic influence on the life of man.

The Chinese bite their lips in anger when they see the "red-haired barbarians" desecrate the holy mother, Earth, by opening up her guts and taking out coal and metals. Or by creating telegraph poles that throw shadows on their ancestors' graves. Or by laying down railroad tracks, constructing bridges, building factories without consulting the soothsayers of the land about the will of the spirits. And even worse: "The ones with the big nose" (another nickname for the Whites) kill the infants, put out their eyes and use them to make photographic plates and films. . . .

The Chinese don't believe in the gods very much, but they find it more advantageous to worship the gods than to be atheists. They say, if there are gods, it is always good to offer them sacrifices, and if there are not, the damage is not great. It is safer to behave as if there are gods. "Offer sacrifice to your ancestors, as if they were present!" Confucius taught. "But do our ancestors see our sacrifices?" he was once asked, "and are they pleased with them?" But Confucius avoided revealing his thoughts. "If I say yes," he thought, "all the sons can be destroyed offering all their property as a sacrifice to their ancestors. If I say no, all the sons may neglect the sacrifices and end up being atheists. I will not say anything." And Laotze, the great mystic of Tao, derided Confucius for his logic and scolded him: "Cleanse your mind, make it white as snow; deny your science; throw up your logic! The passing of man through this earthly life resembles the jump of a white horse that wants to pass over the abyss but falls down!"

The relationship between the Chinese and God is a commercial one: give me something, so that I may give you something. They offer him food and prayers, they build for him temples, but he must also help them in their business. Otherwise, they punish him: if he does not send them rain and their crops are withered from thirst, they burn bricks and irons and make him sit on them so that he may also burn. Often they deceive God by fraud: every year on New Year's Eve, the kitchen god goes up to heaven and reports how the family is doing. What do the Chinese do then? On that day they smear his lips with sweetened dough so that he cannot open them and tell what he knows."

When a child is born, they put in a small sack two

chopsticks, two onions, two pieces of charcoal, the hair of a dog and of a cat, and they hang this with a red string at the door of the mother. They also hang the trousers of the father with the sign: EVIL SPIRITS, GET INTO THE TROUSERS AND LET THE INFANT ALONE! No marriage can take place without having the astrologers say whether the horoscopes of the groom and bride complement one another. The astrologer will set the date for the sewing of the bride's clothes, and the "pillows of longevity" that the bride will embroider. The Chinese year is governed by twelve signs of the zodiac: rooster, hare, tiger, monkey, pig, snake, dragon, dog, ox, lamb, mouse and horse. The astrologer must define under the protection of which of these animals the wedding should take place.

There are, however, two main superstitions that regulate the entire life of the Chinese—their joys, griefs, works, holidays, weddings, births, and deaths. They are the *Feng-shui*, and the Dragon. *Feng-shui* is one of the terrible scarecrows of China. It is made up of the ideograms for wind and water and means "place," so that this genie of the place is an omnipotent and vindictive genie whose will the Chinese must ceaselessly struggle to guess and follow. They cannot build a house or dig a grave without consulting the soothsayer of the land who will tell them what *Feng-shui* wants them to do.

Feng, or wind, the invisible; *shui* or water, the visible. The wind and the water bring good or bad fortune; and the wretched Chinese is in agony searching to find what he must do to charm the good fortune. And the whims of *Feng-shui* are unpredictable and incomprehensible! You build on this lot and all the fortune comes running to you; whereas, when another builds in the same spot, *Feng-shui* is angry and destroys him. But the greatest agony is this: when one of the relatives dies, what is the wish of *Feng-shui?* When should he be buried? Where?

How? The smallest deviation from his wish can destroy you and all your family, because the dead live much more intensely than the living and they revenge themselves relentlessly. The Chinese do not think of their dead either disinterestedly or tenderly; every dead person is a tornado of invisible forces and one must placate him with sacrifices and prayers in order to make him a protector. The corpse often waits for weeks and months under some hut covered with a straw mat or with branches until the relatives collect enough money for a good funeral. The soothsayer comes with his tools: a pair of compasses or a mirror. He searches for hours, or for days if the dead one is rich, to find in exactly what place the grave must be dug so that no star may be found above it; so that no dragon may be found beneath it; so that no wind may hit hard; so that the color of the earth and the silhouette of the mountains around, especially their shadows, may be comfortable. And most important is the current of the world that represents the Tiger passing to his right and the current of the Dragon to his left.

The Dragon is the other terrible scarecrow of China. Everywhere, wherever you throw your glance, you see on banners, on doors, on embroidery, on paintings, on marble and on wood, this terrible fantastic monster: half-crocodile, half-snake, with five-nailed, clawing feet. The dragon has no wings, but it can fly to the clouds. That's why it symbolizes everything high: the mountain, the big tree, the emperor. The dragon is the symbol of power; all the great physical phenomena are his own works—fires, floods, thunders, earthquakes. When the dragon becomes angry, he moves his tail and the earth is shaken, or he rushes at the moon and the sun, opens his mouth and swallows them. And then, as the earth begins to darken, the Chinese tremble; they beat the gongs and the drums, they throw rockets to scare the Dragon and force him to throw up the sun and the moon.

Sometimes in order to placate the Dragon, they resort not to force but to prayer and begging. When the river overflows, or when the farms are burned by a drought, the magicians run and find a viper or a lizard. They declare that it is the Dragon, they place it on a velvet pillow, they beat the gongs and the drums around it. They fall and worship it. The Dragon is found everywhere, on the earth, in the sky, on the waters; it is even found inside the houses where he makes himself feel at home. That's why the Chinese build their rooftops tilted upward—so that the Dragon may coil himself comfortably about them. The Chinese are afraid of opening arteries within the earth and exploiting their rich mines or of building bridges. Not long ago, a high governmental official fought against the establishment of the railroads of China with amazing arguments: "Instead of spending huge amounts of money," he said, "to buy machines which come from the seas, wouldn't it be more practical to spend money to study the ancient means of communication which are mentioned by our classical writers, as for example the carriages drawn by the flying winged dragons?"

China is a mysterious country where many contradictory characteristics coexist in the same bosom: the narrow logic, the most austere and practical spirit and, simultaneously, the belief in invisible, superhuman forces full of evil, whimsicality and jealousy. Confucius, the stuffy, practical mind, and Lao-tze, the ecstatic apostle who doesn't care either about good or evil and has contempt for action. "The perfect man does not feel any joy living long or any sorrow dying prematurely. Neither do riches make him proud nor poverty make him ashamed. Life and death, riches and poverty are for him all one. He does not get angry with people, he is not afraid of the spirits. His mind, immovable, strides over the world. And striding over the world, it remains immovable. It has reached perfection. The endless seas can boil without becoming hot. The great rivers can freeze without becoming cold. The thunderbolts may break down the mountains, and the winds may lift the seas without scaring it. The perfect man rides on the wind, rushes up amid the stars, and does not worry about life and death; much less does he care about good and evil!"

The Chinese soul is rich and able to create many admirable, fertile contrasts and an exquisite civilization. The contact with substance would remain formless and incoherent without the intervention of the practical, firm mind. The practical mind would remain sterile, unable to desire great works beyond immediate needs without the incurable mystical craving. And here in China, the two great leaders and collaborators, Don Quixote and Sancho, created the world.

I wander in the temples and monasteries of Peking; I enjoy the empty fruits of this ancient faith. In the blue corners, Buddha, the greatest leader of men, smiles and shines, surrounded by incense clouds. I feel that all the flesh has reached its highest ambition and has become spirit.

I remember that one day the monastery of Lama, at the end of Peking, sighed and groaned in the sun like a bronze calf: drums, gong, flutes, psalms, the entire vast temple to its foundation echoed the morning rites. Child monks on rows of benches, with long yellow robes and yellow *tricado*, chanted their own tunes. An old priest, full of wrinkles, all shaven, also in yellow *tricado*, went back and forth among the adolescent monks and murmured prayers. He held a rosary with thick black beads in his left hand and an incense burner in his right hand. All the air was full of the nauseating smoke; and in this religious fog you discerned statues and paintings and carvings and plump child monks and indolent gourmets, and unfaithful monks.

The Chinese don't love the often shameless, reveling

monks. They have caustic popular songs satirizing them. And it sounded to me as if this wrinkled monkey with the censer murmured one of the prayers that the people might have created to mock him: "Buddha, have pity on me, a wretched monk, help me to leave your temple, because men have lost their faith and no longer come with hands full of offerings. Help me, Buddha, to leave so that I may not be hungry and cold any more. Help me to marry a beautiful girl and throw the robe away!"

And the "Laughing Buddha," a colossal statue, is enthroned in a chapel of the monastery, and his huge ears hang farther down than his chin and stick up above his pumpkin-like, gleaming skull. His belly, three feet high, shines bare, satisfied, full. He holds a rosary of human skulls passed through a red string. He smiles, he bursts out laughing, he listens to the prayer of the monk, he sees the child monks, he gazes at Peking through the open door. And in front of him, rows of multicolored paper prayer wheels grind the air.

In another chapel a gigantic statue represents Buddha as a wild Mongol, like Tamerlane, with black tassels which represent his hair leaping from his chin, his temples and his nostrils. This one does not laugh, he does not face the spectacle of the earth as a reveler god. Nor does he look at the troubles of men with irony. He is the great conqueror who has fallen upon China; he holds in his hands all the gifts that God brings to man—earthquake, fire, flood and war.

■ THE CHINESE AND DEATH

■ ONE DAY ON A narrow street in Peking an amazing Shakespearean spectacle leaped up before me. A riotous assembly: drums, gaudy colors; two tall and husky Chinese who blew long trumpets like huge funnels ran in front. Behind them, two groups of rag-clad urchins holding white paper candles. And between these two groups, a flabby clown powdered with flour, holding by the head a life-size painted paper figure of a girl that moved rhythmically, right and left, in the air. Behind the clown, a stretcher with a longish case on it was carried by sixteen gay Chinese dressed in green. And at the tail of this colorful rag-clad crowd, a multitude of carts with women dressed in white with indifferent callous faces, moving their hands hastily in the air. They passed by very quickly, sounding their trumpets, and disappeared.

"What is it? A circus? Masqueraders? An advertisement?" I asked my companion, a German professor at the University of Peking, who had been living in China for twelve years.

"No," he replied laughing, "it's a funeral. A girl died. Didn't you see her paper effigy?"

"A funeral? So gay? And why are they in a hurry?"

"Because at the end of the funeral a dinner will be given. All these poor people with the trumpets and with the green tails will eat, after God knows how many days of fasting. The relatives of the dead girl, in order to save face and placate her soul so that she will not become a vampire, will spend all their savings to give an opulent funeral dinner. These stingy creatures become prodigal out of fear."

"But are the Chinese so much afraid of death?"

"They are not afraid of death at all; they are afraid of the dead. After death the Chinese acquires a terrible power, and all his relatives tremble before him as before a demon or a god. Just before he passes away, they lay him on a plank and take him out of the room, because they believe that the soul of he who dies on his bed does not follow his body but holds onto the bed, and no one dares live there any more. The room must be destroyed from the foundation as well as all the furniture, so that the soul will come loose and go away. Therefore, they put the moribund person out and dress him in his best clothes; then they bury under his pillowcase a white cloth that represents a rooster. Sometimes they tie a real rooster on the foot of their dead. This bird will bring him good luck in the nether world, because the words for rooster and happiness are pronounced alike. The coffin also plays a very important role; woe to him who will die and descend to the earth without a coffin—he will definitely become a vampire and will ravage the living. For that reason, one of the best gifts that you can give a Chinese is a coffin!"

We walked quietly, talking about death and looking at the entangled multicolored carvings on the doors of the stores and the red and green banner-signs that waved in the air. At every threshold, in all the yards, where there was a little water, the poor women washed, deloused, combed, cleaned their children and their husbands. As you looked at them you were overcome by pity for them; you forgot their ugliness and misery and you respectfully thought of their difficult sacred task. If it were not for these humble workers, lice and filth would have eaten up all the men. They are the valets of men.

My companion, however, was accustomed to these Chinese spectacles and could continue his thought undisturbed:

"Neither Buddha nor Confucius nor Tao. But the one true god of China is the ancestor. The worship of the ancestors is the oldest single religion of the Chinese. The dead man who descends to the earth acquires dangerous powers and we must cajole him lest he exterminate us. Only one can intercede: the son. The son must offer sacrifices every day: flowers, food, prayers; and he must faithfully follow his father's traces in life. 'Don't take a step, don't say a word against the established order,' Confucius commands. 'The slightest straying can bring an irreparable catastrophe—not only to you but to your whole family, the visible and the invisible.'"

I turned, surprised.

"The visible and the invisible?"

My friend smiled.

"The Chinese family," he replied, "is not only visible, it does not only consist of the living ones. It has two other invisible stories: the floor below, the cellar, where the ancestors in full armor dwell, and the floor above, where the unborn descendants still wait. The salvation or the destruction of the entire building hangs from the action of the living.

"Woe to the family that does not have a male descendant. It is lost, because only the son can offer the necessary sacrifices and cajole the dead; the women do not count, they are only the 'receptacles,' nothing else. The eternal element, the immortal water is held by the man.

"The dead govern China; they count incomparably more than the living; they do not die, they live and rule inside every man and push him to his every act. The past leads the present and creates the future. For that reason, we have a supreme duty: to listen to the old voices with religious awe and execute all, even the least important, formalities. Because the formalities are not empty forms, they are the necessary manifestations of a deep emotion; it is the body of our soul.

"If there were no formalities, the inner essence would not have something to be held down by and would be lost.

"The dead, not their bones but their spirits, are the foundations of China. The day on which worshiping begins to shake, China will fall down."

"I am afraid," I said, "the China whose psychology you describe to me will soon break down. The 'light of science' will soon arrive here."

The voice of my friend was blurred, sad.

"It has already arrived," he said. "The day before yesterday I read a manifesto in one of the Chinese magazines that some young scientists who recently returned from American universities wrote in order to 'enlighten' the people. 'We, the young,' declared the manifesto, 'are positivists; we prefer a basket of good manure to a basket of holy offers for our ancestors.' " My friend abruptly stopped.

In a grocery there were many people and policemen. Someone had stepped on a box and unhooked a rope hanging on a hook at the top of a door.

"Someone has been hung," my companion said. "Surely out of vengeance. I am going to see."

Shortly he returned.

"He has worked it out well. This grocer had lent some money to a coolie and put a mortgage on his little house and sold it on auction. What did the shrewd coolie do to avenge himself? He came tonight and hung himself at the door of the grocery!"

"But why didn't he kill the grocer?"

"He was not stupid. If he had killed the grocer, both he and his family would have gotten into trouble. And when he in turn had died, they would not have buried him accordingly, with the necessary formalities, and his soul would have suffered eternally. Whereas now, all the troubles will fall on the grocer's head. He will be grabbed by the courts and will have to pay indemnity to the family of the coolie. And the most important thing is that the coolie will descend to his grave in glory. He saved face. Then, don't forget that suicide often is committed to escape punishment; women kill themselves to escape from the nails of their mothers-in-law; men commit suicide because of jealousy, vengeance, pride, poverty. Sometimes a beggar kills himself in front of your door if you chase him away in a bad manner—and then, woe to you! Courts, fines, humiliations. Two merchants compete: one, who feels that he will be defeated, goes and hangs himself at the store of his adversary; thus the adversary is lost. Another one loses his case and asks a rehearing, but in vain; he then goes and kills himself at the threshold of his adversary. The trial is reviewed and nearly all the judges, dazzled by the splendor the dead man acquired, find him right.

"The most usual means of suicide is hanging; then comes the big dose of hashish and the razor. Whoever commits suicide in order to be sure that his death will destroy his enemy writes on his skin the reasons for his suicide and accuses the responsible. Thus the Chinese trembles lest you retaliate by committing suicide. One night someone robbed a peasant, took his purse and left. 'Have pity on me!' cried the peasant, 'Give me back my purse!' But the robber ran faster. 'Have pity on me,' the peasant cried again, 'If you don't give me my purse, I will kill myself!' The robber, frightened, immediately returned the purse to the peasant.

"The Chinese are strange and incomprehensible to us. A different world. Virtues that are elementary with us the Chinese does not have. For example, the feeling of kindness. He measures everything only in terms of his own interest. He does good only when it is of interest to him. If you fall on the street, if your carriage breaks to pieces, the Chinese gather and look at you indifferently, or even laugh; only if you pay them do they rush to help you. If you ask directions on the street, they lie to you in order to force you to pay them. The word kindness in Chinese is written with an ideogram that has no relation to the ideogram expressing emotion and having as its root the word for heart. The word kindness is written without the symbol of the heart.

"Also the Chinese does not know gratitude. A missionary once cured a blind beggar who, as soon as he saw light, asked compensation from the missionary because now that he was no longer blind people would not pity him and would not give him alms."

Quietly the professor looked around him at the colorful spectacle of Chinese life and became silent. And I exercised my senses in order to withstand a mysterious charm, dangerous, shameless curiosity, a dark craving to touch all this body of earth. . . .

My friend interrupted his silence, laughing.

"For a while it's difficult," he said, "to live here in China. Difficult and dangerous. The Chinese are hard, vindictive, stingy, filthy; nevertheless, behind every Chinese extends the whole of China, endless, full of mystery. Here man has depth, his roots grow down in the mud and filth. . . . And the deeper they go, the higher the flower leaps up. The flower, the civilization of China, has an indescribable charm. Because you feel that the filth—man—is transubstantiated and has become spirit; you rejoice that stinginess and cruelty are defeated and that a most tender union with the universe has taken place.

"And thus we see the most unexpected sight, a Chinese sage, Chuang-tze, ordering his fellow Chinese who are energetic, calculating and full of logic: 'Rest in inertia and you'll immediately see how good the world is. Throw away your skin as the snake does. Spit your brain through your mouth. Mingle with infinity!' And elsewhere he says: 'There is nothing under the dome of heaven which surpasses in grandeur a little leaf in autumn!' And when Chuang-tze was near his end and his disciples wanted to give him a magnificent funeral, he laughed: 'The earth,' he said, 'will be used as my coffin, and the sky as my tombstone. The sun, the moon and the stars will be nailed on my grave, as adornments. What thing more beautiful can you add? Leave me without a funeral. I don't want a grave!' 'But the vultures will eat you up!' protested the disciples. 'If you leave me unburied, the vultures will devour me; if you bury me, the worms will devour me. Why should I show a preference to the latter and not the former?'

"The Chinese, who so rapaciously hold on to the things that they want to eat, drink and make their own, gave birth to a poet who wrote these verses expressing ideas that Shakespeare arrived at only at the end of his life:

> *I dream and I see that I am a butterfly.*
> *I wake up and I see that I am a man.*
> *Which is the dream?*
> *The man? The butterfly?*
> *Perhaps neither the one nor the other.*
> *I say: 'I woke up.'*
> *Should perhaps I have said: 'I was transformed?'*

"And in the tenth century another Chinese poet, Su-Kung-Tu, sang:

> *Let us build a hut under the pine trees*
> *And there with a bare head let us complete*
> *verses*

*Without caring either about the sunrises or
about the sunsets!"*

This transubstantiation of the thickest mud into the
lightest song constitutes the invincible charm of China,

A PRINCESS AND

THE YELLOW PSICHARE*

■ PRINCESS DAN-PAO-TSAO wears a tight golden silk robe and long green earrings. Her eyes are black, full of shadows. She lived for years in palaces, and now that the imperial courts have been deserted, the princess has withdrawn to this out-of-the-way house with its fresh, enclosed garden. You feel that her hands and her face and her neck are watered with many lotions and aromas and secret cosmetics. She is slender and svelte and still dangerously beautiful. She has written a book about love. As I ask her about contemporary Chinese literature, her velvet eyes are shadowed by nostalgia.

"We have nothing any more," she said. "Our creative power was lost together with our empire. Our young men are lazy and shameless. They do not believe in the classics any more. They do not study them, and when they write, their language is vulgar. You feel they do not write; they write the way they talk. Then a cursed leader appears who wants to throw down our old intellectual gods and change the language and force us to write the way the coolies and the peasants talk!"

I was glad; I let the animated, mature, slender princess talk on; she lit her aromatic cigarette, and as she blew

---

* Ioannis Psichare (1854-1929), the leader of the Demoticistic Movement in Greece and a Professor of Medieval and Modern Greek at the Sorbonne. In 1888 he published the first important prose work in Demotic, *My Journey;* since then Demotic has gradually become the only language used in Greek literature.—G.C.P.

the smoke from her nostrils and mouth, she reminded me of the exquisite bronze birds at the entrance of the palace, which symbolize the empress and are filled with aromas that burn as the Son of Heaven passes by. Likewise our princess burned and smoked in anger.

"But how is it possible," she cried, "for educated men to write the way the people talk? How can they express noble feelings and lofty concepts in the language of my servant? You tell me, is it possible?"

Ah! how I recalled at that moment the fearless fighter at the borders of our Greek language, Petros Vlastos,* at the other end of the world, in Liverpool! How he would have burst out laughing listening to this purist, this "blue-stocking" with her little mouth wrinkled in contempt.

"It is as if someone came out in your country and supported the idea that you must write not in the language of Plato but in the language which the peasants and fishermen speak. What would you do to him?"

And I laughed.

"What would we do to him? We would send him in exile far away from Greece; we would insult him and call him 'bought' and 'traitor' and we would never allow him to set his foot in the Academy. And we would do whatever we could to make him die of starvation!"

"Then, we should do the same to that cursed Dr. Hu Shih!" said the princess animatedly.

The tea, flavored with jasmine, came. The blue evening began to enter through the tall windows. A blossoming peach tree shone red as blood through the window glass. The princess glowed in shadowed light on the divan, like an oriental idol loaded with evening stars, gold and

---

* Petros Vlastos (1879-1941), one of the leaders of the Demoticistic Movement, was the son of a rich Greek family living abroad. He was born in Calcutta, India, studied law at the University of Athens, and was a successful businessman living in England. He has written poetry, essays and linguistic treatises, using an uncompromising form of Demotic, for which he was admired by Kazantzakis.—G.C.P.

aromas. Her voice was warm, and I listened to her talking with joy about the Chinese language:

"We have two languages: the written and the spoken. Our written language is not alphabetical, its words are not sound combinations (represented by letters) as your languages. We have thousands of ideograms; each ideogram represents an idea or a thing. Our first ideograms were gross drawings representing the sky, the earth, man, the domestic animals, the dog, the cat, the ox, and still others for birds, trees, fish and metals. There were all together 214 of them. But these ideograms were not adequate for our intellectual wealth. Our system of writing had to be perfected. A new means of writing had to be found, because, naturally, it was impossible for us to go on writing by drawing every object. How could you distinguish an apple from a peach tree or from a cherry tree? And then, how could you express abstract concepts or sentiments—wrath, love, hope? It was a difficult problem and it never crossed our minds to solve it the way you did, by alphabetic or syllabic systems of writing. What did we do then? We combined the first 214 ideograms and we formed new signs, arbitrarily, of course, but very handy and expressive. Our every word is a little riddle, and only the educated can solve it. And the more educated you are the more riddles you can solve. Therefore, we divided the animals and plants into categories. The type of carnivorous animals are represented by the general ideogram of the dog; the ox is the general ideogram of the ruminating animals; the mouse of the rodent; the pig of the pachyderms. When we want to write the word tiger, we write first the general ideogram of the carnivorous and next to it a small sign which, combined with it, represents the tiger."

"But what about the abstract concepts? How were you able to represent them?"

"It was very difficult," the princess replied, laughing,

"but here appeared the wisdom and shrewdness of our race. In order to express wrath, we draw a heart with the little sign of slavery on top of it; two women under a roof mean quarrel; a hand with a balanced scale means historian; two similar pearls mean friendship. You understand now why for us calligraphy is considered equal to painting? In order to be a good sage, you must also be a good painter. When our race was at the peak of its growth, our writing was a sacred art. You had to bathe your body and put on clean clothes before you held the paintbrush. You had to hold your arm parallel to the paper so that your elbow might never touch it. The top of the paintbrush had to form a triangle with your nose and heart. A very difficult task. Many Chinese sages in wintertime, when they did not have a fire to warm themselves, began to write, and after ten minutes they were soaked in perspiration. When you are angry or sad, you write and your anger and sadness disappear. And think how out of 214 ideograms that we had at the beginning, we now have thousands. Our famous classical dictionary which was written two centuries ago includes 44,449 ideograms. But no one knows all of them. We learn as many as we can; five, six thousand are enough."

"And the spoken language?"

"That's simpler!" the princess replied with contempt. "It consists of 450 monosyllabic utterances which with different tones add up to 1,600 words. The Chinese words are divided into categories of homophonous utterances which, in order to avoid confusion, we combine when it is necessary with a word of similar or opposite meaning. As you see, our spoken language does not have the difficulties, the subtleties and the nobility of our written language. And now comes this demon Hu Shih. . . ."

On the same night, in a small restaurant, I had dinner with the demon who wants to make the Chinese write as they speak—Dr. Hu Shih. We spoke about the princess and we burst out laughing; we became friends at once because the same idea united us at the two ends of the earth. Hu Shih was about forty-five years old, full of life and force, his eyes sparkled behind his glasses. He studied philosophy and philology in America; there his mind was enlightened. He saw the leprosy that ate up the mind of his race, and he threw himself into the struggle.

As soon as he returned from America, he published in Shanghai, together with a friend of his, the *Manifesto of the Chinese Philological Revolution*. The classic Chinese language, he declared, is useless for our present-day life; it has been for fifteen centuries incomprehensible to our nation, an impediment to our intellectual advancement. The only language which can save our nation is Pai hua, the spoken popular language. A living people cannot express themselves by means of a dead language. "No dead language can create a living literature."

"I had sworn in 1916," Hu Shih told me, "not to write any more prose or poetry except in our spoken language. We took on our side a few professors of the University and many students, and we established the magazine *Youth*, written exclusively in the spoken language. In two years, from all the provinces, the young responded to our movement. Our idea spread throughout China like fire. In 1920, our first great victory came about. The Ministry of Education for the first time after thousands of years introduced the spoken language to the first two grades. In 1928 the National Government of Nanking introduced the spoken language to all the grades of the grammar school and to the lower grades of the high school. Three-fourths of the books that were printed in the last five years were written in the spoken language. A triumph! Our greatest adversary, the old Lin-Su, who translated over two hundred European books into our classical language, is at a loss! The only argument he presents is this: 'I feel that we should write in our classical language; I feel it, but I cannot say why.' "

Hu Shih laughed, glowing.

"And what about you?" he asked.

I told him about the epic struggle of our Demotic movement. The names Psichare, Pallis, Palamas, Eftaliotis, Filintas, Vlastos echoed triumphantly in the small Chinese restaurant. And the yellow Psichare listened to the distant echo of our fight and laughed.

So we, who have lived abroad for a long time, fellow fighters of the same struggle, laughed and talked until midnight and did not want to separate. It was as if an army were waging war and a messenger from one end of the field and another from the other end, both bringing tidings of victory, met, exchanged their cheerful news and did not want to separate.

▪ CH'I, THE BLACK MANIA

▪ THE RITUALISTIC RULES of Chinese nobility number three hundred, and the commandments of etiquette three thousand. You play chess with a Chinese, and you hear him speak with contempt about his pawns: "Allow me to move my insignificant tower! Allow me to attack your glorious tower with my trifling pawn!" And the Chinese woman, when she speaks to you about her husband, out of politeness, will not say to you: "My husband." She will always use a roundabout expression which means my master, my teacher or, if he is a barber, she may say, "my barber shop" and if he is a grocer, "my grocery."

When a stranger comes to your house, politeness demands that you offer him tobacco. The Chinese, even though he knows that his tobacco case is empty, nevertheless opens it and offers it to you. You, out of politeness again, pretend that you take the nonexisting tobacco and bring it to your nostrils, and you even sneeze! Politeness, worship of formality, conviction that the material act of giving is not of such a value as is the inner intention of donation. It is an endeavor to surround the concept without expressing it directly, a light, delicate contact, a secret, restrained discipline of the mind and hand. . . .

The longer I breathe the air of China, the more dense the mystery becomes, and the mechanism behind the chest of the Chinese seems to me darker and more complicated. What do those sly, slanted black eyes, moving as those of a monkey, mean when they look at you? And when the Chinese bows deeply and submits himself to your voice, you shudder because you feel that this silence of his is terrible, full of wild, silent wings. I look at the waiter who serves me; I have never seen more dexterous hands, more silent submission, more flawless intuition— anticipating what I want before I ask for it. "What a happiness," I say to myself, "to have such a faithful and willing servant in your life!" I raise my eyes to smile at him and I am terrified; I catch his glance fixed on me like a dagger. The Chinese is quiet, patient, obliging. He gathers and stores in his heart all the insults, the humiliations and the bitterness. He does not talk. He does not make the slightest movement that will betray his heart. You look at him and say, "He did not understand." But he sees everything, he hears everything, and puts it down on his memory. He charges you. And one day, surely, you will not escape him.

I remember when I went to Shanghai for the first time; I took out of my pocket the money to pay the coolie who had brought me in his ricksha down to the port. The coolie had opened his two palms and I counted into them the heavy copper dimes and waited to see when he would nod that it was enough. When his hand was filled with dimes, he put them in his bosom and extended his hand again. An Englishman stopped and looked at us; I started again filling his hand when suddenly the Englishman gave the coolie a strong blow in the belly and said something to him angrily. The coolie fell back, holding his belly from the pain, but said nothing. About thirty Chinese, silent, stopped and looked at us. "You gave him too much!" said the Britisher full of anger. "You should not let them get used to that."

I laughed. "It doesn't matter," I said. "He is poor."

"It does matter!" protested the Englishman in a dry

tone. "It does matter! Don't forget that you are in China!"

"But why didn't you tell me to stop, without kicking him?"

"Because he would begin insulting and threatening. My blow scared him. That's the way it should be!"

That's the way it should be. Five hundred million Chinese on one side, one Englishman on the other. But for how long? I looked at the Chinese that had gathered around us; no one spoke, no one moved. Their faces remained immovable as masks. The Chinese picks himself up, gathers and deposits the kicks, the blows, the insults, the injustices, the laughs: and one day his anger will overflow. I wonder whether the ships will then be in time to save the white necks?

Likewise in his everyday life, the Chinese gathers his wrath and swallows his tongue. But suddenly his eyes blur and he is seized with a mania like rabies: that is the *ch'i*, the black mania. You can see children, women and men fall down and foam. A woman often faints or takes a knife or a stone or a pot of hot boiling water and kills her husband or her mother-in-law. Sometimes out of this hysterical crisis their throats are so tightened that they can no longer swallow and they die of starvation. This black mania, the *ch'i*, sometimes captures the Chinese in groups. And then horrible slaughters take place and their white masters are in danger. . . .

On May 20, 1920, the *ch'i* had suddenly befallen the Chinese. Red letters covered all the walls of Peking: KILL THE WHITE BARBARIANS! THROW THEM TO THE SEA! CHINA FOR THE CHINESE! Inflaming manifestoes were distributed among the yellow multitudes: "The Christian religion insults our gods, has contempt for Buddha, angers heaven and earth, and thus rain does not fall on our farms. But eight million warlike spirits will descend and cleanse our country from the foreigners. Be sure, it will not rain if we do not slay all the Whites!"

Frenzied, they took rifles, guns, swords, crowbars, sticks, whatever they found, and rushed upon the section where the embassies were. Those who saw them say that their bravery and disregard for death were fantastic. They had wrapped their heads with red kerchiefs on which the word *fu*, which means happiness, was written. Their force had become ferocious; they climbed the trees, jumped from big heights; their frothed lips uttered incomprehensible oracles. A fanatic, in his ecstasy, chopped his daughter with a knife and threw her in small pieces to his loyal followers. Such was their psychosis that when the bullets tore their hearts, they continued to march on, holding their swords or banners. . . .

In all my tour of China, passing through cities and villages, traveling along the rivers, I looked at the multitudes of yellow ants with terror. Now the Chinese sit down with crossed legs, they smoke hashish quietly with half-open eyelids, they dig and cultivate the earth, they carry the Whites on their rickshas. But the day will come when these straws will catch fire and will enfold the world in flames. The *ch'i* might suddenly take over not only a few coolies but the half-billion Chinese who may be armed, not with bars and rusty swords but with tanks and airplanes and educated generals, and who may change the fortune of the world.

I wonder whether the Japanese will be the tanks, the airplanes and the generals of the future "black mania."

■ THE CHINESE THEATER

■ THE NOBLEWOMAN Lau-Lee celebrates her ninetieth birthday today. Her great-grandson, the diplomat whom I met at the symposium of the old mandarin, called me early this morning.

"There is a great opportunity to see a Chinese family holiday. My great-grandmother celebrates her ninetieth birthday. I'll come and take you to greet her. She has a long artificial tress and tiny little deformed feet. Don't forget to tell her a nice word about her beauty; she will be very glad and may offer you as a gift a silk fan!"

The house of the old noblewoman was immense, only one floor, like a big Turkish house. As in all Chinese houses, you see at the entrance a small folding screen-wall that stops you from seeing deep into the yard. It is the famous *yg-pei*, the shield that stops the evil spirits from entering the house. Because the evil spirits follow only straight lines, when they meet a wall in front of them they cannot go sideways and they go back. Which are these evil spirits? Certainly the glances of passers-by trying to see the women in the yard are stopped by the miraculous *yg-pei*.

We, however, passed by the little wall and found ourselves in a huge, elaborately adorned yard. Broad red stripes, like flags, with big golden letters were waving everywhere, on reeds, on poles, on walls, in the windows, in the trees.

"They are the congratulatory notes the old lady received," the diplomat explained to me. "They write to her: 'Eternal Youth!' 'May you see a son of your great-grandson!' 'Long live the fruitful vine!' "

First her old sons, then her grandsons and her great-grandsons came to welcome us.

"We all are eighty-two branches of the old vine, a whole vineyard!" the diplomat whispered to me.

We entered the living room. Large tables, small tables, chairs, drapes, curtains, divans. How far we are from the divine Japanese simplicity! On a throne staffed with pillows sits the old noblewoman—a charming yellow little woman, whose face resembles a shrunken apple. Her great-grandchildren hold a fan of ostrich feathers and fan her. At her feet sit two old friends, two wrinkled old men with blurred eyes. But the freshly painted eyes of the old lady glow gaily, and her curly hair waves across her forehead and temples in a playful manner as the fan blows it.

"He is a Greek," my friend said when he bent and bowed to her as if she were an old wooden idol. "He came especially to greet your flowered old age."

The old lady said something.

"She asks," my friend explained to me, "what is a Greek?"

"Tell her," I said to myself, "they are a type of Chinese purist, followers of the old calendar, and cannibals at the other end of the world." But at that moment, a sort of bagpipe sounded and strong drumbeats were heard. My friend opened a door in the background into another larger room in which there were many seats, a multitude of guests, a platform with curtains like a stage.

"What is it?" I asked. "A theater?"

"The old lady is not able to go to the theater; therefore, the theater comes to her. They will play some comedies to make her laugh. And then we will have dinner in the courtyard and fireworks to chase away the evil spirits. But let's go sit down; the performance begins."

The trays come and go: tea, pastries, fruits, lemonades. In front of the multicolored stage there is a sign in black letters: TAKE THIS PERFORMANCE AS YOU LIKE—TRUE OR IMAGINARY. BUT SUCH IS LIFE.

The curtain opens; two boys dressed in girls' clothes meow cheerfully. A youth with a long sword and with feathers on his head enters. The girls rush upon him and embrace him; a fast love play begins to see who will win his heart. The one is slender with thin feet like a stork; the other plump like a seal. The poor youth—like the donkey who was hungry and thirsty and died unable to make a decision between water and grass—did not know which to select. When he looks at the plump girl, he craves for the slender, and when he bends over the slender, he is tortured by his desire for the plump. Until finally, desperate, he draws his sword and commits suicide. Thus he escapes.

The flexibility and grace of the actors are indescribable. There are no people in the world with more flexible bodies than the Chinese; they are natural-born jugglers and acrobats. They have defeated the law of gravity. I have seen a woman with mutilated little feet leaping comfortably along a stretched rope.

"The Chinese have four great passions," my friend told me. "The lucky games, the pleasure of the flesh, the hashish and the theater. And all these passions spring from our desire to escape from real life, to give wings to everyday banality. The life of the Chinese is enraged by necessity; what other joys remain to him beside that of getting drunk? Being intoxicated with the hope of wealth or with woman or with dreams or with poetry. For this reason, when a theatrical troupe passes through some village or small city, all leave their work, close their shops, bring straw mats, tables, stools to the square where the stage is set. They forget their daily cares, half close their eyes, and surrender to the words, music and colors, to the sacred illusion of the stage. The schools have no classes, all the children from the neighboring villages dress in their best clothes and run to attend the performance. The houses of the happy village where the theatrical troupe arrives open hospitably and welcome their guests. No chicken is left alive, all the watermelons are cut, and all the yearly savings are spent in one week. But the Chinese tolerates all this waste because the joy of attending the theater overcomes his stinginess. He forgets logic because within him leaps up the other great Chinese soul, the mystically passionate, the Oriental, which sees everything as a spectacle. He knows that this world is a theater where everyone plays the role he was created to play. One plays the woman, another the man, a third one both; others play the idiot or the hero or the beggar. . . ."

As my friend continued talking, a multitude of spectacles that I had seen on the Chinese streets were clarified in my mind. The theatrical craving is deeply rooted within the Chinese: two Chinese quarrel on the street, and many spectators run cheerfully to see the fight. The protagonists look proudly at their audience, throw their caps in the air, roll their sleeves; the performance begins. Everyone passionately cries out, beats his chest, kneels, asks for justice. But he does not care so much about justice as he does about a deeper necessity that the Chinese have: "to save face." To appear that he is right and receive the applause of the people. Once a mandarin had been condemned to be hanged; what did he ask as a last favor? To wear his best clothes in order "to save face." That is his self-pride, his self-esteem, or what the Greeks call *philótimo*.

Intermission. In the yard of the old lady, the trays come and go. The women shine, the naked knees sparkle. The twilight enters quietly through the open door like a child monk of Buddha in an orange robe.

The bagpipe sounds again, the drums beat. An unbearable music, instruments that shriek over your head like enamored cats. I get tired and sit in a corner in the yard. Then one of the two old men who sat at the feet of the old lady comes out with his fan to take some fresh air. As he sees me, he approaches, smiling. We chat. He speaks strange, archaic French. He was once the ambassador of China to Paris. I ask him about China. In those days, disquieting telegrams arrived: the Communists advanced in the distant province of Se-Tswan in the north, toward Peking. The Japanese also advanced southward from Manchuria directly for Peking.

"Aren't you afraid?" I ask the old man.

But he smiles.

"Communism is ephemeral," he says. "Japan is also ephemeral. China is eternal."

He remains silent for a while, then he says:

"Do you know that the elephant has in the wrinkles of his body a lot of parasites? Some birds come and sit on the elephant and pinch him and eat the parasites and clean him. China is the elephant."

"Aren't you also afraid of its other enemies, the bigger ones, let's say the spirits or the flood? A few years ago, the Yangtze flooded and thirty million people were drowned."

The old man looks at me, smiling, and shrugs his shoulders.

"And what is thirty million people?" he says. "China is eternal."

■ IN A CHINESE VILLAGE

■ CHINA IS ETERNAL. An endless fertile plain, emerald green in spring, gray-silver in summer, compassionate, overflowing with milk like a mother; innumerable swarms of ants. Her children in blue cotton pajamas bend over to suckle her.

Rice, cotton, sugar cane, mulberry trees, tea; huge rivers water her, moving in a heavy rhythm. Everything here in China is quiet, slow-moving and simple, without gaudy adornments. You don't feel here the frenzied outburst and the impatient, unsteady haste of the tropical places that seem governed by an impetuous rage of destruction and creation; here in China the rhythm is patient and deep; it does not hasten, it acts as if it were immortal. It knows that the quick, nervous movements are ephemeral and do not fit the seriousness and eternity of the earth.

Generations come and go, men and soil and water collaborate peacefully in the safe, ruminating rhythm of fertility; you think the true god of China is the wise, the perfectly balanced practical mind, Confucius. But suddenly this amazing thing happens: the abrupt fury that comes over the Chinese and makes him leap up, foaming, on his roof, cursing the street, also captures the landscape. Tornadoes uproot cities, pull down forests; rivers change their routes and bury thousands of villagers in mud, drown millions of people; behind this calm mask of Confucius springs up sarcastically the wild, blood-licking god, the dark ruler of China, the Dragon with the green scales.

But the tempest passes away, the little men appear again from the mud, they rebuild their huts, they open fresh new streams, they dig the earth again. The mask is patched up, and Confucius appears quietly smiling, as if nothing had happened. He knows well that it is not to his interest for a man to think of the abyss.

I wandered in the Chinese plains for many days thinking of the rivers of sweat and tears the Chinese have shed in order to create China. Very old songs praise the ancestor who cleared the wild Chinese deserts, burned the thistles, opened with a sharp stone the guts of the earth and entrusted the seed.

> Big armfuls of thistles
> Why did our ancestors burn them?
> So that we, the grandsons, may sow.
> Let the floors be filled; let the carts be over-
>   flowed!
> Abundance! Abundance! Let the homes of the
>   people be satisfied!

The *Tseuli*, the very old Chinese Bible that was written over a thousand years before Christ, regulated for thirty centuries the incessant cyclic collaboration of man and earth. All rise from the soil and all return to the soil. The universe is the mystic snake that bites its tail, forming a holy circle. All are sacred because all are transubstantiated and circulate within this huge snake. Head and tail mingle.

Whatever comes out of the earth must return to the earth, and the earth will assume the responsibility of bringing it up again in a new form. And we read with nausea in the *Tseuli* amazing commandments about the stinking—but holy in the Chinese Bible—excrements of man: "The inspectors of agriculture will take care so that the smallest drop of human excrement should not be wasted; the salvation of our people depends on it. You will collect it in receptacles where it will remain for six days so that it will ferment; then you will mix it with water and fertilize the farms with it. You should put it at the root of each plant with great care so that there will be no great waste. Only if you use human dung with economy and knowledge will you have rich harvests and will the people be happy."

That's the reason the whole Chinese earth has a certain very definite sickly stink which you can hardly get used to. That's the characteristic smell of China. Truly, you need to have strong nerves or a deep understanding of what Tao is and of what the *Tseuli* says in order to endure walking in China.

One day I went to a small Chinese village in order to try my psychic and physical endurance. Low houses built of mud and straw crowded in the middle of an endless mud-colored plain and through them passed the river, moving slowly. Half-naked men and women dipped in the river up to their waists and brought water in pails to water their rice fields. Pigs and children happily wallowed in mud. A corpse of a dog at the end of the water rotted, full of worms and crabs. And next to the corpse in the flaming sun, the Chinese slept with their mouths open, and between their sparse yellow teeth flies went in and out.

I go on in haste, holding my nose, and reach the middle of the village. Sprawled on straw mats, about ten Chinese smoke hashish. Their eyes are blurred, their slender hands glisten; no one talks; they are all sunk in a blessed annihilation. Amid such poverty and misery the hashish is the only door to salvation—as for others is the religion, the idea, the sexual love, the wine. They forget their miserable life, they mingle with a better world, they turn the horrible reality into a happy, slow-moving dream.

Death certainly comes fast, but the hashish has enough time to give them their only solace, the only joy that they ever experience in this world. If they missed this, their life would be an incessant martyrdom. Hashish is their poetry, their dream. It provides the only moment in which they don't curse the hour in which they were born. "Why do you smoke hashish?" one day I asked a coolie who drew me on his ricksha. He looked at me with his small sad eyes that had already begun to blur and answered me. "Life, boss, is hard."

Life is really hard, I think, as I walk in this ghastly village where you can't see even a single person laughing, not even a flower in a pot nor a bird anywhere. Outside of every door there are two pails full of human excrement. Sometimes at the door yellow figures appear, anxious to see that the pails are still there and have not been stolen by the neighbors. When they are filled, they hang them at the ends of a thick cane; they take them across their shoulders and empty them on their rice fields.

Naked children, like erect piglets, covered with mud, make a circle around me; others deride me and touch me; others hold stones in their hands. Their glance is full of poison; if looks could kill, I would be lost. Red papers with thick black letters on the walls. The urchins point them out to me and look at me hard. I wonder what these letters say. I secretly unglue one and put it in my pocket. When I went to Nanking I showed it to a Chinese whom I knew. "What does this paper say?" I asked. "Death to foreigners!"

While I am in the village, I think: here is the moment to try my endurance. To see if I can defeat the horror. To stay one or two years in this hideous village. To have neither books, nor paper and ink, nor a letter from a friend. To seclude myself from what I love, to live in this mud, to breathe all this stink. Patiently, simply, bravely. After two years of such a trial I would have come out either a beast or a saint.

The sun sets, the ragged beggars crawl on the streets, dig the garbage, look secretly from the doors, seek to find something to eat or to steal. Others, naked, covered with straw below the waist; others heavily loaded with all their rags. Whatever they own they carry; whatever they find they pass through their belt—old shoes, cucumbers, pen-knives, cans, bells. Old men and women, tall and husky young men, girls seven and eight years old, naked. Lame lepers with missing hands. The blind go one after the other, they make up gangs and pass through the villages; they clear the streets; many fall dead of starvation on the way. Stench and hunger—these are the two greatest deities of China; Confucius, Lao-tze and Buddha do not have so many followers.

"Don't feel sorry for them!" a Chinese once told me. "They are not so unfortunate as you think. You should see them in the evening, when they sprawl down on their farms to sleep; what laughs they have, what songs they sing, what love they make as they take their hashish! And with what passion they throw themselves into the lucky games all night! They gamble whatever they have: a handful of rice, their rags, their women, their children. And when they lose, they even gamble one of their fingers or a piece of their flesh." I thought hell has its joys, perhaps a little warmer, but nevertheless more human than the joys of paradise!

Night had already come, and at the end of the village I saw a small wooden pagoda of Buddha. I said I would lie down in this temple and sleep. I had a few bananas and two apples. I sat at the steps of the temple and I distinguished in the background, at a corner, the small gilded wooden statue of Buddha. About twenty hands sur-

rounded him like rays; some hands blessed, others threat-
ened and others prayed. I sat at the steps, and I thought
with compassion of how many ways man has found to
turn his hunger into satiation. Buddha, this empty,
hopeless air, nurtures millions of souls. And the hashish
is a sort of Buddhist escape, a gross but quick union
with dreams. You can sink into ecstasy and forget your
"hated I" in many ways: the first, the lowest degree of in-
itiation, is the wine and the hashish; the second is love;
the third, the idea; the fourth, faith; the fifth (the highest), literary creation. Everyone follows his own way.

"What are you thinking of?" a hissing voice was suddenly heard saying behind me.

I turned; it was a lame monk with one tooth. He spoke
a little English and we started chatting.

"What are you here for in our village?"

"To see things."

"What to see! Dust, poverty, lice. . . ."

He entered the sanctuary and returned shortly, holding
a black, glistening gong.

"Have you got money? I will sell this!"

He took the round bar and knocked at it; a very sweet
deep, serene sound spread. I tuned my ear and listened
to it in ecstasy as it slowly faded away and vanished. I
took the gong in my hands and caressed it. Smooth like
ivory, rhythmically wavy, it gave an inexpressible pleasure as I held it in my hand.

The monk looked at me slyly; he felt his bait had succeeded.

"It's an old gong of the temple. Such are not made any
more. In the old days, molding metal was a religious act.
The ironmongers were holy persons, hermits. They mingled various metals, male and female, and married them.
Boys and girls worked on the bellows. Now the ironmongers have fallen; no one believes any more and no

good gongs are made. This is one of the old that the hermits made; take it."

"But it is not yours; how can you sell it?"

"It belongs to Buddha," replied the sly monk. "We all are one, as the Scriptures say. I am Buddha. The gong is mine. Take it!" I bought the gong with rapacious joy, and at night I used it as my pillow on the straw mat of the temple.

It took me a long time to fall asleep. Leaning on this sounding pillow, I thought of—and it seemed that I heard it—the broad rhythm that the water and soil make in China, the winters and the summers and the souls of men.

The cheerful spring holidays are still described in the old Chinese songs: *Spring came, the boys and girls ran in the flowered fields.* The girls invite the boys: "What do you say, boys? Shall we go over there?" "We're just coming from there!" answer the boys. "Well, then, come now, let's go again!" "Let's go again!" the boys say. And they begin, two by two, the games of love.

The girls, the old Chinese sages assure us, fall in love in the spring and boys in the fall; for that reason, they become engaged in the spring and married in the fall.

All winter long they sit hibernating and waiting, locked in their low houses. The soul wrinkles there.

But as soon as spring sends its first smells, doors open, chests expand; all go out in the sun and the sacred spring orgy begins. Girls and boys wrestle, run, compete to see who will come first and who will dance and sing best. They carry whatever food and drinks they have, the miserable stingy Chinese become prodigal in spring. The ants grow wings and throw themselves into feasting and reveling.

And when the couples are selected, the great symbolic ceremony takes place: before they mingle in the flowered fields, the girls fall half-naked into the river and swim from one bank to the other. The souls of the ancestors swim on the waters, rush upon the virgins, and the future brides feel the breath of the immortal dead impregnating them. Before they give themselves to the young men they have selected, they give their virginity to the ancestors; only they can fertilize the women; the living men transmit the temporal body; the ancestors, however, transmit something immortal—the soul.

The spring passes away, the summer comes, the work begins, the reaping, the threshing, the harvest. Where now is the time for love games? But the good autumn arrives, the storehouses are filled, the men are relieved of their worries; they only think of the heavy winter that is coming. Company is good in the long cold nights; the weddings take place. A girl takes the hand of a young man and recites the ritualistic words of the wedding:

> *In life and death*
> *I shall be your companion.*
> *I put my hands into your hands.*
> *I want to grow old together with you.*

In life and death, in war and peace, the Chinese woman for thousands of years is yoked next to her man, a faithful companion, full of fearlessness and perseverance; old womanly voices that have been saved in a few songs tell of her pain. An unknown poet—or was she a newly-wed housewife?—sighed centuries ago, and her sigh was saved because it had time to enter into verses that still fill the heart of man with bitterness:

> *The general's horse, impatient, knocks the earth*
> *with his foot.*
> *His little wife stands under the pillars.*

She extends her hand and gives him a silk shawl
  —red with gray embroidery,
"How many tender words have I not woven, my
  beloved, among its threads!
Read it when you are alone under your tent.
And when you look at the full moon high in
  the sky,
Think of me, of me and my tiny world!
And, oh, do not take long to come back to me,
Come back to my bosom!
Think of the full moon
That is wasted night in and night out
And how one day it will hang in the sky like a
  frosted little old woman!"

Distant voices, sighs, roars of wild wars and erotic bell ringings are left by the bracelets on the Chinese hands and feet. All night, with my head leaning on the gong, sprawled on the straw mat of the Buddhist temple, I have been hearing China humming quietly, endlessly, sweetly, as when no wind blows at all and the quiet sweet night rain falls on the endless plain.

■ THE HIGHEST PREY

■ THIS WAS A quick impatient glance that was
not satisfied. It became light and I saw at a moment the
huge yellow body of China; the lightning died out—and
all the Far East sank again in the dark. What has remained? I'd like to take inventory of my losses and gains,
like a merchant at the end of every spiritual undertaking.

What has remained out of all this? Multitudes of men,
women and children, the roar of a silk factory, deserted
palaces full of grass and deformed feet of women, stench
and flowered wisterias, monasteries and floating brothels,
and a thick, sticky aroma of jasmine, incense and human manure.

And behind this firm mask which I touched, a long
tender face, old sayings, sad songs, and voices that died
out. Old hermits who sit with crossed legs, quietly smiling
at the fringe of the abyss and gazing at the endless blue
Nothing. Once they lived on real rocks and smiled with
fleshy lips; now they have been reduced to paintings on
silk and their lips are a slight airy, yellow, brush stroke.

My eyes are filled, my soul rejoices, my mind sifts carefully and throws into oblivion the superfluous and dangerous and only keeps what is able to change anarchy into
a narrow disciplined area. The mind is the merchant,
the terrible bloodsucker, who seeks to make a profit out of
every trip in which the soul was endangered.

We throw to the mind a few copper dimes so that it
won't cry out, and we keep for the selfless, proud, hope-

less soul a prey—the highest prey—the alabaster Buddha which we saw one day in a temple of Peking.

You climb high stairs, you reach an elevated garden, you hear from far away the bells that hang at the roof of the temple sounding sweetly like running flocks; you advance a little; a low wooden temple rises in front of you. Darkness. You move on, prying about; you see nothing. You only feel your body getting cool; outside, a burning sun, clouds of dust, wild incoherent voices; beggars, wounded and stinking, pursue you; men who shamelessly dirty the streets—all the holy and foul breath of man. And suddenly inside this temple, fragrance, silence and coolness. "And if Buddha is only this, that is enough!"

But at that moment, a monk whom I had not seen was in the corner. He turned on a small electric light. And suddenly at the back of the temple, Buddha, all freshness and smiles, appeared sitting with crossed legs, carved on precious, transparent alabaster, in the flower of his youth, in a crimson tunic that left uncovered his fleshy chest. Never has a statue given me greater joy; not joy, deliverance, freedom, in the sense that I escaped from my hated self, but joy that I broke the fence and was united with the endless transparent Nothing. That which only dance, music and the sky full of stars can give, is given here by this precious, immovable crust of earth. The first wave that captures you facing this Buddha is the joy that the swimmer feels when he joins his hands, stretches and balances himself on his toes for a lightning instant before throwing himself into the sea.

You feel as if you swim noiselessly in a dream, in transparent green waters, and there is a full moon. For the first time I understood the teaching of Buddha. What is nirvana? The absolute disappearance or the immortal union with the universe? For two thousand years the philosophers and the theologians have quarreled, commented upon, analyzed and struggled to find the meaning of nirvana. You see this alabaster Buddha and your mind is overflowed with certainty. You live in nirvana. Neither disappearance nor immortality; time and place vanish, the problem changes form; it reaches its supreme form that surpasses human reason. You look at this transparent Buddha and your body becomes cool, your heart is sweetened and your mind becomes a quiet candle inside the chaos. Until now the mind was shipwrecked by the passions; it fed on glories, interests, beloved persons, homelands. And suddenly you see this Buddha and your mind vanishes. It does not vanish; it becomes Buddha.

I remained immovable for hours and I gazed at this alabaster center of the world. I felt that here, at this self-illuminated phosphorescent marble all the beams of the earth and all the efforts of man end up.

When I came out, the sun was about to set and the air began turning a golden green. I stopped for a while at a garden; I leaned on a tree to filter the joy within me. My mind was like the golden scarab that dawn found in a lily and that now got away from the lily and was sprinkled with golden pollen. Suddenly, as the world danced around me, I distinguished in the middle of the garden a multicolored marble pedestal—green, violet, white and rose. I approached. On it was carved a passionate hunt—wild boars, horses, dogs. This colorful marble had once been the pedestal of the alabaster Buddha. But there was not enough room for both in the little chapel and they separated them. And now the pedestal is rooted in the middle of the garden, and from it only the air rises—the final, complete statue of Buddha, carved on Nothing.

I looked for a long time, disturbed, at the invisible presence on the pedestal. I recalled the soundless, immaterial concert that I had attended the day before last at a noble Chinese house. In a large, dimly lit room, about ten guests sat silently. In the background was a platform covered with gray silk. The musicians came, greeted us, and sat down. Some held small drums, others Chinese lutes with seven strings, the *ch'in*, others a primitive kind of lyre. They put down a huge harp, the *se* that has twenty-five strings. And two boys held long flutes.

The old host extended his hands, made the motion that we make when we want to applaud, but his palms did not touch each other; they stopped a hair before. That was the signal to begin this amazing dumb concert. The bows were raised, the flute players brought their flutes near their lips without touching them and began to move rapidly, the tips of their fingers on the holes. The bows played in the air without touching the strings, the sticks stopped quietly just before touching the skin of the drum, the harpist moved his hand in the air and sometimes stopped and listened ecstatically to the immaterial sound. Nothing was heard. As if the concert took place far away, in the shadows, at the other bank of life, and you saw only the musicians who played and the bows that moved in an immovable silence. I was terrified. I looked at the guests around me; all, with their eyes nailed on the musical instruments, had sunk deep into the dumb harmony. Everyone followed the motion of the conductor and completed the music within himself. A signal was given, and everyone let his heart loose to complete the incomplete and to climax the pleasure.

When the mute concert ended, I bent to the guest next to me and posed my question. And he smilingly answered me: "For trained ears the sound is superfluous. The redeemed souls have no need of the act. The true Buddha has no body."

To be sure, the true Buddha has no body. I look at the empty air in this garden on the pedestal and mold the invisible statue of Buddha with the most quiet, inexpressible boldness of my mind. I think that when a people reaches, after thousands of years, the highest stage of human civilization, such statues will be erected in the squares: a pedestal, and on it carved a name. Nothing else. The superior spectator will carve the statue with his eyes, using the marble of the air.

Invisible statues, silent music—these are, I thought, the highest flowers of the muddy root of the body. They will sprout when man succeeds in clearing himself from the beast.

Blessed be this muddy China which is the only land in the world today that can give you the clues to the future, the more distant mankind.

TWENTY YEARS AFTER:

AN EPILOGUE*

BY HELEN KAZANTZAKIS

* Notes from the journal of N.K., edited and with commentary by
Helen Kazantzakis.

■ It has been raining all day today, a thin, silent rain. The cocoon, our little golden-yellow home, is now cold and empty. It seems like a cenotaph. Alas, the master silkworm who wove so much silk is gone, he has grown wings. . . .

I would rather have a wild storm break and hear the thunder groan and the sea beat upon the rocks of our castle. The silence envelops me like a winding sheet.

Eight o'clock in the evening. I turn the radio on at random. Someone is speaking. A soft, emotion-filled voice speaks hesitantly, in English. It is Charlie Chaplin. At Villefranche near Nice he has seen the little chapel of the fishermen in the harbor and is now explaining to Cocteau, who painted it, how much he likes it. His daughter translates his words into French. Charlie corrects her. "Much feeling—yes, much feeling . . ." he says. Now Picasso speaks, very fast, with his harsh Spanish pronunciation. He thanks the Minister of Education and the city officials of Antibes, who had made him an honorary citizen.

Yes, I remember when we were there with Picasso; he was wearing shoes for the first time, instead of shuffling about in his worn-out woolen slippers full of holes, and a beautiful loose jacket with big white and black checks. . . . He is very short, and his entirely round black eyes keep spinning around greedily and slyly. . . . Robert Santoul announces that we are about to hear the voice of the Great One who has just left us.

253

And soon comes the beloved voice:

"Nikos Kazantzakis," asks Robert Santoul, "what single thing has had the greatest influence upon your life?"

"Dreams and travels," unhesitatingly answers Kazantzakis.

Then he starts a new sentence, abandons it before he finishes the first two words. You can feel from his agitation that it is his first time on the air and he does not yet feel at home.

"Yes," he says after a little while, "an ancient Egyptian said, 'Happy is he who has seen the most water in his life.'"

He laughs, takes a breath, and then very quickly, in a voice choked with emotion, "You see, that's what I'm trying to do myself, to see as much water and earth as I can before I die."

Oh yes, Nikos Kazantzakis saw much water before he closed his eyes forever. For an entire week we sailed on the muddy waters of the Yangtze—fifteen hundred kilometers of water from Hankow to Chungking. For no other travelers did the Chinese prepare this trip up the Yangtze with as much love as they did for us, "the poets," as they called us. They took good care, even in the smallest details, so as not to tire Nikos Kazantzakis, because we were to pass through the famous landscapes which had been sung by the greatest poets of China. . . .

He saw much water, but it did not quench his thirst— how well he understood what his Cretan grandfather one day said to him in anger: accursed be he whose thirst is quenched!

Water was even his last word. Water! He wanted more water. It seems as if Fate had wished to punish him for his audacity and would not let him quench his thirst. . . .

But let me try to take the events in order, one by one. We left Antibes for Bern, Prague, Moscow, Peking; we came down to Hankow in China; we went up the Yangtze as far as Chungking; we lived for one week by the eternal spring of Kunming, beside the great lake at an altitude of two thousand meters. We made excursions to hot springs and to forests; we went up to temples cut into the cliffs; we then left for Canton where, unfortunately, the little Chinese doctor vaccinated Kazantzakis with smallpox vaccine. Three professors in Athens had said that he could take as many vaccinations as he wished. From there, without any care or suspicion, not knowing we carried death in ourselves, we flew across to Japan—Tokyo, Kyoto, Nara, Kamakura. After two weeks we flew to Alaska over the North Pole where, by a hair's breadth, we escaped falling and drowning among the icebergs after our plane had been damaged. Finally on to Copenhagen and to Freiburg, where the Asian flu had made an appointment with us. . . .

"What do you intend to write?" I asked Kazantzakis when I saw him writing in his little red notebook.

"I'm not going to write a travel book this time. All this will become a story."

But later, in the clinic, when he gained back his full strength, he said, "You will see. I will write an epilogue, Twenty Years After, and in it I will tell what great and profound changes have taken place in China. No statistics and factories, they don't interest me any more. . . ."

Alas! Nikos Kazantzakis has left us and will never again return to sit at his desk and write. We said that the silkworm had grown wings and departed. . . . And now I, another Sancho Panza, can only copy with reverence the few notes from the little red notebook and add whatever else I remember from that last trip of ours. And to be honest, I will do this not only for your sake, dear reader of Nikos Kazantzakis, but also somewhat for my own, so that I may have the illusion that I am again taking the road, hand in hand with the beloved companion of my life, and again taking with him that last trip of ours to China and

Japan. Let these few inadequate lines which I have dared to write stand as a memorial to Nikos Kazantzakis.*

---

* In the pages that follow, all text in *italics* is by Helen Kazantzakis. Sections of text in *roman* are from Kazantzakis' notes.

—H.K., Antibes, 1957

BERN.
We left at half past eight in the evening on June 5 from Antibes for Bern. We are going to Bern, Moscow and Peking.

"This trip will do him good, you'll see!" Madame Sou, *the beautiful bookseller of Antibes, tells me." It seems you have bad omens because you're afraid. You shouldn't be afraid. I believe in palm reading. . . ."*
Many years ago, a palm reader, the manager of a hotel on a high mountain in Austria, without knowing Kazantzakis at all, and without Kazantzakis knowing that it was he who also told Hitler's fortune, said many correct things about Kazantzakis of his present, past and future. He even told him: "In your seventieth year you will suffer a great illness. But you will be cured and you will reach a very old age." Because what he said had come true, this lady, and we ourselves, I confess, had been influenced by his prophecies.
Our friends at the station brought us red roses. All night they smelled sweetly by our pillows.
"A good omen," said Kazantzakis, pleased, when the trip started.

The next day in the morning, in Lausanne. We saw the Alps. We ate together.

June 6, in Bern, at the Hotel Beren ("bears"). In the evening Chrysos Evelpides* arrived.

We wandered about the old Bern. Under the vaults untold riches shone in the small shops. We went to the tower with the clock and naturally to the Bears. The taxi driver seemed to have lost tourists before and did not let us out of his sight. I felt that Kazantzakis was tired and I worried. We had not even really begun our trip.

June 7. Chinese Embassy, visa, etc. Greek Embassy: the ambassador, an extremist, narrow-minded, sure that he held the truth by the horns, ironic, antipathetic—a nightmare. Russian Embassy: most polite. We ate at the Casino at noon. At the Chinese Embassy in the evening. What politeness, what elaborate dishes, what a difference from the Greek Embassy where they did not even offer us, for one hour, one chair to sit on. . . .

Tonight I learned a Chinese proverb: "If you have two shirts, sell one and buy a rose."

I reminded Kazantzakis about the Greek lady on the train from Batum to Moscow. It was in 1929. Terrible poverty, especially for the middle class. Under her seat, this lady had placed a small case. Every now and then she bent and caressed it as if she wanted to be sure that it was neither very cold nor very hot. We had a bright sun in Batum and snows in Moscow. It was fall. "What do you have in your little case?" Kazantzakis asked her on the spur of the moment. "Oranges?" I volunteered, because I had spent hours and hours in the orange orchards of the Black Sea. "Roses!" the Greek lady said, smiling. "Roses?" "Yes, I have a girl friend who has lost all her

---

* A Greek writer and friend of Kazantzakis who accompanied him and his wife on this trip and who wrote the book, *India-Tradition, Japan-Evolution, China-Revolution*, dedicated to Kazantzakis.

fortune. The Bolsheviks took it. What could I bring her from Batum? I know that she likes white roses. . . ."

"She, too, is an Oriental, like the Chinese proverb," sighed Kazantzakis.

The Chinese Embassy in Bern is very beautiful. It is full of plants and of thick, softly colored Chinese carpets. Tea and Chinese cigarettes were offered before we had the time to sit down.

We ate, we drank, we laughed, we also learned our first Chinese word: hsieh hsieh ("thank you"), the only word we succeeded in bringing back from China. When you know how to say hsieh hsieh ni, thank you, or just hsieh hsieh, thanks, you know enough. The only thing you will never learn is exactly how you should pronounce it. Every Chinese we met pronounced it differently. Here is a point they have in common with the speakers of the English language.

June 8. We had lunch with the Greek commercial attaché. A simple, good and honest man. He was a poor orphan, he struggled to study and become a lawyer. He fought in Albania. At four in the afternoon we left for Zurich.

We were four; our new friends from the Chinese Embassy came to the station. A railroad employee showed each one of us to a separate compartment. "This way!" "No, not this way!" "But I assure you that it's this way. I am certain he told me number 4!" "And I am sure they told me number 3!"

We all talk at once, become upset; we carry our suitcases from one compartment to the other, we forget the Chinese who look at us undisturbed and smile. Now and then we, too, pretend a smile, but our Greek blood is boiling. At long last we get on the right train and we burst out laughing, we wave our handkerchiefs, we are reminded of the shoeshine boy during the occupation: "Nach Omonia, bitte!" *asked the tall and husky German soldier, clicking his heels. And the little shoeshine boy of Kolonaki, looking very serious, pointed in three different directions, saying:* "Ai sihtir! Ai sihtir! Ai sihtir!" *("Go to the devil!")* "Danke!" *the German thanked him as he picked the most convenient "Ai sihtir" that led to Omonia Square. . . .*

PRAGUE.
We left Zurich at 6 P.M. and arrived in Prague at 9 P.M. A representative of the Chinese Embassy waited for us. We went to the excellent Hotel Alkron, where we had a beautiful room.
June 9. Prague: a beautiful city. In the morning, to the church of Saint Giles with its exquisite stained glass. Especially beautiful is the one which is full of flames. Later, to the palace of the archbishop. Spacious rooms with gilded chandeliers, magnificent riches. Poor barefoot Christ!

Then the Museum of Art: beautiful Gothic paintings, many paintings of Christ on the Cross and of the Madonna; icons, Cranach, Brueghel, Rembrandt, El Greco, Bassano. . . .

In the afternoon we climbed up to Strachova, to the old monastery with its excellent library. Rare editions, three thousand incunabula, tiny editions, vast rooms with frescoes, and a charming and very erudite hunchbacked guide who explained everything to us in perfect German. I will never forget him and I will send him my *Saint Francis.* Exquisite view, greenery. . . . In the morning we went to the Greek Embassy. The ambassador is hospitable, kind. His beautiful wife offered us coffee. His car took us to the Museum of Art. We spent the evening relaxing at the hotel.
June 10. At the Chinese Embassy, a beautiful garden. An insignificant contact for all were vacationing. Tired. I relaxed in the afternoon.

June 11. I signed a contract with a Czech publisher for the publication of *The Greek Passion.* The Czech woman who will translate it is lovable. In the afternoon we went with members of the Greek Parliament (Gonticas, Lemos and others) to see the Greek students who had left Greece because they were leftists. They study engineering, economics, et cetera.

In my own notebook I find the name of a Cretan, G. S., who is studying film art. He explained to me that their studies lasted four years. In the fifth year they had the right to produce a film. They could use the symphony orchestra and any actors they wanted from the National Theater. The picture had to last twenty minutes. They also had to produce a ten-minute short. As a graduating project they were required to produce a Greek-speaking film. The state gave them 600 crowns per month as stipend. I asked him what they paid for rent: 30 crowns a month for a room and 175 crowns for two meals per day. They also received a student's card for the opera and the theater.

"On March 25," he told us, "we presented a beautiful tableau vivant about Cyprus, with verses of Solomos and Sikelianos."

His eyes shone when he spoke of Greece.

I still remember the emotion with which the students' wives waited for us in the small apartments. A baby in their arms, a baby in the cradle; all spoke Greek. They wanted to offer us Turkish coffee and preserved fruits with syrup, the typical Greek treatment. . . .

The Czech publisher of Kazantzakis said: "The ten thousand copies of the first edition will be sold in one week. Here they form a line outside of the bookstores every time a good book is published. We often sell all the first edition in two days. . . ."

"I hope now that you've made the beginning, you will

also translate other Greek writers," said Kazantzakis. "You know, we have many good writers."

What did we see in the stores of Prague? Cosmetics, stationery, fabrics, even nylon nightgowns. . . . The famous Bohemian crystals, china, and at the antique shops many beautiful and different things: silverware, dinner sets, laces, glassware, paintings . . . We bought some small items as souvenirs. . . .

MOSCOW.

June 12. In the morning in Prague we went to the small houses of the alchemists of the Middle Ages. In the afternoon we left by plane, and in two hours we reached Moscow, where we were welcomed by a committee of writers. I was moved to see Moscow again. The high building of the University shone red and black in the night. New apartment buildings with all their windows full of light. We went to the most luxurious Hotel Metropole. Everyone seemed cordial.

(*At the airport, Apletin, the president of the Union of Soviet Writers, came to welcome us. Polevoi and Ehrenburg were visiting Athens.*)

June 13. We made a tour of the city by car. How much it has changed! Its religious character has been lost, the golden domes of the churches and the sound of bells have vanished. Huge apartment houses. The University is a whole town—a superb view from its terrace.

In the afternoon we relaxed, and in the evening we went to the Puppet Theater. A wonderful art, but it lasted too long and I don't care very much about such shows. At midnight we had supper.

How Moscow had changed! Gone were the troikas with the red-bearded coachmen who looked so much like fat monks, the golden cupolas with their huge golden crosses and their hanging golden chains, the small wooden dachas, the private one-floor palaces with two pseudo-Greek columns on the right and left of the door. And the small chapel at the entrance of the Red Square with its Vladimirskaya, its miraculous Virgin icon. There was as long a line for the Virgin as there was for the tomb of Lenin. And the lit candles . . .

Kazantzakis also remembered all these but did not speak. He looked insatiably, he knew that it could not be different.

"One doesn't live with the past, Lenotska," he said to me, and was lost again in his thoughts. "I wish we had a university in Greece where our children could study, eat, drink and sleep for free, and I wouldn't care if it were as ugly as this," I heard him murmur when they showed us the huge University of Moscow, which looks like an American wedding cake.

June 14. We wasted the entire morning in the subway. Heavy, needless luxury; multicolored marbles; statues; excellent ventilation, broad, comfortable halls.

In the evening an exquisite ballet by Prokofiev—*Romeo and Juliet.* Superb music, divine colors.

We didn't mind not seeing Ulanova. Struchkova is wonderful! When she dances, you think she does not touch ground. Faier was the orchestra conductor. The beauty and opulence of this ballet I think are unsurpassable. I cannot compare it with anything, regardless of how hard I keep digging into my memory.

We began to discuss the subway again, annoyed by its luxury. Kazantzakis laughed:

I imagine that there are many who enjoy it. Let's say a group of peasants started out for the first time from their distant village to come to Moscow. With what joy and pride they would wander inside the subway station with their thick lambskin coats, their high boots that have a heavy goat stench. Why shouldn't they ever enjoy statues, golden mirrors, black and white marble, crystal chandeliers?"

The subway is a way of making them forget their bitterness for not having enjoyed all the goods of the upper middle class, I said to myself, completing in my thoughts what Kazantzakis said. And really, why not? They will also one day pass through their 1900s and reach the modern art that we Europeans pretend to love so much. . . .

In the afternoon we left Kazantzakis at the hotel to rest and write. Mr. and Mrs. Evelpidis went to the vast Russian Agricultural Fair; I wanted to see again the French impressionists that I had seen in 1928 in Moscow. I still remembered the "Dance" and the "Red Fish" by Matisse, and one or two blue Picassos.

Before the revolution, two merchants, Schukin and Morosov, the one in Leningrad and the other in Moscow, had the ambition to acquire, each one for himself, a good collection. If I remember well, the Moscovite, in the heart of the East, passionately looked for the most modern paintings and bought as many as he could by Matisse, Picasso, Utrillo, Gauguin, Van Gogh and two very good Marqué. The other collector, in Leningrad, in the "modern" capital, preferred the "classics" and filled his house with Corot, Watteau, Poussin, and others. The revolution came, the Bolsheviks respected the paintings, but asked their owners to turn their houses into museums. They allowed them to live in them, but forced them to allow people to come and admire their collections. When both these enlightened merchants died, the Communists took their collections and placed them in the large museums of Moscow and Leningrad. There I found again this afternoon my old friends, and my heart rejoiced at the French paintings which are the best ambassadors of France.

June 15. In the morning, to the Chinese Embassy, then to the Kremlin. The Cathedral is wonderful, full of icons, exquisite golden domes, a huge broken bronze bell. An extreme opulence in the treasures of the Kremlin: pearls, diamonds, emeralds, golden swords, embroidery, ivory thrones, golden plates, tiaras.

They did not show us the treasures pouring out of sacks like wheat which Kazantzakis and Panait Istrati had seen in 1928 in the cellars of the Kremlin. An English woman journalist had fainted when she saw them. The north wind blew and froze us to the marrow. They showed us, a little farther on from the largest bell in the world, the largest cannon, and then the small cannons of Napoleon. Kazantzakis recalled Tolstoy:
"For me there is no greater masterpiece than Anna Karenina," he said. "We all shall die, but that will remain immortal."

In the evening we had dinner at the Greek ambassador's house, I met a cousin of mine.

This time the Greek Embassy made an excellent impression on Kazantzakis. I still recall with what attention he listened to the richly nuanced explanations that two of the gentlemen of the Embassy, Messrs. P. and Ch., gave him. We stayed there until late in the evening. Kazantzakis had also been greatly moved by the "Greek" dandelions that one of the ladies had gathered. . . . And the others wondered about the many difficulties that the housewives of Moscow had in order to find what is needed for a good dinner.

June 16. In the morning, to the graves of Lenin and Stalin. An endless line. Cold, rain. The domes shone.

We entered the famous cathedral of Basil the Beatified, full of color and frenzied oriental imagination. We found it full of ladders. Young men and women painted silently, hunched in the dim light, at every corner, at every step.

We women had already killed enough time in the shops. The sweets that were abundant and cheap in 1928-29 had become an item of luxury, especially chocolates. What had become of those mountains of rose, white and pistachio halvah? We ate buloktsi—cakes with raisins—and tried to console ourselves. We drank full bottles of cool kefir. Mr. E. and I studied the various items for women: the silk kerchiefs which cost one hundred francs in France cost one thousand here. A pair of good men's shoes cost about eighty thousand francs—ten times more than in France. However, we bought very good and cheap musical records. We kept looking for some souvenir like embroidery or old custari. In 1928 you could still find many such custari, that is, wooden boxes, ladies' bowls painted very beautifully by hand. On these items the last icon painters of Russia painted Saint Demetrios riding on a black horse and Saint George on a white horse, the Lake of Genessaret, and the Apostles fishing. We still have at home two such beautiful boxes. The Russian writers gave me one as a present and the Greeks of Moscow gave another to Kazantzakis. Both are beautiful, but do not look at all like the old ones. Their paintings are romantic scenes taken from Russian folk tales. Looking around at the Russian shops we found out how rare and expensive they were, these present-day custari.

At the jewelry shops there were crowds around the rings, necklaces and bracelets made of stones from the Ural Mountains. . . .

In the evening we went to Gayne, at the Bolshoi. It's a ballet by Khachaturian. We didn't have tickets because we didn't ask for them on time. Mrs. E. suggested staying in front of the theater. "Someone," she said, "may return his tickets." After a long time of standing, we found the much-desired tickets. The show was again excellent. The oriental music, the story an Armenian folk tale. The Bolshoi Theater is always filled to capacity. At intermission they eat oranges and ice cream or drink lemonades. The people are well dressed; no one wears the white blouse and red kerchief, as they did in the twenties. . . .

In the afternoon we visited the Tetryakov Gallery. Excellent icons: the exquisite Vladimirskaya Virgin, the superb Saint Nicholas with the broad forehead, Rubliov, Theophanes the Cretan, the mosaic of Saint Demetrius, Saint George on a white horse with a tunic like fire. . . . At midnight we left for Leningrad.

LENINGRAD.
June 17. We spent the morning in the Hotel Astoria; sunny. Straightway to the Hermitage. A stretch of twenty-two kilometers of rooms, twelve thousand paintings on show and many more in the storehouses. Rembrandt, Cranach, Titian, El Greco ("Peter and Paul"), Van Gogh, Matisse, Gauguin, Cézanne, Giorgione, Picasso . . . Afternoon: our divine walk along the Neva River. Sea, children, sports, What a rhythm! What colors! Flags from all Russia. I was very pleased.

With what joy Kazantzakis saw again his favorite Rembrandt, "The Return of the Prodigal"; how he stood in ecstasy in front of it! I felt that his fatigue slowly began to lessen. He was very tired when we started out from Antibes. He had had to check his whole Odyssey from six to eight hours a day with K. F. And then in Paris the celebration for Saint Francis, the invitations, the journalists . . . "If I knew that this is glory, I would never have desired it!" Kazantzakis confessed.

The "children by the sea" that Kazantzakis mentions

above were the youth of Russia preparing themselves for the big festival. Now they have built in Leningrad a huge stadium, which is surrounded by the sea on three sides and endless meadows with green grass and high trees on the fourth side. And there we happened to see the children doing gymnastics and dances with banners. . . .

June 18. In the morning we tried to go to the Byzantine Museum to see the icons of Novgorod. We knew that it was closed, but Xenia K. had hopes. She would pronounce the magic word "foreigners" and Ali Baba would open the door for us. Nevertheless, this magic word does not seem to have any longer the influence it had, and thus we started out for Petropavlosk, the summer palace of the czar. The Germans had ruined it. The Russians are repairing it. Today they were gilding the Neptunes, the nereids, the gorgons, the frogs from whose mouths run green waters under the terraces of the Palace. In front of us, beyond four rows of trees, shines the sea. A little woman sold us ice cream, good and cheap. The Russians are crazy about ice cream and eat it in summer and winter.

Afternoon June 18. Writers. We talked of Greek and Russian literature. The writers were very likable. I said: Russia has a duty to find a synthesis of Europe and Asia; Greece has the same problem. There are three solutions: (1) to imitate our ancestors, which is impossible—we'll only make monkeys of ourselves. (2) to deny our ancestors and imitate contemporary literature, French, et cetera. This is false and artificial. (3) to find a synthesis: we should not deny our Greek tradition, but we should adapt ourselves to the new problems and try to find their modern Greek expression. . . . I spoke to them about *The Odyssey* and *The Greek Passion*.

In the evening the brilliant pianist Richter played

Schubert and Liszt. He was tall, blond, ugly, excitable. A great pianist. At midnight we left for Moscow.

We will never forget the "white nights" of Leningrad. It took great effort for us to fall asleep. You think you dream of the coming of dawn. . . .

This time we liked Leningrad much more than Moscow. In other times exactly the opposite happened. Leningrad reminded us of Berlin. Order, uniformity, nothing original. On the other hand, in Moscow, then, with every step there was a surprise. Today Moscow is in the process of being rebuilt and one day will be like a modern, Americanized metropolis. It's a pity. But how could it be different?

MOSCOW.

June 19. A journalist representing *Soviet Russia* came and asked me to write about the atomic bomb. Our young guide Vlad told us how the partisans in Vietnam used bats instead of airplanes. They hung on the bats' necks a small sack of powder with a fuse, then the bats would go to nest in the garrets of the houses where the French soldiers lived; the powder would catch fire and the houses would burn.

Another story: only the partisans and their friends had salt; the French would taste the partisans' tongues to see if they had eaten salt, and if their tongues were salty, they would kill them.

Another one: they had trained elephants, and at night they would let them loose in the French camps to cause panic so that the guerrillas could attack.

I met a young Greek poet named Alexis Parnis. . . . The young Russian, Julius Mogdison, who speaks Greek, came to interview me for the radio; I spoke of my impressions of Russia.

June 20. In the morning, to the cemetery where the graves of Gogol and other Russian writers are. In the evening, enthusiastic farewell dinner with Russian writers; presents, warm speeches . . . Today G. came, happiness . . . At 11 P.M. we left for Peking.

At the cemetery we also saw the grave of Stalin's wife. They say that she was still beautiful and young when Stalin killed her. I was pleased that we could talk freely. The Russians laughed; they didn't seem to be afraid.

They told us an anecdote about Chekhov who said: Vodka is white, but it reddens the nose and blackens the character.

"Who, in your opinion, are the most important young writers in Russia?" we asked the president of their society, Michael Yakovlevits Apletin.

"Tetriankov, Obeskin, Antonov," he answered.

"Do you publish many books by Russian authors every year?"

"In 1934 we printed 84 Russian authors. In 1957 we have printed 900 authors, 9,000 editions, in 44 languages. Fadeev is translated into 54 languages."

"I recall that Gorky used to be the best known of the Soviet writers."

"Yes, even in 1934 forty per cent of our editions were Gorky's books. . . ."

PEKING.*

June 21. At 10 A.M. in sizzling heat we arrived in Peking. Welcomed at the airport with flowers. Before coming to Peking, we stopped at Omsk and Irkutsk. A Tibetan began a religious dance at the airport. He danced with slow, harmonious movements, a heavy, silent strut as if he were chasing the evil spirits. We went to the Hotel Peking.

---

* "Here the tourist has very little to see, but the man too much." From a card that N.K. sent from Peking to a friend of his in France.

We ate. In the afternoon, a car ride around the city. How much Peking has changed and deteriorated! No more hand organs on the streets or noisy yellow crowds. Electric lights in abundance, americanization, all the cities have become degraded.

Samarkand, Mecca, Baghdad, Moscow, Peking—fragrant spicy flowers of the Far East! The dream has been crystallized within us, more vivid, more irresistible than the most tangible reality. Our soul stubbornly kicks and denies the present forms. We need time to extinguish the inner vision, to separate the real from the dream. Kazantzakis stands full of life in front of me as when he had returned from China twenty years ago.

"Ah, Peking is the most beautiful city in the world!" he said again and again. "But how it stinks!"

He used to burst out laughing and begin again as if he spoke to himself:

"Never has a city stunk so much. You go out in the morning to take a walk and the wandering vendors wake up the city with their song: Vermicelli! Ver-mi-celli! Rolls, sesame rolls! And what do you see? The householders sit in a row bundled over the open sewer and laugh and chat with the ones next to them, pleasantly smoking their pipes. . . . And their temples and their Forbidden City are the same way. . . . And from everywhere hang the multicolored banners with thick Chinese letters, which look like little men. And at night, thousands of lit lanterns, white, red, yellow, blue, and violet . . . I saw a slender Buddha, without a double belly and double chin, handsome as Adonis, made of white jasper."

As Kazantzakis kept talking about Peking, his nostalgia flamed within him and the irresistible desire to take the road to Peking to see it again caught him. Not only to see it, but to go and live in Peking for a few years. And, indeed, that desire of his would almost become reality. . . .

This day, Kazantzakis haunted the streets with his flaming glance as if he wanted to find the things he knew. Where were the long pigtails and the wild slanted glances and the beautiful Chinese women in their rich silk clothes and the mandarins and their long goatees in their black, glistening robes? Where were the camels, the Mongols in their lambskin coats and the women with the tiny feet who walk tottering like big birds whose feathers have been cut? A modern well-aired city spread before us, with traffic policemen in glass towers, cars, double rows of trees, and thousands of bicycles. You no longer see men doing the work of horses. No! Even the rickshas are drawn by bikes. And those strange coachmen wear white gloves. Fortunately, however, most of them have thrown away their white masks which they wore during the period of their war against the flies, the mice and the germs. Only now and then a young man appears in this heat with his mouth and nose covered with a white gauze, as if he were a surgeon.

How clean the Chinese are now. The peasants and the workers, the civil servants, the clerks, the merchants; and the students, the old men and women, and the little children in the gardens! The Chinese children are certainly the most charming in the world. They go about dressed in their shorts, holding an ice cream in their hand. With a teacher who is no more than sixteen years old, they go to the lake for a walk, or to a museum.

We also took a walk to Pai-Hai, the large park with the Lake of the North; we passed by the bridges, curved like the hump of a camel; we climbed to the Coal Mountain, which is an artificial hill made of coal, because, as the tradition says, the first emperor of the Dynasty of Yüan was afraid of being left without coal and ordered it by the tons. Now it is a hill full of cedars, cypress trees, wisterias and mimosas. And on its peak there is a beautiful pagoda with a triple golden roof.

"Do you see this cedar tree?" Wang said to us. "Here on April 9, 1644 the last emperor of the Dynasty of Ming, the last Chinese emperor, was hanged. A revolution had broken out, the famished peasants had already reached the gates of Peking. The Emperor ordered his wife to drink the most effective poison, slew his daughter, and sent his sons away on the fastest horses. He invited his favorite poets—he was a poet himself and knew how to appreciate well-written verse—and asked their forgiveness, and then he remained alone to talk to his ancestors. On his white sleeve they found written these words: 'We, poor in virtue and worthy of contempt, attracted on our head the ire of gods. Our ministers deceived us. We are full of shame with the idea that we are going to meet our ancestors. I take from my head the imperial crown; with my hair thrown on my face I wait for the rebels to chop me up. The only thing I wish is that they may not torture my people.' The rebels, however, did not enjoy their victory. The friends of the Emperor had invited the barbarians to their aid. The Manchu came and remained until 1911, the sole rulers of China."

June 22. In the morning, to the Temple of Heaven, a wonder: it is built in the form of a Chinese straw hut made for the protection of the crops. More wonders around it: smaller temples, the courtyard, the echo, laurels and vines, marble stairs with carved dragons, phoenix, clouds. . . .

In the afternoon we sat at a beautiful garden over the lake, a cool breeze was blowing; they had boat races. All the Chinese were very clean.

It did not take long for our host and guide, the very likable Chinese philosopher Wang Shen-shi, to love Nikos Kazantzakis. They both worshiped the same gods: freedom, poetry and Buddha, and the eternal and invincible beauty, wherever it was found.

As if Kazantzakis were his father, Wang Shen-shi wanted in every way not only to guess his wishes but also to protect him from the heat and unnecessary efforts.

"I will take you directly to what I love most," Wang said to us that morning with secret pride. "You will see what, in my opinion, is the highest achievement of architecture, the perfect harmony; I don't think that man has ever reached higher."

"He did very well!" I shouted, excited by the perfect beauty of the blue temple.

The sun shone on the marble threshing floors; inside the temple, you enjoyed a blue-green cool light, as if you were under the open tail of some mythical peacock, and you felt relaxed and insignificant next to the enormous wooden columns that were whole trunks of trees. But outside— only on the Acropolis could you be seized by such a sacred intoxication—you wander for hours and hours from yard to yard, climbing the marble stairs, up and down the steps with carved marble covers, passing through the marble bridges and getting lost inside this highest mathematical theorem, which seems as if made of untrodden snow and untamed sun. And above you, very high, a blue sky made of Persian faïence, with cotton-like white clouds . . .

"No, he didn't do well at all," Kazantzakis whispered to me, lest Wang should hear him and feel distressed. "Now you won't enjoy the Forbidden City as you should."

And Kazantzakis was right, as always.

June 23. Forbidden City. What fine roofs, cedars, marble stairs carved with dragons, phoenix, storks and clouds. Ancient vessels of faïence. Paintings of bamboo that symbolize strong character because they endure the wind and the winter. Plum trees that blossom in the winter, an angry clay camel, paintings on silk . . .

At noon we ate as the guests of the vice president of the Committee for Peace, with the Deputy Minister of Education. The old gentleman told us about the play that we would see that night. Quite cordial.

In the evening, at the opera, the harmony, the movements, the opulence and the silks were wonderful and the music sometimes reminded us of Byzantine music. The greatest actor of China, Mei Lan-fang, sixty-four years old, was playing the beautiful young lady. . . .

A rich day; from now on Kazantzakis would never again put down in his little red notebook that he felt tired. His soul rejoiced, and his body rejoiced, too, listening to the soul.

What a pity that he did not have the time to tell you himself what he saw and heard in China. Now I would like to make a brief remark: "Wonder" is for us a bitter repetition, but for him it is a bead of an amber rosary, which he caresses softly with the tips of his fingers and then lets fall and be one with the rest.

Wherever we went, he always asked me to open my notebook and begged me: "Write! Write it! Or you will forget it!" As if he had an intuition that only these crumbs would remain from the entire trip . . .

The Japanese occupied Peking for nine years. During these nine years they stole and burned what they could.

Twenty years ago, Kazantzakis described the roofs of the palaces covered with grass, the doors unlatched, the columns eaten by worms. In the last few years the Chinese with the difficult problems they had to solve—to feed six hundred million people, to repair the roads and bridges and make new ones, to tame the floods, to fight the terrible epidemics of smallpox, typhus, cholera, plague and even worse ones of superstition, illiteracy, filth and stink— have also had to take care of the palaces, the parks and the temples, because that was their heritage.

Now everything is as tidy as the anonymous multitude in Peking. The temples and the palaces are repainted, the walls rebuilt, the doors fixed; the roofs shine without grass; the museums are being refilled. Every shovel, every ax that digs the Chinese earth uncovers an old treasure, as it still does in Greece.

The Chinese even had their Earl of Elgin,* not the same one, but his only son. He caused a great destruction, following the orders of His Majesty. His soldiers burned the summer palace of the empress of China. They stole and killed many people. But this noble Englishman to placate his conscience, every evening put down in his diary: "I thought with bitterness of those who for egotistical reasons destroy an ancient civilization." Or: "May the good Lord help us so that we will not bring poverty and destruction by opening this country to the West. . . ."

A French nobleman, Count d'Erson, writes that they turned everything into dust and crumbled pieces: "My soldiers," he says somewhere, "covered up to their heads in the trunks of the empress, are half dead under mountains of silk and brocade; others put rubies, sapphires, pearls and golden jewelery into their pockets, into their shirts, into their caps and cover their chests with necklaces of big pearls. . . . The men of the engineering battalion have brought their hatchets and break the furniture to take out the gems that are wedged inside the precious wood. . . ."

Another Frenchman, the famous author and naval officer Pierre Loti, left us unforgettable descriptions of the vandalism of the English and the French in Peking in 1900. He had the courage to play Handel and Bach on the

---

* From 1803 to 1812 the Earl of Elgin removed the bulk of the surviving metope of the Parthenon, which in 1816, together with additional sculpture, was purchased by him on behalf of the British government.

organ of the church in Peking while his soldiers killed, looted and burned.

Later, on our tour from Peking to the southern gates of China, we would often remember the horrible descriptions of Pierre Loti, the Earl of Elgin and Count d'Erson, and also other descriptions which are full of admiration and were written by various missionaries—Jesuits or Protestants—before various friends and enemies "civilized" China. Father Hook, a very smart Basque, toured all of China with a friend of his; he was chased out of Tibet and condemned to death; he toured with all the comforts and honors that become an important representative of a friendly kingdom. . . .

He speaks of cities that we also saw on our trip and which we could only describe as terrible muddy villages. They were in his time "first-class" cities, as for example Ichang, along the Yangtze. . . . And more recently, another missionary and professor of philosophy, Robert Payne, describes Kunming and its famous university (where he taught before the last war) with its palaces and its temples with respect and love. . . . We saw only a poor city and a large but very poor university; everything else had been burned to the ground either by the Japanese or during the war with Chiang Kai-shek. Even Chungking was bombed one hundred and fifty times by the Japanese and as many times by the planes of Chiang Kai-shek. . . . What do you expect to be left? Where are the palaces, the temples, the rich clothing stores, the opulent private houses with their yards, the museums, the beautiful public buildings? Everywhere you find ruins. The foreigners—Mongols, Japanese, British and French—and finally the Chinese themselves during the civil war, have left the mark of destruction in the places they passed.

The old missionaries also described the universities, the thousands of roads, the important bridges, the irrigation works, the cultured and beloved mandarins who once were the fathers of their race. But the barbarians came, the Manchu conquerors, who were only a handful of men but enslaved five hundred million people. . . . How did they succeed? They got the idea in their heads that from then on every mandarin would not have the right to stay in the same place longer than three years. He would go from city to city, from village to village throughout his life, and never stay and rule the place where he was born, so that he would not be interested in his "people." Where he is appointed, no one would know him. Thus he would lose his shame; he could steal and lie quite freely.

This devilish psychology succeeded. The mandarins, once fathers of their race, ended up as the greatest enemies of the poor people. What did they care about? They stole, made money and spent their old age well.

It's not a secret that until recently the peasants threw their female infants to the pigs because they were so poor that they couldn't feed them. Or they sold them to their neighbors; they married them with the neighboring boys when they were still in diapers to become the maids of their "husbands" until death. That's why so many suicides take place in China.

Claude Roi, a friend of our guide Wang who assured us that what Roi says is true, writes in his book, The Keys of China, that once he was in a small town and attended a divorce trial. The judge talked with a mother who held by the hand her thirteen-year-old son who looked around openmouthed. Next to them was a young woman—the wife of the boy. Seeing how passionately the mother accused her daughter-in-law you would think that she asked for the divorce: "And when my little one caught a cold last winter, do you think she took good care of him? No. She let him go to school with fever. And when he got lice, she let me wash him with black soap. And at the season the watermelons are plenty, she let him eat too many and he had diarrhea. And then . . ." Claude Roi says the series of complaints went on until the mother revealed that the young woman asked for a divorce. The girl was married to her son when she was seventeen years old and he only nine. Now the girl wanted to marry a young man who loved her and whom she loved. But the mother-in-law cried: "I've spent so much for her and she didn't take good care of my son." To this the judge retorted, "If this is so, then you should be pleased that she wants to leave." "Hum," the old woman readily answered, "she cost us so much. We fed and dressed her for four years. . . . Who's going to pay us for that now?"

At noon we were invited to dinner by the vice president of the Peace Committee. An old gentleman dressed in a black silk robe with a long and sparse goatee welcomed us. He was the calligrapher and sage, Chen Shu-tung who was also the Deputy President of the Parliament.

We sat on comfortable sofas and drank tea. On the walls there were large paintings, mostly of flowers. Wang whispered to us when we entered that the old gentleman had donated his private collection of one hundred wonderful paintings of blossomed plum trees to the State. They introduced us to the Deputy Minister of Education, Dr. Wei Shuen, who told us what we were to see in the opera. When he spoke to us about old Chinese poetry, his eyes shone. They also introduced us to the famous and wise legal authority, Hsu Pao-tsin, a likable small man whose eyes smiled with kindness.

I didn't take notes that day. I only recall that Mr. E. spoke about Nikos and himself to the Chinese, who listened with great interest about distant Greece—Sila, as they say in Chinese.

After the dinner, the Deputy Minister of Education turned our conversation back to the theater and said:

"You are very lucky. Tonight you will see Mei Lan-fang!"

Mei Lan-fang! No Chinese utters this name without deep love, respect and pride. They had already told us so much about him that we were afraid of having one of the greatest disappointments of our lives. . . . A retiring wise gentleman who is sixty-four years old playing the role of an eighteen-year-old girl. . . .

"Tonight he will play only one act from an old classical Chinese fairy tale," Wei Shuen explained to us. "A princess who is about eighteen years old tires of her loneliness. She complains to her governess who consoles her and lets her wander in the garden through the blossomed cherry trees. 'Patience, patience, my little darling, and everything will come in its time. . . .' The girl goes to the garden and wanders free of cares from one tree to another and from flower to flower. She gets tired, sits on the bench, and falls asleep. And in her dream, the handsome prince comes. . . .

That is all. But on the evening we saw it, it seemed to us that a new world opened before us. . . .

The theater was suffocatingly crowded. The heat was terrible. Wang had already equipped us with fans.

A peasant with his little boy on his knees sat next to me. Behind us there was a family with six children. No one made the slightest noise. Only the whispering of Wang was heard in the room. But we were foreigners. No one protested.

They played one act of each of three long plays.

The first was the story of the second wife of the emperor who, in order to save her country from the Mongol conqueror, must go and surrender herself to him. The wife was played by a very beautiful woman. We would swear that a more beautiful woman does not exist. No scenery, only a golden yellow drape. From time to time they brought on a table or a chair like a throne. The costumes were indescribably rich, embroidered, multicolored, and the actors were distinguished by the costume they wore. One was a general with six small flags pinned at the back of his cap; the other, a mandarin wearing a white hat with a black stripe; the young man who held a stick with multicolored rags was supposed to be the horse, and so on. We could not distinguish them, but the Chinese knew not only what everyone represented but also his character— red stood for bravery, black and white for cowardice, and the unpainted was the honest and noble character. They also knew from his conventional stylized movements exactly what the actor meant at every moment.

"You see, now he raises his foot, which means he goes out of his home. . . . Now he raises it again, which means he enters his friend's house." Wang was tireless in trying to explain to us as much as he could, but even without an explanation the show was so rich and harmonious that it enchanted us.

The poor woman cried, a long, monotonous weeping that tore your heart. She did not want to go. She loved her husband. She begged and tried to awaken the shame in men who expect everything from a woman. Cowards, good-for-nothings, who eat bread without earning it. . . .

A chorus of richly dressed girls, silent, surrounded her. Various boys went in and out performing somersaults. Finally the groups started out to accompany the victim. At the borders we saw the sentry of the Mongol emperor. . . .

The people rose quietly and went out to the courtyard to buy ice cream. Wang offered us ice cream. His slender hands trembled. He appeared nervous, as if he were about to go on stage. Would we like Mei Lan-fang? That was his concern and anxiety. He became pale.

When Mei Lan-fang appeared as a thin-waisted princess, you could have heard a pin drop. His fresh oval face, his huge almond-like eyes, his ricelike little teeth, his swordlike eyebrows, and his cheeks like ripe peaches would not let us discern—although we sat in the fourth row—the real face under the make-up. Here was really a case of magic.

His raven hair hung like a thick tassel down his back; his cap was embroidered and full of gems and he had two thin and long antennas made of peacock feathers which moved and bent as he moved his head. His? Let me say from now on her, because I am nearer the truth. She moved her head, laughed, spoke, stubbornly kicked her little foot, sang with a very thin Chinese voice, hissing and lingering but nevertheless attractive. We kept talking about her voice for the rest of our trip. . . . She was the epitome of woman. Naturally, all her gestures meant something which escaped us. The other spectators who could read Chinese were aided by the text that was projected on the wall to the left and right of the stage. We had our indefatigable Wang.

As the fire and the cant frighten you, so do the two delicate hands of Mei Lan-fang. Under the broad sleeve of his robe always appeared a second long white and narrow sleeve, which covered his entire arm and hung down about a foot. That white sleeve, with an abrupt movement, was thrown on top of the other sleeve and the beautiful hand of the actor appeared. His fingers were so expressive and lively that you would forget that they were part of the rest of his body. This is the part of the great actor which often attracts you more than his face, even though the face is very beautiful. . . .

Our princess wore four robes, one on top of the other, which she let fall like the petals of a magic lotus. The first was red with golden dragons, the second blue-green and from the waist down entirely blue like a foaming sea, the third was apricot, embroidered with branches of cherry blossoms, the fourth was violet, full of wisterias. . . .

We went out to the yard and ate ice cream again; we were refreshed under the soft light of the star-studded sky. In the third act, another very important actor very dear to the Chinese, Han She-chang, played a fresh peasant girl sixteen years old. Where does he find all this gaiety and caprice! All the people burst out laughing with his whims. And he, too, is in his sixties. During the nine years of Japanese occupation in Peking he had never acted and had grown a beard, as Mei Lan-fang had. And a friend of theirs, also a great actor, Tseu Hsin-fang, out of fear that the Japanese might force him to act, hid himself, announced his death, and had his friends build a grave for him. . . .

Wang is pure; he doesn't like compromises. At least that's what I think, because he avoided talking to us about another famous actor of the Opera of Peking, Ma Liang-lieng. Although Ma Liang-lieng may be a great actor, he certainly doesn't have a great soul, and Wang is one who loves only those whom he can admire. Ma Liang-lieng, who never plays feminine roles (we saw him two days later playing a terrible general, the kind of hero who makes the earth tremble when he walks on it), had collaborated with the Japanese. And when the Red Army began to win, he left for Hong Kong and was afraid of returning to China.

But Mao knows how to forgive those who are needed. He brought him back, not by force, but by persuasion. He assured him that no one would annoy him as long as he lived quietly and played for the people of China. Today Ma Liang-lieng lives in a rich house in the heart of Peking with his wife, his mistresses, his children and grand children and smokes, as the evil tongues say, his opium pipe.

Ma Liang-lieng is no exception. Mao has forgiven many enemies of his regime.

I recall that at an official reception we happened to mention the wise and amiable ambassador of Nationalist China in Athens, whom we praised highly. The Chinese not only did not attack him, but even said nice things about him and assured us that he was free to return to the mainland of China, if he wanted to, and live freely any way he liked.

June 24. In the morning, visited the old painter Chi Pai-shi, who received the Peace Prize. Ninety-six years old, hard of hearing, not understanding well, but very likable. Stingy, with double locks on everything. Also visited some cool, clean houses in poor neighborhoods.

Chi Pai-shi did not feel well. Nevertheless, he politely invited us to visit. He wanted to meet Kazantzakis. When we reached his house, we found him in bed. Through the half-open door we could see his sons respectfully lifting him out of bed and his daughters-in-law dressing and grooming him. He sat next to us on a patriarchal armchair wearing a beautiful black silk robe and a black silk cap. With his long and sparse beard he looked exactly like the sages who muse under a rock in the old paintings.

Chi Pai-shi, the son of a poor peasant, spent his youth taking his master's oxen to pasture and gathering wood for his fire. But at the same time he tried to learn an art. He became a furniture-maker, but even this art did not satisfy him. He began to carve stamps and became popular in his home town for them and also for his calligraphy. One day, they told us, while carving a stamp, he cut his finger and lost a lot of blood and fainted.

He was twenty-seven years old when he used the paintbrush for the first time. He died in September, 1957. He left behind thousands of paintings. In every house we visited we saw his flowers, his shrimps or his insects, always in an honored position. The Chinese love and honor him more than any other painter.

"I have been painting for seventy years now," he said to his friends, "and still I am not sure about myself. I would like to paint all the animals and all the insects and all the plants that exist in this beautiful world. But if you ask me to paint a dragon, I will not succeed in doing it because I have never seen a dragon."

"In which school can we place him?" I asked Wang when they photographed Chi Pai-shi with Kazantzakis.

"He does not belong to any school," Wang responded. "In his fifties he did not paint at all like he did in his thirties, and in his seventies not at all like in his fifties. He has a style entirely his own: with two or three strokes of his brush he paints the thinnest insect or the most complicated animal. Do you remember his shrimps which you liked so much? In every one of his paintings the love for life is effusive."

"Can you explain to me why they honored him with the Peace Prize?"

"Of course. Chi Pai-shi is not only the best of our contemporary painters but also a man of integrity. When the Japanese came, he immediately took his paintbrush and wrote a sign which he hung on the outside door of his house: CHI PAI-SHI DOES NOT SELL HIS PAINTINGS TO THE OFFICIALS.

"By officials he meant the Japanese occupation forces and their Chinese collaborators. And in one of his paintings he had painted some crabs and wrote on top: 'for how long, do you think, you can rule us?' "

"Would you like to show us your house?" we asked Wang as soon as we came out of Chi Pai-shi's house. "We would like to see a Chinese home where they don't expect us."

Wang was very pleased, because, as we understood later, he was very proud of his house, which his mother had built herself.

"With pleasure!" he told us. "I hope we'll find my mother there who will be very happy to meet you."

Mrs. Wang was there. She welcomed us with great politeness and immediately offered us tea and candy. In the living room we saw a radio and a phonograph. Then she showed us the rest of the rooms. As in all the Chinese

houses, there is a series of rooms around the central courtyard. All the rooms used to be theirs, but now the regime
has taken half of the rooms. The courtyard is very clean,
with the necessary flowerpots and the small tree at the
corner. Two children played alongside the small cistern,
and when they saw us, they rushed inside.

"And where are your wife and children?" we asked our
guide.

"At the hospital. She is an obstetrician; we can go and
see her whenever you wish."

"Is she satisfied with her work?"

"Of course! She had 150 births this month."

The plum tree symbolizes the heroism of China. It blossoms first, it endures in the cold and the snow, and always
preserves its beauty.

In the evening, the performance of the young people
who were to leave for the Moscow festival. Flexibility,
grace, rhythm, colors. Remember the dance of the swords
and of the peacock!

June 25. An excursion to the Great Wall, sixty-two kilometers from Peking. A cultivated plain, new buildings,
mountains, towers on the summits of the wall which is
twenty-two thousand kilometers in length.

We ate at the beautiful pavilion, then went to the
graves of the Ming. What a magnificent sight! A valley
circled by mountains; at the entrance a huge marble
turtle holds a gravestone. Then an avenue with huge
statues right and left: lions, elephants, camels, horses,
generals and ministers. Then a big hall with twenty-four
gigantic columns made of whole trunks of trees (1400
A.D.).

As we left Peking we passed through neighborhoods
with large new apartment buildings. The roads are protected by double rows of trees from the sand that the wind

carries from the Gobi Desert. We passed through poor houses made of mud, with wax paper instead of glass in the windows. Pigs and children, barefoot but rather well fed.

The landscape here reminded me of Greece: smooth hills with only a few pine trees. The Great Wall, like a prehistoric reptile, ascends and descends the small mountains; here you see it, there you lose it. Unwillingly you think of how much sweat and hardship has gone into building this great beast.

The tourist pavilion was clean and comfortable. We ate, drank beer and lemonades, then we lay down on comfortable sofas. In this place there wasn't even a fly.

The valley with the thirteen graves of the Ming covers an area of forty square kilometers. We counted the columns in the largest grave: twenty-four columns in the middle, each made from one piece. The colors we knew: red, blue, green. The tiles are golden yellow. Wheat is planted in the plain.

To reach the first grave you pass through a gate of white marble. The heads of the columns are flames and leaves of cactus. A second gate is as red as the walls of the Forbidden City, and then there is another red gate, inside of which is the huge turtle with the gravestone. In front of you now you see a pagoda with terraces and marble railings. Before the marble stairs, as in the palaces of Peking, are flowerpots with roses and pomegranates. And at the ends you see big, picturesque cedars and a few old pine trees.

Finally we got to the grave itself—three stories high, marble terraces, golden yellow rooftops with existing and imaginary little animals on their four upturned ends.

"The top of every grave," Wang explained to us, "has its exact counterpart under the earth. There are still many which we have not found yet. But I am sure we shall find them sometime."

As we left, we passed again by the ministers, the generals, the horses, the camels, the elephants, the lions—this strange caravan that has been turned into stone in front of the graves of the Ming, and we came to the exit with its magnificent white gate which looked like a Greek capital Π.

June 26. In the morning, the doctor. Analysis of my blood (good, forty thousand white blood cells). In the afternoon, the first meeting of the Chinese Parliament. Chou En-lai spoke for three hours. Then we saw the great sage, Kuo Mo-jo, president of the Academy. And then we spoke to Chou En-lai in the garden. Charming, cheerful, we spoke about Cyprus.

In order to understand the meaning of the speech of the Chinese prime minister we must remember that Red China has already passed through two stages: the first, absolutely Communistic, during which even literature had to be subjugated to what was considered politically advantageous. And when the chaos began to take on a face, Mao gave the signal for self-criticism, the so-called Three Anti, Five Anti and Chen-feng, that is, "the leveling of the line." It's time, he declared, to take the beam from our eyes, and then we'll see how we'll help our adversaries take the splinter from theirs.

But man is always the same regardless of whether he is white, yellow, black or red. As soon as you give him your little finger, he will try to eat up your arm. And behind the country's interest is hidden almost always the individual's interest. Some believe that this was not the case with Mao Tse-tung and Chou En-lai.

When the leaders of Red China had given the people some of the much-desired freedom and had asked the people and the local leaders to voice their complaints clearly, the fanatics of the two factions—the rightists and the leftists—took the opportunity to attack their adversaries. The rightists attacked the leftists, but the fanatic leftists did not only accuse the reactionaries but also some old Communists who did not happen to be as fanatic as they. And if it were not for Mao Tse-tung and Chou En-lai no one knows where this turmoil would have led.

They, without losing a moment, condemned the extremists and hit hard at the trouble spots without shedding any blood.

But let's hear Chou En-lai himself speak about it:

> China is an agricultural country, a poor country, politically and economically retarded, with a large population and relatively little tillable earth. . . . As things stand, our standard of living is very low, if you compare it to that of other countries where industry is well developed.
>
> We have six hundred million people. If the purchasing power of every one of us increases by one yen per year, that means that the country's purchasing power will increase by six hundred million yen, and consequently the government must also increase the goods of the country by six hundred million yen.
>
> Therefore, we must advance very prudently and slowly. . . . Some say that there is a big difference between the standard of living of the peasant and that of the worker. Is that true? Naturally, we must accept that there is a difference; but when we compare the conditions of the two types of life we must not forget the difference in living in the country and in the city. . . . In the old times most of our peasants wore rags and starved. . . . Now, twenty-five to thirty per cent of them have a little more than they need, over sixty per cent have as much as they need and only ten to

fifteen per cent do not have as much as they should, and we must help them.

In the future, when we decide the workers' wages we must be more careful to make the worker understand that he cannot live without the peasant. . . . And as long as the standard of living of our peasants cannot be raised, the workers must not ask for quick improvement of their lives.

Immediately after the liberation, the system of wages in our country was chaotic—big gaps between high and low wages and between what seemed important and unimportant to us. As far as the system of apprenticeship is concerned, it would have been right to throw away the bad feudal laws, but there were many good things in those laws, as, for example, the period of apprenticeship, the various techniques of teaching, the wages for the apprentices and the remuneration for their teachers. We should study these things carefully and we should adopt them.

Some of the apprentices took on airs. They think it is easy to possess technical knowledge and they do not have enough respect for the technical experience of the old men who acquired it through hard work and practice. They are sometimes too proud to ask the opinion of the old workers or to learn something from them. This tendency prevented the unity of young and old workmen and marred the relations between the craftsmen and their apprentices. . . . We must patiently teach these young workers. . . . Our old workers are one of the treasures of our country; they have a wealth of technical dexterity and also political and social experience.

In the villages we should also teach the young

peasants to respect the old men and to learn humbly from their experiences what is needed for the cultivation of the land and for the political life of our country.

Now, let's come to the question of education. China is very retarded. . . . Over seventy per cent are illiterate. The pupils in the elementary schools increased from twenty-four million in 1949 to sixty-three million in 1956. . . . The money that the Government spent from 1951 to 57 reached 4,900,000,000 yen; that is over fifty-four per cent of the money that generally has been spent for education. Nevertheless, we still are not pleased. . . . At the beginning we made unwarranted efforts for the establishment of gardens in public schools, and the building of more schools. Now we correct our errors. Great progress has been made for the education of our people and for their future on the principles: "Let a hundred flowers blossom" and "Let's learn to create the new from the old." We shall do even more to increase the initiative and the creative genius of our people.

We have done more than a little in the last few years for the improvement of medical care and the health conditions of our people. . . . Some of the most dangerous diseases—plague, cholera, smallpox—are today under control.

Nevertheless, we sometimes observe that unity and mutual respect are lacking between the doctors and the nurses.

If we want to throw away poverty and ignorance once and for all and build a socialistic China with modern industry and agriculture where our people will be able to enjoy a happy life, we must fight very hard for a long time. Victory is not a question of a few years; decades are needed. . . . From the leaders to those in the lowest rank, we must select a way of life characterized by hard work and strict economy. . . . And we of the older generation must teach the young and help them understand that the good life can be achieved only through our ceaseless effort.

Intermission. We went out to the cool yard with the trees and the refreshments. We relaxed, we enjoyed the fresh air, we reentered to hear the rest of the speech. Now Chou En-lai spoke about the crisis that was created after the last Chen-feng, when friends and enemies were invited to say their opinions clearly and honestly.

The People's Republic of China is directed by the working class and is based on the alliance of the worker and peasant. In our country almost all the power belongs to the people. . . . The people exercise their power through the National People's Congress and the local People's Congresses on all the levels.

Our system is based on the socialistic and economic relations of our country. With this system we had great triumphs in the establishment of socialism in our country. . . . We must continue to believe in our system in order to succeed in the establishment of a socialist society in China.

Consequently, there is no reason to allow aimless discussions on the basis of our electoral system. However, this does not mean that we cannot improve certain points of our government organization. On the contrary, improvement and development are often necessary. We should not forget that the socialist organization in our country is still in its cradle.

Our system is based on democracy and dictatorship. Some think that after the final victory of the socialist revolution there is no reason for the existence of a dictatorship. That is not correct. It is an error, because there are still remnants of entire revolutions in our country that are trying to find an opportunity to fight us. . . . There are those individuals who come from the class that used to exploit our people. And there are still many others: thieves, crooks, killers who violate law and order. And we must not forget Chiang Kai-shek and the American imperialism which send spies and provocateurs to us every day.

Nevertheless, I must stress that bureaucracy still exists to a serious degree in our government machine on various levels. Socialism has just been established in our country. The personnel of the government machine is still infected by the customs of the old society, especially by the middle-class ideas.

They accuse us of placing walls and ditches between the Communists and non-Communists . . . They say the Communists do not have enough respect for the non-Communists, individuals and organizations. . . . That is a serious fault of sectarianism. There is still a class of non-Communists who do not show enough interest, who are even indifferent about their work. They look down on the Communist Party and its members. Nevertheless, the Communist Party tried to help them. These last two cases require great care and we must make every possible effort to correct them.

Studying these cases I see one solution. First,

the members of the Communist Party must follow with all their heart the policy of the united front in order to help defeat sectarianism, and they must learn to respect and help the non-Communists and humbly listen to their opinions and criticisms and benefit from their technical ability and experience and thus improve themselves.

The campaign that we began to correct the "line" of the Communist Party aims to combat bureaucracy, sectarianism and subjectivity. For that reason, we must welcome every constructive criticism, even if it is excessive or unrealistic.

However, some rightists say that the three evils I mentioned above have been brought about by the people's dictatorship. These are unjust accusations and we cannot accept them. Socialism is in the general interest of all the people, especially the working class. A socialist country must and can mobilize the great majority of its people to participate in the organization and administration of the country. Consequently, there is no place in a socialistic country for bureaucracy, sectarianism and subjectivity.

Comrades, deputies! In his speech of February 27, 1957, Mao Tse-tung said that we must learn to distinguish two types of conflicts—the conflict between ourselves and the enemy and the conflicts among our own people. But it is not impossible for the one type of conflict to be mixed with the other and take its place. Those who are still under surveillance—when they become "new men" after they have been corrected through work, then they can enjoy their political rights and also become members of the people. And, on the other hand, certain individuals or groups who

are now members of the people may become enemies of the people if they continue to insist on
their antisocialist ideas, if they resist the socialist
reform and want to blow up the socialist structure.

The rightists of the middle classes, although
they still are among the lines of the people, resist
socialism, and even commit acts which are against
the interests of socialism. Because of this, we
must draw a sharp line between us and the rightists, politically and ideologically, and start a campaign against them in order to enable the large
majority, the true patriots, to see that the criteria
and the acts of the rightists are erroneous. . . .
We hope that after we isolate them, they will
think it over and will recover and will "re-enter
into the right mold". . . . The door of socialism
is still open for them. But a small number of the
rightists may insist on a reactionary view and refuse to "re-enter into the mold" and even commit acts of sabotage against the socialist states. In
that case, they will be removed from the people.

Comrades, deputies! The international situation is favorable for socialism. If we stand on the
brilliant principles of our President, Mao Tse-
tung, and handle the conflicts among our people
correctly, we, the Chinese people, will forge with
our struggle a still stronger unity fighting the
rightists, the anti-socialists. . . . When we continue our endeavor to strengthen our national
and international unity and to achieve increase of
production, economy and reconstruction of our
country through a ceaseless struggle and a strict
economy, no force in the world will be able to
stop the victorious advance of our great socialist
idea.

After Chou En-lai finished his speech, he came out in the yard where they presented to him the various groups of foreign visitors; first the Japanese, then the English, and others. He spoke and laughed with all. . . .

Kazantzakis asked him to change his attitude on Cyprus. . . .

I asked what exactly the rightists had done.

"They have not yet understood that our country can be saved only if we all remain united," answered the indefatigable Wang.

At this point I reread my notes. Unfortunately they are not clear. Therefore, I prefer to say briefly how the well-known right-wing socialist and former premier of France, M. Edgar Faure, who left China at about the time we arrived, saw and explained the situation:

The San fan, the campaign of Three Anti, had begun in 1951 and the Wu fan, the campaign of Five Anti, soon after. What were those campaigns about?

The first was directed against the functionaries of the Communist Party. The slogan of San fan was "Down with bureaucracy! Down with waste! Down with corruption!"

There was even a sensational trial which was broadcast by megaphones in the public gardens, the universities and the government offices. . . . Seven "big shots" were brought to justice. Two of them were condemned to death. All those who made special favors, accepted bribes —the incompetent, the flippant—were severely punished.

The Five Anti, the Wu fan, was directly mainly against the merchants and not only against the big businessmen, as one would think. Down with their five basic shortcomings: accepting gifts, avoiding paying taxes, stealing from the state, sabotaging the work, and selling inferior products. . . . (We were then at the period of the Korean War.) "War against the tigers, big or small, according to their illegitimate profits."

The campaign of Wu fan had one sure result: it lowered

the prices by five per cent, because the merchants, in order to save their heads, were pleased to sell their hidden stock.

As soon as we arrived in China, we heard the new slogan. It seemed new to us, but Mao had thrown it to the people for the first time years ago. "Let a hundred flowers blossom and a hundred schools contend. . . ." Pravda had announced the Chen-fang in April, 1957.

When, however, the displeased got up and started expressing their opinions openly and the most hot-blooded youths flooded the streets and started riots, Chou En-lai decided to change policy and deliver the speech we happened to hear.

And here is what Edgar Faure learned, which our likable guide, Wang, naturally did not tell us.

On June 12 and 13, in Hanyang (Hupeh), over a thousand students got into the streets and began to sing and shout anti-Communist slogans. They entered the city hall and wanted to tie the mayor with ropes; since they did not find him there, they took with them two municipal employees. The authorities suspect that their professors not only did not restrain them but even encouraged them.

On June 17, four days before our arrival in Peking, a medical student, twenty-three years old, threw a bomb at the secretary of the Communist Committee of the Medical School at Peking.

On June 25, four days after our arrival, the mayor of a town was assassinated. Seven persons were assassinated on June 12.

We went to the agricultural fair of the whole of China. The most luxurious pavilion had been built and donated by the Russians who had used it once in one of their own fairs. Similar pavilions, almost exactly alike, we were to see later in other cities. Charming Chinese girls with pointers in their hands explained statistics to soldiers and peasants who listened to them openmouthed. Huge potatoes which weighed forty to fifty pounds each. Beautiful, round eggplants; strange, longish cabbages, like Greek lettuces. Only two kinds of grapes. Tiny brown chestnuts, squash, green peppers, pineapples, cacao, grapefruits, soya beans, corn and many other products. . . .

June 27. I wasted the morning in the hospitals. In the evening, to the opera. They played the *Divine Ape*, who is a terrible rebel who fights against every authority, and only Buddha defeats him. I admired again the amazing flexibility, harmony and grace of the Chinese. Somersaults, juggling, dances, song, joviality—all perfect!

Yes, the show was again excellent. The Divine Ape and the other demons made double and triple somersaults. They would take a running stretch and would dive from all four sides of the stage like dolphins—with head down, the one on top of the other, as many as four deep. Noiselessly, without breathing heavily. Drops of perspiration as big as chick peas ran from the wig of the Divine Ape.

"How old is this amazing actor?" we asked Wang.

"He is not yet twenty!"

And Wang licked his lips in enthusiasm about the impression the young actor had made on us.

Chang Chuen-hwa is a small man who looks like a boy of fifteen and is flexible like a monkey. He climbs on trees and rocks; he jumps on the imperial throne, he enters the caves, he steals the apples of immortality, eats them rapidly, spits the seeds on the ground—imaginary apples and imaginary seeds; he bursts out laughing, he rejoices, he does somersaults, he fights with the bad demons, he defeats the double-crossing greedy ministers, but Buddha's disciples come and chain him. . . .

June 28. The university. Simple and low, outside of Peking. A likable professor. A female student's room. A crowd of charming, smiling female students encircled us;

many of them spoke French and German. A petite girl, Foot Looree, continuously held me by the hand, fanned me with her fan, and smiled at me. I shall never forget Foot Looree.

The most beautiful water deposit in the world. A high tower made of green and red pagodas, the one on top of the other. . . .

Yes, we shall never forget the real face of China.

Only once did I have to tell our Chinese friends that Kazantzakis should not eat salt. From Peking to Hong Kong, if we ate from ten to twenty different dishes, wherever we were invited, Kazantzakis saw them bring to him these different dishes without salt. . . . And now, at the university, our friends had informed them that Kazantzakis was coming, that he was a little sick, and must not be tired. And the president of the university with great love and care selected Foot Looree to fan him, to hold him, to help him sit down. . . . Oriental politeness that combines kindness with beauty and joy. At a moment I turn and what do I see? Foot Looree has bent over the chest of Kazantzakis; she unbuttons his shirt quietly, opens it as much as she can, holds with one of her small hands the collar so that it won't close again and with her other hand she fans him. Everybody began to laugh.

"Yes, I know very well that I am not sick," Kazantzakis shouts enthusiastically, "but I can't help it because I am enjoying this."

If the Russians, by building the huge University of Moscow, decided to give all the possible comforts to the students of the Soviet Union, the Chinese started from an entirely different principle and built a very simple university that has everything that is needed, but absolutely no unnecessary luxury, lest the student who comes from a distant poor village get accustomed to it and not want to return to his village.

"And what can we do with the doctors if they all gather in the large cities. We need them," the professor who showed the university to us explained, "to go around in the villages and small towns and spread joy and knowledge everywhere in China."

He is right, and thus we were not surprised when we saw the very narrow beds that looked like the berths of a ship. We also observed that their laboratories and libraries were still very poor. Everything must be built from scratch. However, the park of the university was very beautiful with its high trees, evergreen bushes, flowers and brooks.

We ate at the summer palace of the empress. In its two-story theater they had presented two different plays simultaneously. The empress looked through her glasses and when she was tired of looking at the play below, she raised her eyes and attended the play on the upper floor.

Then we had an excellent walk, saw the lake, the frozen boat, a tunnel half a kilometer long with a carved and painted ceiling. In the evening we saw acrobats, a miracle of strength, grace and flexibility.

The tunnel under the lake led us to a good restaurant where we ate delicious Chinese food. We recalled another dinner: shark's fins, black eggs, bouillabaisse, ravioli, roast chicken which as soon as you touched it with the chopsticks broke as if it were made of glass, soup with ham and squash skins, green peppers, every kind of seaweed, various pickled vegetables, boiled bread and blancmange, with pineapple syrup. We drank black sweet wine and rum made of rice.

At the hotel we went up to the terrace with the jasmines where the Europeans used to get drunk and then go down, as Simone de Beauvoir says, and piss on the Chinese policemen.

It was a beautiful cool night, the sky was full of stars, the jasmine perfumed the air. And Peking spread like a garden city at our feet. Only those ugly chimneys which they build now to install central heating, and which we thought were factories at the beginning, made the panorama of Peking somewhat ugly beside the lake and the blue Temple of Heaven.

Our guide, Wang, always becomes more encouraged and opens his heart to us. He speaks to us of the bamboo which is obstructed by stones, but defeats them; farther on appear its roots, which go deeper as it tries to overcome the stones. Such must be the Chinese people.

He speaks to us about the lotus, the immaculate flower which grows in mud but doesn't have even one dirt spot. Such must be man.

June 29. Wang came to our room in the morning. We took a walk along the streets; we saw engravings. They gave me one. It was very hot. We returned to the hotel at noon on a ricksha.

We took another walk along the streets with Wang: big bookstores, a lot of magazines, young men who leaf through and voraciously read periodicals.

In the afternoon, to the temple of Lama, which is filled by the gilded statue of Milarepa bursting into laughter. There is a motto on the top saying: "In order to materialize the divine, you should clean your heart."

Later we saw the exquisite statue of Buddha made of white jasper with a golden tunic on his left shoulder; he smiles with abundant sweetness. I shouted to him "Nevermore," and I bid him farewell.

We visited a clothing factory, the second largest in Peking: 100,000 spools, 2,436 looms, 240,000 meters of fabric a day (cotton gabardines and cabot), 36,000 kilos of thread,

5,600 workers, 500 mechanics, 200 apprentices, et cetera.

The cleanliness and the good cool air impressed us most. In the winter it is heated by the same system. The working girls see the manager and they are no longer afraid. They sit quietly and read or work, depending on their hours. A little girl sprawled on a sack of threads is reading. She does not get up to stand at attention as the manager passes by. She only smiles.

They also showed us the nursery where the children of the workers play or sleep in their cradles. After working hours those who wish can be educated. There are seventy classes and the lessons are attended by three thousand workers. The classes range from grammar school to junior high.

We asked if the machines were Russian-made.

"No, they are Chinese. We have higher production rates when we use Chinese machines. Now we even export them."

No one under sixteen is allowed to work. They give fifty-six days off to the pregnant women. And after the seventh month of pregnancy, they make the work lighter.

We knew then why the women are very satisfied. They used to be eternal slaves of their father, their brother, their husband, their mother-in-law, and later of their son. Slaves until death. "The chicken does not crow in the morning," the old folk used to say. "Stupidity is her only virtue." That's what they used to believe, and they never let a woman talk like a human being. And the only thing a woman could do was to commit suicide. Or wait until she became a mother-in-law so she could torture, in her turn, her daughter-in-law.

June 30. A winter palace, courts, pavilion, gilded bronze censers. Porcelains, exquisite art, colors, finesse. *Bleu de Chine* . . .

During the entire afternoon, rest; I read de Beauvoir. I

plan to complete my book on China: *Twenty Years After.*

The turtle, oracle: they touch the shell of its belly with a burning iron and from the way it cracks they foretell things to come.

Mr. E. left for Manchuria. Kazantzakis read and talked avidly with Wang. Mrs. E. and I went again to the big covered bazaar where you can find books, clothes, knickknacks, preserved fruits, des olives coufites, corals, jade, fans, silverware, incense, sandals, umbrellas of wax paper and everything else you can think of.

The emperor could have thirteen official wives and as many mistresses as he pleased. Everyone of his official wives had her own pavilion, a small palace with a yard covered by tiles and fenced with high red walls. The furniture was of carved ebony or lacquered in red and black. We saw a few huge cabinet closets as high as the ceiling. Beds, short and wide, covered with brocade; carved thrones like the famous miniatures made of jade . . .

In the museum, their terra cottas reminded us very much of the Greek ones. And their vases are white with black geometrical forms. Later we come to the well-known Chinese colors, dark red, light pistachio, yellow with flowers bleu pervenche. The white craquelé, the cloisonné. We liked best of all the solid color vases with the delicate carvings, the white ones and the blue-green, which are barely distinguishable from white.

We also went to visit the musicians. We met the Chinese composer and violinist Ma Sa-chung, who is the general director of all the conservatories of China. He has written a great deal of good chamber music; we listened to one of his quintets. Very interesting. He played an Amati. The Chinese do not make famous violins. But in the past they made very good pianos. They even exported them.

Mrs. E. is very interested in the musical activities of China.

"How many orchestras do you have? How many conservatories? How many years does one have to study in order to graduate, et cetera?"

Mr. Ma Sa-chung and his colleague Ho Lu-ting, director of the Conservatory of Shanghai, gave us all the information we wanted. "We have two orchestras of over sixty instruments each, and four of about forty or less instruments each. In our conservatories, in Shanghai, in Tientsin, in Hankow, et cetera, the students study for seven years and then if they want to become soloists, five years longer. The Union of the Musicians has 588 members."

We listened to some popular songs of the minority groups. They pointed out an instrument, the erh hu, which looks like a violin, that Confucius used to play. In order to hear its sound, they gave us a record, a popular song of Yünnan. They also drew for us the p'i p'a, which has only two strings and a bass sound and which reminded us of the lute.

Our conversation about music changed to one about the theater.

"Do you know how many groups of amateur actors there are in China?"

"Thirty thousand! Seven thousand alone in the province of Szechwan."

"We couldn't imagine that there are so many, although we knew the love of the Chinese people for theater, music and poetry."

"There was a time," said the tireless Wang, "when all the people wrote poems—from the emperor and the prime minister to the street sweeper and the drunkard of the village."

"And the women too," added Mr. Ma Sa-chung, "in the good times. Do you know any of our old poetesses?"

"Yes, we know some, we have even translated one or two of their poems into Greek."

ALONE IN THE NIGHT
by Li I-Yan

The lukewarm rain and the fresh air
For the first time have freed the willow trees of
*   frost.*
I have looked at the peach trees and I have
*   already felt*
Spring in my heart.
My thoughts are disturbed by the wine,
And my poetry; who will share them with me,
Mingling his tears with mine?
My make-up has faded;
The adornments of my head are very heavy.
Still wrapped in my double garments
On the piles of my golden embroidered pillows
I lie and caress the pins in my hair.
In my loneliness I enclose in my heart
A bitter and heavy melancholy with no good
*   dreams.*
As the night advances, I cut and arrange
The flowering flames of the candles.

FATIGUE
by Chu Shu-cheng

Oh, blossoming spring! autumn moon!
Flowers that float on the lakes!
How you manage to draw along my heart
As if it were an unmoored little boat!
I no longer feel either bones or flesh.
Would I be able to endure once more such an
*   emotion?*

"I will give the Chinese authors the rights to my books,"
Kazantzakis told me. "I must pay back in some way the joy
they gave me."

"Which books do you think will interest them most?"

"I suppose *Freedom or Death*, *The Greek Passion* and *Zorba the Greek*. Bring me some paper and ink, please, and let me write a letter to them."

In two minutes the letter was ready. Kazantzakis gave his three novels to the writers of China.

July 1. In the morning I read de Beauvoir. In the afternoon, to a Buddhist temple. In the big red hall a monk in white welcomed us. We sat, had tea, and spoke a little until the Deputy President Biku Su-chan, a young man with bright eyes, came noiselessly, smiling. I mentioned how much I loved Buddhism; in my youth I sought the most heroic discipline and found it in Buddhism. But I am a Greek; I love and believe in the visible world and I put aside the invisible. But Buddha taught me that the visible world is also an illusion. Consequently, the struggle between Apollo and Buddha; love of the world and simultaenously of *nada* (nothing, chaos). That's why my youth was tragic. I struggled, I still struggle for a synthesis: to love the visible and simultaneously to know that it is a self-deception; and thus, knowing how ephemeral the world is, to love it with passion and tenderness.

Now I see with a free eye, I welcome everything. Three paths lead to superior wisdom: meditation, good deeds and beauty. Even a flower may lead you to the superior wisdom.

Biku said then: at the end of his life Buddha took a lotus, looked at it, and smiled. Only one of his disciples understood the meaning of that smile. And Buddha made him his successor.

And then I told him about the leaf of a tree: Christ crucified and Christ resurrected.*

---

* Here Kazantzakis refers to a Greek mystic who said that in one leaf of a tree you can see the entire world, Christ crucified and Christ resurrected.

Then I narrated a legend: Socrates wanted to learn from a wise Oriental the laws that govern a city. Buddha smiled at him; Socrates did not understand a thing and returned to Greece empty-handed.

A quiet, deep discussion. I told them that the Westerners can never become true Buddhists, because Buddha commands the denial of everything, while the Westerners want to conquer everything. I said to them that of the three paths of wisdom, I followed the path of beauty; and then Biku got up and brought me an English book.

"Here you will find," he said, "the method you selected."

We parted.

"You are the first Greek I've met," he said.

That evening, to the opera. Once more a wonder: the rhythm, the song, the movements, the costumes. But tonight, a new joy: the heroine wants to get across the river; she calls a boatman who comes holding an oar. And then an amazing pantomime begins: the woman is reluctant to enter the boat, then she enters—she shakes, totters as if she had entered a real boat. This is indeed a wonder; this stylized scene is much more realistic and much more expressive than if the boat were real. The spectator works with his imagination; he creates, makes the invisible visible, as he wishes, in the way that it would move him most. A real boat would limit his imagination and his emotion.

July 2. In the morning, relaxation. In the evening, reception and dinner at the Writers' Society. The Minister of Education, Mao Tun, professor at the university, a dramatic writer, poet, et cetera. Rich Chinese dinner. We spoke cordially of literature, of the theater, of progress in China.

Mr. Evelpides returned from his tour in Manchuria. He was very pleased. What he had seen he decided to include in a book he intended to write on China and its progress. Collective farms, factories, ways of work, et cetera.

July 3. Last day in Peking. Tomorrow morning we leave for our trip along the Yangtze with our dear friend Wang Shen-shi.

Paintings at palace: finesse and sensitivity, horses, a camel, flowers, exquisite bamboo. Then Ming Period. Later, decline, copying, overloading.

Divine yards with pine trees as those in a painting and with blossoming laurels and pomegranates. Many pomegranates . . .

Nikos gave the letter giving the rights to his books to Mao Tun. They did not expect it. All seemed very enthusiastic and moved.

"All the other writers," Wang whispered in my ear, "have accustomed us to expect the immediate question, 'When and how much?' and to figure out on paper their royalty percentage. . . ."

"Yes," I whispered in his ear, "but don't forget that Kazantzakis is not one of those others."

When we first came to China a cold sweat overcame us —how were we to distinguish one Chinese from the other and remember their names!

"Do you recall who were the ones we saw tonight or yesterday?" I asked our friends and Kazantzakis with true anxiety. "I still cannot distinguish the Chinese from the Japanese. . . ."

Kazantzakis laughed, but I was not sure that he managed any better than I.

That day, however, what a joy I experienced in recognizing unhesitatingly Mao Tun, the President of the Academy, and Hsia Yen, the well-known playwright, and Deputy Minister of Education, and Lo She-yi, who directs the literary publications.

"All three have worked with Lu Hsün, the Gorky of China, who died at the age of thirty-six," Wang told us.

We talked about spoken and purist Chinese, about the simplification of writing, the use of Latin characters; about the theater, whether it should continue following the ancient tradition, and of the leeway Communism gives writers to write what they wish.

"How come you don't know our slogan about 'the hundred flowers'?"

"Yes, yes, we know it, but we want to hear from you that you are free."

"Free," they shout with one voice. "But don't forget that art for art's sake is not valid for us any more in China. Because first of all we have one aim in our mind and our heart: with our writings we want to help our people free themselves from their old sins, their prejudices, their superstitions, their ignorance, their slavery, their fear, and from now on to live a more dignified life. And you, what are you doing in Greece?"

Our friends have many questions. They know the classic Greek writers fairly well, but they don't know a thing about modern Greek literature.

Here are some of the things I've put down in my notebook on what was said that evening:

"How do the writers and artists live today in China?"

"Our people love their writers very much. Their life is now more secure and gradually becomes easier as education and interest in the arts spreads in our country."

"How many copies of a good Chinese novel are printed?"

"From sixty thousand to eighty thousand. But when we want to popularize a book, we print four million copies. Nevertheless, remember that at the time of the Kuomintang our best authors, Lu Hsün, Mao Tun, and Kuo Mo-jo, were not printed in editions of more than two thousand copies."

"Does the government help the writers?"

"Special sums have been appropriated for those who are in financial difficulties. The workers, clerks, civil servants and, generally, every Chinese who has the talent and feels the need to write but cannot because he works to earn his living, has the right to take special leaves. Many of our writers today are deputies and members of the people's committees who participate in the government of our country.

"Before the liberation, the life of our authors was very hard. They led a miserable life and lived in attics and cellars. Today not only is their life not in danger but our people honor and respect them. Naturally, if an author loses his mind and thinks that only he exists and no one else, he will draw upon him the anger of public opinion. Because no one in our country has the right to think himself superior to the others."

"Which works do the Chinese people like best?"

"Those which describe the new man, those which speak of the new conquests of science and of art and which give courage to our people to create something beautiful and useful. The reading public of China loves a rich and broad literature that deals with all the problems of the contemporary man."

"Are the people and the writers of China interested in foreign literature?"

"Of course. The Chinese people never refuse to recognize other people's important virtues and take them as models. This happened, for example, with the Buddhist art, which has a tradition of two thousand years, and with the European literature of the nineteenth century, and with the Russian and classical Greek literature. From the day that Mao Tse-tung in 1942 spoke in Yenan, socialist realism has become the most important trend in Chinese literature; our reading public does not like the anti-realistic literature any longer.

"The General Society of Literary Writers of China had

705 members, 12 local associations and 1,115 followers in its entirety.

"According to the last statistics, which are not complete, from 1950 to 1956, 28,370 literary works were printed, and of these, 18,347 were original and circulated in 711,000 copies. In these numbers are not included the literary works which were published in popular editions in 1950 and 1951."

"Are the Chinese books expensive?"

"Not at all. After the liberation we lowered the prices of the books three times; from five to ten per cent in 1953, from four to twenty per cent in May, 1955; and once more from eight to twenty per cent in April, 1956. Now a book does not cost more than a yen, and consequently, everybody can buy books."

"Are there many magazines in China?"

"Fourteen in Peking alone. Literary Translations, devoted to foreign authors. Chinese Literature, which is published in English and aims at making our literature known to the foreigners. The Magazine of Poetry, which only publishes poetry. The Philological Periodical, which publishes theories and reviews. The Monthly Magazine, which publishes dramatic plays. Art, Letters of the Army, et cetera, each having a specialty, as the titles indicate. Such magazines are published in all the large cities of China and in most of the provinces."

"Are you free to write what you wish?"

"Yes. Our constitution is clear on this question. But if an author resists socialism and propagandizes for war or attacks the equality of the various races—in other words, if he impairs the common interest—then, naturally, he will lose the right to express his opinion freely.

"Some writers, however, raise objections, but they are honest and well-disposed, or they have certain shortcomings which can be corrected through free discussion. Then a public discussion begins; those who do not agree with them tell them directly. The writers have the right to answer and, if they can, they are free to prove they are right."

"Did you translate many foreign works?"

"Up to June, 1957, we translated 4,258 artistic and literary works from forty-six foreign languages. Among them, first came the Russian and Soviet books. Now we have made a plan to translate the greatest masterpieces of world literature.

"We have also translated and published Gorky, Chekhov, Ibsen, George Bernard Shaw, Molière, Kalidasa; most of their plays have been presented in the theater and have had a great success. Our people love tragedies and comedies."

"Which are the most famous Chinese writers, novelists, poets, playwrights?"

"Novelists: Mao Tun, Lao She, Pa Chin, Liu Pai-yu, Chou Li-po, Chao Shu-li. Poets: Ku Mo-go, Tien Tsum, Ping Hsin, Hsiao San, Emi Siao. Playwrights: Kuo Mo-jo, Lao-Se, Tsao Yu, Hsia Yen. The oldest are our guides because they have a great experience and because they want to help the young writers."

"Who are read most? The best or the worst?"

"The best."

"Will you simplify your system of writing?"

"We are studying this question very carefully. We have already begun a certain simplification and thus we save the people from extra pain in learning to write and to read our difficult ideograms. But we have not yet made any decision about the adoption of the Latin alphabet. We must thoroughly discuss this before we make any decision, because the entire nation is interested in this question."

"Is there a difference between your spoken and written language?"

"Yes. In China, writing is a means of helping all the people, regardless of dialect, to communicate by means of written signs, whereas speech is a means for everyday communication. Where there is an alphabet the difference is not so great because writing renders speech phonetically to a certain extent. Chinese writing is based on ideograms. Over eighty per cent of the Chinese characters are half phonetic and half pictographic; they express the meaning and the category to which the word belongs. For a long time we used to write in a literary language quite different from the spoken one. That's why there is still a difference between the way we write our ideas and the way we express them orally."

"Would you like to have a common language which can be understood by every Chinese?"

"Of course. Now we are trying to create a common language based on the pronunciation of the dialect of Peking, especially where the Han live. Although the language of the Han is the same, the pronunciation changes so much from province to province that often two Chinese who speak the same language cannot understand each other.

"The pronunciation in Peking is already widely used. In the last two years we made an effort to introduce it in the elementary and secondary schools of the Han territories, and we had satisfactory results. In other areas of China where minorities live, the people continue to speak and write their own dialect; but in order to be able to communicate with the other Chinese they have begun of their own volition to learn the language of the Han."

"Which foreign books are read most?"

"The Russian, and, naturally, the French. For example, Balzac and Maupassant, even Stendhal . . ."

"How many copies are printed of a good foreign novel?"

"Two hundred thousand. But we have literary magazines that circulate in three hundred thousand copies, others in one hundred fifty to two hundred thousand copies for the youngsters, and others for the soldiers. We also have specialized periodicals; sixty-four for the natural sciences, eighty-seven for applied sciences, thirty for medicine, thirty-nine for educators, and one hundred seven for the fine arts and letters. . . ."

We had asked Wang to show us a good Chinese motion picture. On that evening they presented especially for us the beautiful and sad film of Lou Hsun, The Sacrifice of the New Year, with a screenplay by Hsia Yen. We refrained from crying with difficulty. The fate of a poor woman was horrible. She either had to destroy herself by committing suicide, or destroy her daughter-in-law by living.

"Why," I asked Kazantzakis, "doesn't the Chinese mother-in-law follow the humane commandment: Do unto others what you would have them do unto you? Why does she forget what she suffered before she became a mother-in-law?"

Kazantzakis lifted his eyes from the book he was reading, gazed at me silently and sighed: "Bottomless is the heart of man, my dear. . . ."

"I will try to find for you The Girl with the White Hair," Wang told us that evening, pleased that we liked the Chinese film. "It's a very old Chinese movie; the whole of China has cried watching it; you will too. I only hope I can find it; I am not sure. . . ."

We were sure he would. You could never ask anything of a Chinese that he would not give you. They had told us that in France; now we saw it for ourselves. Indeed, after a few days Wang got hold of The Girl with the White Hair and presented it to us in Chungking. But we were not lucky. Just as the presentation started, the projector went out of order. They could not fix it. Two or three "specialists" came but they did not succeed in repairing it either. At long last we got tired of eating ice cream and waiting in the empty hall, and we returned to our hotel to sleep.

HANKOW.

July 4. We leave at seven o'clock in the morning by plane. The day is beautiful. China is rose-colored; the Yellow River begins with a multitude of branches. Endless plains, a few trees, the Yangtze appears broad with a lot of water, lakes. Seeing its windings you understand how the dragons were born. Below us, beautiful white clouds.

Landed at eleven-thirty. Welcomed by the Chinese in automobiles. We drive through endless roads, greenery on both sides, poor houses, noise, broad straw hats; we enter Hankow, vast, full of little houses. They show us the "concessions"; they tell us about the capitalists' feeling of superiority, about how the British kept their shooting up until the moment of their departure, and about the shameless exploitation of China.

In the afternoon we visited the famous bridge which was about to be completed (seventeen hundred meters long—on it, twelve thousand workers worked day and night).

Then to the exhibition paintings of the Sung and Ming. Some of them excellent: landscapes, horses, portraits, the wild cat that plucked the peacock, its feathers scattered on the ground and the peacock plucked on the top of the tree. A dried-out branch and on it two lonely birds and the signature of the painter: a drunken idiot.

Around the concession on the bank, a garden with the sign: THE ENTRANCE IS PROHIBITED TO THE CHINESE AND THE DOGS.

Never forget the rhythmic, plaintive melody of the porters who carried the big stones for the bridge: the eternal voice of China.

Our friends, Mr. and Mrs. E., would have liked to take the familiar trip to Tientsin, Nanking, Shanghai.

But Wang had guessed the secret desires of Kazantzakis and prepared a surprise for us.

"We will not take the usual route of all the tourists. We will follow the traces of the poets," he told us with a sly smile one morning.

"Speak out, Wang, speak out!" we all said in unison.

"Here is my plan, we will go to Hankow by plane. And from there to Chungking by boat."

"How many days will it take us to go by boat?"

"Six. At the beginning you might not like it. But after Ichang, you will see some of the most beautiful places in China. High cliffs, gigantic rocks, and between them the river."

"And then?"

"Then Chungking. And from there by plane to Kunming, to the eternal spring."

"To the capital of Yenan?"

"Yes, it's two thousand meters high. There you will relax, after the great heat of Chungking."

Wang stopped to see whether we liked his plan. We applauded him.

"Bravo, bravo, Wang! And then?"

"Then," Wang continued less exuberantly, "we'll take the plane to Canton. And there we will separate. That is, if you want me, I can accompany you up to the borders."

Wang was supposed to leave us after we left Peking. But we felt very sad about it because we doubted whether we could find anyone else to put up with us and do for us all the favors Wang did.

"Do not be afraid," he consoled us. "We'll send word ahead so that you will be met at the airport, in every city."

But we were very perturbed and afraid of losing him. Finally word came that he could accompany us up to Canton and even up to the borders, if we wished.

Good Wang was among the first to write to me, and his first thought was to come to Freiburg when he learned of our misfortune. And his letter gave me courage: "My sister, withstand your pain, try to emulate Mme. Sun Yat-sen; you are not alone, the Chinese and the Greek people and all mankind are by your side. . . ."

On the plane Nikos and I tried to guess what the Blue River would be like. Images from the past came to mind, a blue river, wide as the sea. The Volga. With bleached sand at its banks, barges heavily loaded with watermelons, the washed clothes spread on clotheslines, the rooster on the roof. The beautiful and comfortable riverboat with its two big wheels, its red velvets, even at the time of the czars. The peasants with the unkempt beards on the deck, chewing pumpkin seeds and spitting day and night. The chickens, the goats, the pigs. The golden cupolas reflected on the blue waters. The fishermen drawing their nets and singing in the moonlight. The huge fish, the belugas, from which they get the black caviar, which they served to us in abundance with soup spoons.

"And Panait?"

"Panaitaki—that's what he wanted us to call him—always had with him throughout the trip a teapot full of honey and, in his pockets, a small bottle of olive oil, a green pepper and a lemon."

In Hankow the heat was terrible. We slept for the first time on straw mats. Everything was very clean. There were neither flies nor mosquitoes. Everywhere in all the hotels they had boiled water in big Thermos so that we could prepare tea in our room when we wanted it. They also had good tea in a box, as well as Tien Amen cigarettes. In our hotel they showed us the line that the waters had left during the terrible flood of 1932; it was higher than one and a half meters. These floods are public enemy number one of China.

Our boat was to leave in twenty-four hours. Program: the next day, early in the morning when it was still cool we

were to go to a beautiful lake. There was an excellent hotel
where we would eat and relax at noon. In the afternoon we
would go to a tea factory; and then we would kill some
time in Hankow.

The lake was very romantic; pink and white lotuses. And
a pagoda on the opposite bank. Far on a hill we could see
the university, big and beautiful. . . .

All alone today, in my little death-stricken house in Antibes, I sip the fragrant tea of Peking and remember how
we went to buy it with Wang in a little shop covered from
top to bottom with endless drawers where they had myriads
of blends of tea sold at all different prices.

"Don't buy the most expensive," our guide advised us,
"you must be a 'specialist' in order to understand the difference; take this here, that's what we drink at home."

It smells like jasmine and it does not sweeten only my
body but also my soul; joyful images come alive in my
memory, like the huge, clean tea factory where we were
amazed to see how much work was needed so that we
might enjoy a cup of good tea. . . .

I leaf through our notebooks. A Chinese signature which
looks like embroidery from the Island of Rhodes is the
name of the Chinese engineer who supervised the construction of the first bridge over the Yangtze. His name is
Yo Kuan-lo and he is thirty-four years old. The bridge is
1650 meters long; it has nine vaults and eight columns under the river. It has two floors, one for the railroad, and another for the cars and the pedestrians (eighteen meters
wide for the vehicles and two and a half for the pedestrians). It was to have been completed by 1958, but it would
now be completed by October 1, 1957—that's what they
told us then, and Wang wrote to us in Freiburg later and
confirmed it. "The bridge has been completed. We celebrated the Moon Festival; we had almond sweets and saw

319 / AN EPILOGUE

Mei Lan-fang performing again. Pity you were not here to
see him. . . ."

We remained silent to hear the plaintive song of the
porters. I hope that the trucks and cranes and everything
else that modern man needs will reach this place soon so
that no more blood and sweat will be so unnecessarily
shed. May China one day become independent, tame its
rivers, sow its plains, plant its mountains with trees, be
able to feed its children, and not be occupied by any conqueror, white, yellow or red!

After we visited the museum, we returned to the river:
it's wild, muddy and very wide. We waited for the river
ferry to take us to the opposite bank. It drizzled. . . .

"From here Mao Tse-tung swam across the river twice
last year," said a young Chinese.

"How old is he?"

"Sixty-three. The year before last, he crossed it four
times. Nothing scares him. Do you know the songs he
wrote about the Yangtze? One in 1947 and another this
year?"

The young man began to recite them for us. Later Wang
helped us translate them.

YANGTZE-KIANG

1

Upon the Chinese earth
The River Yangtze with its nine sheafs,
That flexible cut,
Separates the North from the South in our land,
And the snake and the turtle
Look at each other, look at each other without
    end.

From up high, from the top of the tower, I, the
          vagabond poet,
Let my glances fall down. . . .   (1947)

2

But the snake and the turtle
Keep their eternal pose,
And the images of the future years
Are revealed before me. . . .
From the southern to the northern bank
Men will build an iron bridge,
They will forget that
An impassable chaos was once there.   (1957)

YANGTZE.

July 5. At 6 P.M. we enter the river ferry and depart. It is raining. The river, huge, full of mud. At the quay, the Chinese wave to us for some time in the rain.

Our cabin, painted green, is very clean. Very hot. The Chinese meal is nice. Wang with us, protector and friend. Excellent. I slept well.

July 6. We sail along Yangtze. All mud. Near the land small villages, greenery. Relaxation. I read.

Kazantzakis forgot his blue jacket in Hankow.

"Don't worry, it will be found," our hosts assured us.

We were not sure, although we had never lost anything in China.

Just before the ferryboats started out, a little Chinese, running, waved the blue jacket like a flag. Wang, to whom we had offered a chocolate, remembered to throw it to the young Chinese, who immediately ate it and licked his chops. Chocolate is a luxury in Hankow.

July 7. Sunday. We sail along the Yangtze, it is raining, the radio is horrible. I read dull old Chinese stories. Climate damp, heavy. At five-thirty we reach the small town of Ichang. It is pouring. We will stay here until midnight.

We persuaded Kazantzakis not to come out in Ichang in the rain. Wang rolled up his trousers; he found two large paper umbrellas. We went out. We climbed many broad steps. When we reached the top, the children became aware of us. At the beginning it was only the children. In a little while we looked like a lump of sugar surrounded by ants. Thousands of ants. We pretended to be serious but the smile of the Chinese is catching. The more we smiled at them, the tighter they closed in on us. At any moment now, we'll suffocate. Wang was worried. He raised his weak arms and moved them; he wanted to say something. We did not understand. The men were separated from the women, as if we were in a boiling caldron. . . . Fortunately, the main street ended. In front of a wall there were two rickshas, the first ones we saw without a bicycle. Wang managed to get out of this jam, and asked us to get on the ricksha and return to the boat. We did as he said, but unwillingly. We did not understand anything during this walk. We only saw that their houses were wooden booths, the entire front of them open; the men sit and smoke in the coffee shop, or rather in the chainaya, as the Russians call it, and the women in their living room around a low lacquered table play cards and drink tea. The children and most of the young men walk in the streets in the rain.

Our eyes tried to see inside the houses: in one of them there was a big wooden bed with four bedposts and a mosquito net; in another one the "bedrooms" were separated by drapes; farther on you saw a blanket, a stool, the sky or the small garden in the back through the wooden boards. How can we help recalling the enthusiastic descriptions of

Father Hook? Where are the palaces, the private big houses, the temples, the stores and the beautiful hotels?

It is pouring. We are all in a bad mood. I hear Kazantzakis sighing for the first time: "If I only had water from my fountain. . . ."

No one can understand you better than the Chinese. We did not say a word to the chef, but he arranged everything to our liking. He called us to dinner after the others had finished. The tables and the floor were freshly washed. Everything in the dining room was shining. In the morning and the evening he served us delicious compotes and marmalades; the tea was always at our side, ever since the time I said how much I liked it. And it was always the same blend with the jasmine aroma.

The swiftness of the Chinese impressed us a great deal. You give your clothes to be washed in the morning and in the evening you find them pressed in your room. You order a simple meal and in half an hour they bring you a variety of dishes, the one more delicious than the other, and they laugh and are pleased if you eat everything. The cook in the boat even made fritters to please us. We remember the waiters in Moscow and we laugh. What a contrast. The Muscovite waiters take about an hour to bring you a glass of water. They first take down the entire order and then in their own good time wait until all the food comes from the kitchen and only then they bring you the water, in large portions. About ten bottles! And the only thing you had requested was one glass of water . . . Da, da, syeitchas! syeitchas! But by the time it gets to you, you could die of thirst. . . .

Wang gave us a key. Now we had a private bath at our disposal.

The landscape slowly changed. We had not yet reached the narrow ravine with the abrupt high rocks which made such an impression on the Chinese poets. Green hills with pagodas often on their peaks, which in old times were temples or private villas, but now are schools, as the large red signs over the doors indicate.

We often saw peasants with fans and big straw hats ascending the narrow path and fishermen drawing away from the bank in their beautiful curved boats with their straw sails. . . .

We had not yet seen any fish. The Yangtze does not resemble the Volga, despite the fact that both are called blue. The Volga often resembles the sea. The Yangtze is red, deep and narrow, coiled like a boa, and our ferryboat went from one bank to the other, and we could never guess which was our route. We felt as if we continuously sailed in a small closed lake.

July 8. We enter beautiful dells. Hills, houses, greenery, rocks, beautiful villages, fishermen, boats with beautiful sails, green mountains to left and right. Little by little the landscape becomes wild. High rocks, bare, abrupt. In the evening we stop in a small city. Helen and the E.'s went out and were encircled by the Chinese who were seeing their first Europeans.

Choung-Sien is a little town. It still does not have electricity. They carry muddy water in buckets from the river. I hope they don't drink it.

We again ascended innumerable steps. As soon as we reached the top, the children came after us. Children, teen-age boys and girls, and young women. All very clean. In two minutes we were prisoners again.

But today Wang was prepared. "I beg you," I said to him the day before yesterday, "to help us come in contact with the Chinese people. When we go out again, let us select five or six young men and young ladies and ask them how they live."

This day, as soon as we came out, Wang picked the oldest of the young men and told him what we wanted and he explained it to the rest.

However, we, the women, were surrounded by girls who fanned us with their small fans and smiled at us and asked with the few words of Russian they knew whether we were Russians and if we wanted to write to them. Da, da pisát we said, as we had understood only three Russian words of what they said: pismó, pisát, rúski ("letter," "to write," "Russian").

We came to a beautiful garden. Wang called; the girls stopped, laughed, and asked us something, talking all at once, but we didn't understand them.

"Pick out the ones you want to take with you!" said Wang.

"We are selecting them!"

And we took by the hand the three that were near us: one, a likable, homely girl with braids who told us she was studying engineering, and the two others with the fans. We also selected about five or six young men. We entered the garden, the gates closed, the crowd remained outside. It was already night. The moon shone and the flowers smelled beautiful. We sat first before the large room of the city hall, on comfortable armchairs and chatted. We first asked the girls:

"What are you doing?"

"I study electrical engineering."

"And now during the summer vacation?"

"I help build our school."

"And you?" we asked a dainty, well-dressed girl who looked as if she could have come out of the pages of a fashion magazine.

"I want to study to become an actress. But now I do gymnastics."

"We all do gymnastics," said another girl, "because we'll have a contest to see who will go to Peking for the festival."

"Do you also help build the school?"

"Of course. This year we build the school. Last year we helped in the construction of the road."

"Which road?"

"The one that goes to Lhasa!" (Thousands of kilometers.)

"And where did you find such an elegant dress?"

"My mother made it for me."

"Do you help your mother?"

"No, she works far away from here, in X, in a public nursery."

"Do you help your mother?" we asked another girl.

"Of course, when I go home in the summer. . . ."

"And now where do you live?"

"We live in the school."

The boys also tell us their plans. They study to be agriculturists and engineers. They are pleased and want to offer us tea and ask us questions in their turn. Instead of tea they offer us warm water as they do in all the poor villages; they light their petrol lamp, we enter and sit around a large long table.

When they hear that Mrs. E. plays the violin, they applaud, laugh and speak secretly. In two minutes they bring a violin which passes from hand to hand and comes to Mrs. E. It's very old and has only two strings.

"Please play for us! Play for us!" they all cry and beg, putting on their sweetest smiles.

Mrs. E. does not disappoint them. She manages to play on the two loose strings the national anthem of Greece. What cheers! Now we ask them to sing their anthem. Mr. E. speaks to them about Greece. A lot of applause.

We take the three girls into the boat. All the way they hold our hands lest we slip. At one moment Mrs. E. felt a little hand in her pocket. Yes, she was sure, a little hand had been in her pocket, she was not mistaken.

We offer carbonated drinks to our new girl friends; we

take down their names and promise to write to them. They had never drunk carbonated drinks before; they don't like them at all; they make funny grimaces, but they swallow it; they laugh and they are very pleased that they came aboard the boat. They had never been on a boat before. . . .

When we were alone, Mrs. E. remembered her pocket. She put her hand in and what did she find? A tiny pen-knife, an anonymous gift. And on our bosoms shone the little pins, their school emblems, that the girls gave us as souvenirs.

The Yangtze is one of the largest rivers in the world. We were going only sixteen hundred kilometers, from Hankow to Chungking. Its waters are very dangerous and require a good captain.

One morning in the fog Wang brought us to the bridge of the ship and said:

"Do you see that village with the old walls? There for two years lived our great poet, Tu Fu."

WARRIOR

My childhood was spent in a city of the North,
I lost my youth in a war,
The hoofs of horses stamped on my body;
On the hour the earth had split open to devour
      me,
The hairs on my face were like the porcupine's.
Now the white clouds
Rush to the straits of Lungki
And the red ones sail beneath them.
I will not return before they release me.
I will never see again my wife in Fung-Tien,
My wife who sings and dances to the music of
      the lute,

Who sings to the Mongolian flute
The charging songs of the warriors in battle.
O tears of warriors that run like the rain!

TO THE RIVER CHOU

My boat quickly sails on the river and bending
    over, I look at the water.
The clouds sail on the sky.
The sky is reflected on the river when a cloud
    rolls by,
I see it pass by in the water.
And it seems that my boat slides on the sky
And then I think of my beloved reflected on my
    heart.

THE HOUSE IN MY HEART

The wild fires have turned to ashes the house
    where I was born,
I boarded a golden ship to dissipate my pain.
I took my carved flute and played a song to the
    moon.
But I made the moon ache and it was covered
    by a cloud.
I returned to the mountain, but this did not
    relieve me at all.
It seems that all my childhood joys
Had burned in my little house.
I longed to die and bent over the sea.
At that moment a woman in a boat passed by.
It seemed that I saw the moon reflected on the
    water.
If she were willing, I would rebuild my little
    house inside her heart.

Wang later showed us Tse Kuei where the great poet Ch'ü Yüan was born twenty-three hundred years ago. Unfortunately, we did not find any of his poems to translate.

Tonight a friendly chat with Wang. I was speaking to him, at first reserved; little by little he lost his bitterness. And at the beginning we were the same, but little by little we understood. Especially when he spoke to us with such passion about the bamboo, the plum tree, and the lotus. And then he said that in wretched China corpses were cheap.

He told us how they conquered the "reactionary" villages. There were a million and a half robbers and pirates in southern China. They got into the ships, they caught prisoners, they cut ears, they sent messages to the families and asked for ransom money. The Communist propagandists went to the villages, where they stayed and slept in the poorest homes and spoke to the villagers about the situation and tried to unite them. If they did not at first succeed they left a committee to continue their propaganda and they went to other villages. They showed tact and patience. They knew that every man longs to acquire dignity.

July 9. The beautiful landscapes continue. Small villages against a green background. At the peak of a hill a single tree. Two, three birds like gulls. Boats. Fishermen with broad straw hats. Under a big tree, outside a "temple of ghosts," a multitude of men and women pray for a better future life.

Sweltering heat. In the evening somewhat cool. We arrive in a small town.

A lot of men, innumerable children, the Chinese bring forth children abundantly. Men and women, with a vat on either side of a stick yoked across the back of the neck and held down with the wrists, descend to the river, fill the vats and with heavy steps climb up the rock and go to water fields and animals. And the eternal voice of toil, the sigh of China: *Ei-ho! Ei-ho!* A little girl, also yoked with vats, carries water. What a struggle! What swarms of ants! What poverty!

The last village was Loch-Chi. Many recently built store-houses filled with crops. The harvest was good, they said. We all went down to see the storehouses and the vegeta-ble gardens with their eggplants, tomatoes, squash and peppers. The children ran naked. They lived in shanties. What poverty! The streets, however, were clean.

July 10. Wang tells us anecdotes of the life of Chou En-lai. We hear of his zeal, self-sacrifice and love for the people. He was hungry, but would not eat so long as the people were starving. Tomorrow morning we will reach the end of our route. . . .

"If I only had water from my home fountain." Kazan-tzakis' sigh is still humming in my ears.

"But why, Nikos dear, do you say this again and again?" I asked him. "What do you need?"

He looks at me and smiles.

"Nothing. I'm happy!"

Surely it was not he who sighed, but someone else within him. The other one who knew what awaited him.

We wanted to give a good present to the chef, although we knew from Peking that they didn't like tips. We decided to tell him that with this money we begged him to buy a book—we had seen him reading a lot—because we did not know what to buy for him. Nikos put down the answer the cook gave us.

"The time of tipping has passed. I am an employee on the boat; I am not the servant of the passengers."

We asked his pardon. He laughed kindly.

"You are badly trained," he said, "Never mind!"

CHUNGKING.

July 11. We arrive in the large city of Chungking. End of
our journey. The Committee of Peace welcomes us at the
pier, suffocating heat; we reach a magnificent hotel which
reminds us of the Temple of Heavens in Peking. A luxurious palace. Living room, bedroom, bath, all covered with
velvet; fruits, cigarettes, paper and envelopes, all the comforts, and in addition, oriental politeness and service.

Museum: carvings on stone of the paleolithic age, exquisite horses. What elegance! Vases . . . And among the
lot the horrible rags the peasants wore, and in the showcase opposite, the fur coat of the landlord. And everywhere
the instruments he used to beat, torture and kill with. And
the weights—with the small ones he made loans and with
the big ones he collected his loans.

Remember the poet Li Po, a fat, well-dressed man with
high boots, drunk, held by two eunuchs who took him to
the emperor.

FROM THE HIGH TOWERS

*The moon rose out of the mountains into the
  sky.
It livens the clouds on the sea,
The wind groans ten thousand miles away.
From the gates of Yun-Mer rises a choking hiss,
The sons of Han advance on the broad road,
And the Tartars arrive at the shores of the blue
  sea.
Here they battled in the old days and never did
  a soldier return alive.*

*With eyes nailed to the horizon, all the soldiers
  seek their distant home,*

Their heart is full of fear and trembles.
Tonight from the high towers they see nothing,
But the endless road of an endless pain.

THE YOUNG WOMAN

She who has never been touched by grief
Paints her face today, a spring day,
She climbs up to the emerald tower,
Surprised she sees two new branches on the
    willow tree
And sighs,
Because her husband is at war.
My country is nothing but ruins; you no longer
    see anything
But corpses and rivers.
At this city, in this sweet spring, you see nothing
    but grass
And moss on the trees.
To weep for our age the flowers shed tears,
When the birds went away my heart fluttered,
The beacon lit the sky three times.
A letter from my parents is worth thousands,
    coin in gold.
Despairing.

July 12. Stifling heat. Excursion to a green place, tropical, with banana plants, lemon trees, bamboo, green, red, orange, and yellow reeds. Passing by, we stopped at the house where Mao Tse-tung lived behind bars for many years.

In the car I started a profound discussion with Wang. I told him about my spiritual and bodily exercises, my asceticism. He listened to me moved and in the end cried: "I worship you!"

The small house where Mao hid is on a hill among trees. On the opposite hill were the headquarters of Chiang Kaishek. At that time they were supposed to fight the Japanese together. Mao was allowed to have a staff of eighteen men, but in his house two hundred men were hidden. They showed us the secret story, the attic without windows; Mao's bed, a board on tripods; his table. In front of the house there is a big tree which they call the Tree of Good and Evil, of Victory and Defeat. Here they told us we lost many men. . . .

On the way they showed us the Chinese Auschwitz.

And whom do you think we met at the opera in the evening? The sympathetic chef on the boat, Liu Lin.

The voices in the opera seemed more European, but the actors that night did not compare with those of Peking.

July 13. In the morning, to the writers. There were about ten, an old actor, the director of the opera, very sympathetic, lean, smiling, with a thin goatee, seventy years old but he looked one hundred seventy. I spoke about the struggle of my life and my work and my effort to convert slavery into freedom. I mentioned what a difference there is between Chinese finesse and Western barbarism: the Chinese use chopsticks, they caress the food and invite it to enter and become one with them. The Westerners nail their food with a fork and force it to come to their mouths. Mao won the revolution because he used the chopstick method, caressing and persuading the masses. The entire Chinese revolution was fought with chopsticks.

Then we spoke about the film *He Who Must Die* (based on *The Greek Passion*). I said that those who fight in the beginning to save people for generations are crucified, killed. Evil always prevails in the beginning. But at long last, this is the great law: a savior is saved and saves the people. Such is the adventure of China's struggle to become free; for centuries the leaders who fought met with death. . . .

In the twilight it started raining. It became cooler.

The contemporary Chinese poets and authors fought during the war and the revolution, and now they work together with the peasants and the workers, building houses, bridges, schools. During the intermissions of manual labor, they write. Their words are changed into stones, they have become the foundations of New China. They are perfect, complete poets: word and action are one in their work.

In a beautiful old house with a big terrace laid with tiles, one of the very few that has been saved, the Chinese women waited for us. They offered us tea, hot, damp, small napkins to wipe our perspiration from our faces, and fans. They sat around us in the dimly lit room, smiling and ready to answer our questions. There were many problems before the liberation. They were slaves to their families and their men. Even at the time of the Kuomintang, which was an improvement over the old China, the taxes were high. Factory workers were sometimes hungry. They had to sleep in the factory. They were given permission to go out only twice a week. And when they went out, they were searched as if they were thieves.

They put their children in soap boxes. Nearly all of them were sick, covered with boils. Many died.

Before the revolution there were only ten nurseries in Chungking. Now there are three hundred, besides those in the factories and the mines. Twenty thousand children spend their day pleasantly in them.

"What are your responsibilities?" we asked the women. They answered:

1. To organize a good life in our homes.

2. To find a way for our families to get along with our neighbors and live harmoniously with them.

3. To bring up our children.
4. To learn what we need for our work.

"How many of you are now organized?"

"Seventy-one hundred and eighty-nine staff members, eight thousand volunteers. Six thousand are working exclusively on organizing the neighborhoods."

KUNMING—YÜNNAN—FU.

July 14. We leave at 10:15 and arrive at noon. Plateau two thousand meters high. Here is eternal spring. A cool, light breeze, beautiful landscape, greenery. At the airport the Committee for Peace waited for us. They were very nice. We reached the hotel, had lunch. In the afternoon, a walk in the beautiful park, a lake, a flock of ducks, boats returning from fishing, bamboo, blossomed Arabian reeds.

Shops, children like ants, a pleasant, light fatigue.

A writer of the Yee minority is with us. They had a dialect with only five hundred characters. Now they use a Latin alphabet. In the evening, to the opera: how they sacrificed a girl to calm the Yangtze. The actors are mediocre. When you've seen the very best, such as in Peking, it's senseless to see mediocre ones.

We had left Chungking in fog; as soon as we stepped into Yünnan we felt cool. As we flew we saw from the airplane thousands of small lakes.

July 15. Clouds, coolness, you feel that you are on a height of two thousand meters. Botanical Institute, sympathetic director, one hundred scientists who are devoted to the study of the flora of Yünnan; garden, glass house, coffee and quinine trees, deformed tree trunks, as the Chinese like. . . . A divine white flower of magnolia smells like lemon. White shining lotuses amid the swamp.

A little farther, the pavilion of the Big Dragon. What sweetness in the light foggy air. And in the middle, a very high cedar tree from the eleventh century (the Sung period). And I won't forget the exquisite roofs—raised at the corners, and among the tiles the grass of abandonment begins to grow.

In the Botanical Garden we saw camellias which blossom as big as dahlias in the spring. Begonias of every color, lacy and long. A tomato as high as a three-year-old tree. And another very rare tree that has been preserved for a thousand years.

July 16. An excellent excursion to the Kungming Lake. We climb upwards, green hills, tranquil landscape, and suddenly the lake full of fishing boats. We leave the cars and ascend the rock; we mount a great many steps, we pass by the Tao pagoda, a carved wild bird with green flames holding a book. The door of the Dragon on the mountain is beautiful: the Sleeping Beauty. Here lived the king of Liang. The Temple of the Dragon, Lon-Men, is mentioned in the ancient poetry. Above it, the Temple of the Three Purities. Here they dug into the rock for nine years. On the summit, the pavilion of the Leader of the Erudite: a gilded young man like Buddha; he holds in one hand an inkwell and in the other a pen. But the pen broke when the sculptor Chou Kiang-kuo was working on it, and from his grief the sculptor committed suicide—because the pen was his highest aim and it broke. The pavilion is called "the temple that touches the sky." The Leader of the Erudite is surrounded by clouds and peaches. He holds the pen like a sword and runs. Behind him, animals, plants, men, saints, mountains, trees. . . .

Returning, we stopped at the famous Buddhist monastery where famous monks lived and where Buddhist congresses took place. The temple has beautiful huge Buddhas and the walls are covered with five hundred broken statues, symbolizing the five hundred human characters. It was built in 600 A.D., but it was destroyed five times. The present statues were made in 1927.

In the yard, a rare tree, the tan; it has big white flowers in August which open up at five in the afternoon and close around seven. The yard is ideal for meditation.

The vice president of the Committee for Peace, a wholesome man. I took him for a badly dressed peasant, sixty-eight years old. He used to be a general under Chiang Kai-shek. He said: "I could neither sleep nor eat in the previous regime. I saw the people starve. Now they do not starve any more. I am not a Communist, but I hope one day I will be worthy of entering the party."

He has eight daughters and five sons, all university graduates. He is a poet. He has been working on his poetry and the study of Buddhism for fifty years. He speaks of poetry with passion and understanding.

The University for the Minorities—which comprise 32.55 per cent of the population of Yünnan (seventeen million)—is in a large park. All the minorities of Yünnan have not yet been classified; they know of two hundred. The Yee have only twenty branches. In other times, the Hans persecuted and despised them. They lived in the mountains under terrible conditions. Now New China wants them as friends and allies. Here in the university there are separate small temples and chapels for the Catholics, the Protestants, the Moslems, the Shintoists, the Buddhists, et cetera. Those who faithfully follow the commandments of their religion eat separately. They sleep separately, they wash themselves separately; they have wide freedom.

They waited for us at the entrance, dressed in their national costumes, which were very beautiful. Beautiful girls with elaborate hairdos and gems in their hair, necklaces, bracelets and wonderful embroidered dresses. The Tibetans wore big fur caps.

July 17. In the morning a brilliant rainbow circled about in the waters of the lake opposite my hotel window. All night it was raining hard and thundering, but with the dawn came the sun.

We started out for the Petrified Forest, 120 kilometers away. An exquisite, tender place, all-red earth, full of greenery. Men and women buried up to their knees in the rice fields pull the weeds. We passed by a very beautiful blue lake. It was cool. We came to a pavilion and from there we entered the Petrified Forest on foot. Astonishing, unique in the world. Huge black rocks, titanic stalagmites in fantastic patterns, a moon landscape; it reminds you of Aeschylus and the Apocalypse.

A real labyrinth, the forest, rocks—not petrified trees— are dangerous, and without a guide you can get lost.

In the evening we attended an official dinner where we spoke about peace and brotherhood.

If you scratch the Chinese, you will find the Greek. If you scratch the Greek, you will find the Chinese.

We embraced each other very moved.

July 18. Because of yesterday's bad weather, no plane will depart today. We shall rest one more day here.

Rest, a beautiful walk around the lake, water lilies, children swimming. All the small children with their pants torn for ease. Insignificant shops, poor, uninteresting.

The vice president gave me his hand-written poem.

Tomorrow morning, to Canton, and our pilgrimage to New China will end.

Tien-Hen was a Chi prince who lived in the third century B.C. and died after he fought and was defeated by the emperor of the Han. His five hundred faithful followers, although they were aware of the danger, did not desert him but stayed and died with him in order to declare with their death how sweet it is to die for freedom.

In the temple of Chen-Chou the vice president of the Committee for Peace of the Province of Yünnan, Chao Cheng-go, wrote these verses in 1937:

> Every man has his heart filled
> With anger and with happiness.
> The dusty wind rises from the mountain
> And from the ancient forest.
> The apostles are innumerable inside the temple
> of Buddha
> Where they are carved
> As were the five hundred brave men of Tien-
> Hen.

CANTON.

We flew for five hours from Kungming to Canton. We landed in Nanning. Rain, heat, humidity. For a long time we were passing over cultivated red land, all squares of every shade of green. They reminded one of the stained-glass windows of medieval churches. A typhoon had broken two days earlier. Because of that, we saw for a long time nothing but flooded villages and roads. I did not wake up Kazantzakis to see the flood. The rivers of China surprise you as you see them from the plane. Like spiraled snakes. All the villages in southern China have a tower, from which the sentry guards the harvest.

From the first time the Chinese took a brush and paper to narrate his joys and griefs, the Yellow, Yangtze and Sungari Rivers have taken in his imagination the form of man-devouring dragons. Voracious beings which could not be appeased easily and always sought new victims to soften their rage. No ruler until now, native or foreign, has yet tried seriously to chain the terrible beasts. They only made litanies, prayers and offered sacrifices—even at the time of Kuomintang.

I remember when I was still a child and the Yangtze flooded over forty million Chinese. Forty million (the whole population of France) is not a small number of people to be in danger, but China was far away, and we had other worries and we were absorbed by other preoccupations.

However, as we passed over the flooded plains on our way to Canton, we saw many refugees from the flood sleep on sidewalks with a bundle next to them. We asked, we read, we understood. . . .

When the Sungari River flooded last summer, Harbin was in danger of being destroyed again. The waters of Sungari rose over the banks of the river by four meters. The level rose fifty-eight centimeters higher than the floods of 1956. The waters remained at that height for twenty-two days. It rained uninterruptedly and the wind blew with relentless rage. The new dams were in danger.

Then a miracle: all the people of Harbin and the neighboring towns were roused. Only the old men and the children stayed at home. The army, the factory managers, the university professors, the bank executives, in short, all who did not absolutely have to stay in their offices, started out for the dams. Their wives also came to wash and mend the men's clothes. Even a group of volunteer dancers came.

The struggle lasted for twenty-four days and nights. In these twenty-four days they carried eight hundred eighty-five thousand cubic meters of soil and raised the dam seventy centimeters, and in some places one meter. Three hundred thousand men worked on the dams.

For a time, the waves came close to tearing down one dam. They had neither sandbags nor any other materials. Then about a thousand soldiers and officers went into the water and stood up body to body, forming a living wall for six whole hours until the others repaired the break. The pictures that I had in front of me on our trip were really moving. They reminded me of another brave people who fought the same enemy. But Holland is near us, and so we all learn of its struggle and its victories. While in China the bamboo curtain makes it so easy for us to close our eyes and pretend that we know nothing about it. . . .

July 19. We leave at seven-thirty in the morning, we climb above the clouds, sunny. Feeling tired, I slept. While arriving, I saw the exquisite landscape, river, cultivated plain, red earth, yellow fields, great sweetness.

At the station we were welcomed by members of the Committee for Peace. A huge hotel, a room on the twelfth floor; from the balcony I see the beautiful River Pearl, junks, ferryboats, superb view. Big crowds on the streets.

In the afternoon a stroll to the Mausoleum of Sun Yat-sen with its horrible statue and a huge room with five thousand seats.

Later, to the banks of the river, where families live permanently in junks. They cook, they have chicken bins covered with straw mats. Innumerable children. A lively city, a huge village of two million people. . . .

July 20. We rode in a ferryboat along the River Pearl. *Jonques,* people galore, we entered the covered compartments where about sixty thousand people live permanently with their children and chicken bins. . . . All cheerful, and clean, but very poor . . .

In the afternoon, to the mosque, Arabic minaret; the *imam* kneeling on the crystal-clean floor prays in a thin voice; a few faithful come and kneel behind him.

The temple of Buddha; in the entrance, wooden statue of Milarepa. Inside the temple an old man was rhythmically pounding a big drum. Later he moved near a bronze bell, struck it with an iron rod and prayed. It is pouring. In the hotel I am vaccinated for smallpox and cholera.

The rivermen of Canton were the pariahs of China. Before the liberation, they were not allowed to come on the land. They lived by smuggling things from Hong Kong. They even had a school for their children on a junk. Now there are many wooden narrow paths that connect the junks to the land. Their junks have many flowerpots. Dogs and children swim around and the women draw water and pour it into the shining copper pots and boil their meals. The junks, however, are very clean. We also saw a man taking a shower behind a straw cover.

The present government is trying to move these people out of their navigable houses. It is building small houses for them and rations them land. But not all of them are eager to change their lives.

The tradition states that during the Yen Dynasty the ruler treated his wife badly and she secretly left him, followed by the poor people who did not have land of their own.

We also passed through the European section. They showed us where the English killed the Chinese in the war for opium.

"The Moslems," Wang told us, "came to China at the beginning of the seventh century. There are three thousand in Canton and six thousand in the province of Canton, and ten million in China."

The New China had a great success with the Chinese who live abroad. Wang had spoken with great emotion a number of times about them and we told him of the great things that the Greeks who live abroad did for Greece. Today he took us to see a garden city on a hill where the Chinese who live abroad build their new houses. Most of them come and go, they don't yet live entirely in China. But they send money to their old parents and their little children. Unfortunately, their villas are typically European. You get the impression that you are somewhere in Europe.

Many trees, newly planted parks, swimming pools, schools and nurseries.

"Imagine," Wang had told us, "that in earlier times all the shores of South China looked like a desert. Sand, and as a backdrop mountains of sand. Terrible dryness. This land didn't produce even a handful of rice to feed the old men. And as if the troubles of poverty were not enough, there were pirates too. . . ."

No government has been interested in the fate of south China. For this reason there are so many emigrants from southern China. They went wherever they could—to Japan, to Indonesia and, most often, to Java. And wherever they went, they made progress. Because no one knows how to be pleased with so little as do the Chinese.

And so we learned from Wang about the new factories that the state builds with money sent by the Chinese from abroad, about the irrigation works, about the artificial lakes, about the rice they succeeded in harvesting three times a year instead of two in these areas that before were barren. Instead of making the émigré Chinese mortal enemies as the Russian Bolsheviks made the White Russians, Mao made them friends and allies and now they prepare their homes to come and live and die in their country.

Whoever has a nostalgia for old China, with its colors, its noise, its smells, let him take the ship to Canton. And let him, when night comes, take a walk on the streets. And then, if he wishes, let him go to the river. I don't think his eyes will ever have seen such a spectacle.

Multitudes come out, as soon as night falls, on the streets and spread their merchandise on the ground—here fountain pens; there shoes, a little farther down, a liquid that erases ink; a few steps on, fans. And what voices crying: "Roasted pumpkin seeds!" "Watermelons!" "Fritters!"

And what smells that burst your nostrils! And how noiselessly and with what dexterity circulate the rickshas, opening up a road in this crowd. And how exotic are the long Chinese signs that hang down from every door like strings of living crabs, like creepers. And the multicolored lanterns, and the hot air smelling of the sea.

And where do these antlike multitudes go? To the Cantonese Tivoli,* to the Public Garden, with the Luna Park and its thousand and one entertainments. We also enter it with a few coins, following the crowd. If you care, you see; if you don't, you don't have to. We listen to a current hit song; the chanteuse is very attractive; we stop a few steps farther on in order to see what is playing at the movie, we don't like it and we go on. The clown is more exciting. . . . But we want to see everything! Now we are in front of two famous chess players; it seems they have been playing for a few days; a projector marks their movements on a white screen. The chess fans stand gaping and smiling. We are not interested in it. We come into a rich pavilion where the most beautiful carved ivories are exhibited. What a delicate work! How is a human hand able to carve this foam, these laces, the trees with the thousands of small leaves, the little figurines, complete human forms no larger than a grain of rice? We don't linger even before these display windows; we always follow the current. We pass by an elegant coffee shop with a terrace covered over with blossomed wisterias. We enter another pavilion where furs and loomed fabrics are exhibited. Complex designs, rich colors, we select what we would like to have and go on to see everything; we stop shortly before the jugglers, we leave again. We enter a third pavilion. Here are the various porcelains and the best faïence of China.

And when we get dizzy from standing up and feel tired, we follow again the crowd and go toward the river. We throw curious glances around us. No one seems to feel tired; no one looks nervous and irritated; all are calm and cheerful. The boys and girls stop for a moment to buy or-

---

* The famous garden of Copenhagen.

ange drinks or ice-cream; the old women chew peanuts; the infants lick with their little tongues the cool watermelon. We reach the river, full of lights, as if it were a big holiday, like July 14 on the Seine in Paris. Only the fireworks are missing tonight.

In Canton nearly all the women wear the local glistening black silk slacks with a closed jacket and a high collar. And their wooden sandals knock on the tiles. They laugh, stop short, chat with their girl friends; I don't know if all of them wait for their lovers.

In the morning we went aboard one of those gleaming junks of joy and we spoke with a siren who had surely passed her thirties. I must stress, however, that during our entire trip we saw nothing that would shock us. In the universities and in the schools and the factories the directors explained to us that the Chinese women today avoid the men, because the change is very recent and because they still remember the old tortures and the bitter life that women suffered. They remember what their mothers, older sisters, aunts, and cousins told them. Poor grandmother, if only she was still living. . . . And there are many girls in China who have sworn never to marry and they see it as a misfortune if a girl friend of theirs is deceived by love and believes in it and gets married.

July 21. I didn't go out. I wrote a note of thanks to the Committee of Peace. I looked at the river, full of sampans and junks. The evening lights, like brilliant luster on the waters.

The vice president of the Committee for Peace had prepared for us a surprisingly rich and fine dinner, abundant precious food, and, at the end, soup of shark's fins. Unforgettable.

We went up to the room and I admired for a long time the night and the river.

Tomorrow early in the morning we leave for Hong

Kong. *Say your farewell to the Alexandria that you're losing. . . .* *

In an ancient temple of Confucius which is now a museum, we drank green tea seated on large armchairs of ebony with backs made of marble. Choice Chinese marble was in the courtyard, covered and separated with bookcases made of glass, on which were also some exquisite jade and porcelain pieces. Behind us there was a tiny fountain. We had never seen a more beautiful patio, not even in Córdoba.

"In 1923," the director of the museum explained to us, "the Kuomintang collaborated with the Communists. Then they established two schools, one in Hankow, the military one; the other here, in that temple, the agricultural one. This school was directed by Mao Tse-tung for some time. It had then 327 students who had come from sixteen provinces. . . ."

"And what did Mao teach?"

"The problems of the Chinese people's revolution. And the problems of the peasants and of propaganda."

"Is it true that Chou En-lai also taught here?"

"Yes. Chou En-lai gave military courses. In 1926 we were forced to break with the Kuomintang; the school closed; the Red Army reached Hankow. In 1953 we made the school a museum. Do you wish to see how the students and the professors lived then?"

We left the exquisite opulence of the porcelains of the Ming, the Sung, and the T'ang and the rare plants and fine furniture, and we reached the wooden huts where the present leaders of China lived, ate and slept. It was the same sight we saw in Chungking. A bench, a wooden chair, an old table. And on the wall, the photographs of the slain.

"Most of our professors were killed," the director tells

---

* The last line of C. Cavafy's poem "God Forsakes Anthony."

us very calmly. "You see some young, others old, all working for the same idea, always with the same renunciation. . . ."

On a small sheet of paper folded in four, already yellowing from time and humidity, I found the very concise outline for the epilogue that Nikos Kazantzakis would have written for his book about China. It was to have as its title "Twenty Years After."

    I. The difference between China of twenty years ago and of today.
       1. Then: filth, epidemics, open sewers, stinking streets, many beggars in rags, annoying and dangerous. Political anarchy, civil wars. Corruption in government. Illiteracy, poverty, feudalism.
       2. Now: clean streets, railroads, clothes. No epidemics, flies and mice. No beggars. Sanitation and literacy spread, thanks to the enthusiasm of the people. The beggars either work in the farms or stay in the hospital or in the poorhouse, if they are unable to work. Government, strong and disciplined. Ruler-apostles of economy, no waste, no luxury. Ascetic.
   II. Agricultural reform: The peasants share the land.
      Agricultural communities or "communes" still beginning; they will not progress until they acquire farm machines.
  III. Industry: great effort because they know what it means for China.
      The human beings are still the machines of China.

Mukden. The bridge of Yangtze River. Dams.

IV. Reconstruction: schools, hospitals, houses for the workers.

V. Liberation of the Chinese woman: no longer tyranny of father; equal rights with husband, equal salary (and work); she acquires her own personality.

VI. Discipline, order, at last the feeling of some security, punctuality—in the trains and appointments.

VII. Method of reform: right balance of daring and prudence.

No longer force, but instruction and persuasion. When a government act is not accepted by the people, they change it. They know they can succeed only through propaganda and not through force.

VIII. Motto: virtue and success.

General thirst for honesty. No tipping.

IX. Politeness: they welcomed us with smiles. Dove of peace in their hearts. Peaceful people.

X. Tradition continues. Later, script with Latin characters.

HONG KONG.

July 22. We leave at seven. I was moved as I bid farewell to our dear friend and guide Wang Shen-shi, a very sensitive, intelligent, honest and patient man. I will not forget him.

In Hong Kong, a different atmosphere. At the Hotel Golden Gate, a cool breeze, very pleasant. At the bar, the barman tried to induce us to take an *apéritif*. A young Englishman with an elastic spine leaned with his chest on the bar and they filled him up with a green drink.

At the tables, well-dressed Chinese and Englishmen played dice. Repulsive faces, without sweetness, without politeness; where is the noble smile and the pale face of China!

The train was very clean. All the time the clerk with boiling water for tea passed by. Wang kept us company and held for us a basket full of sweet and juicy litchi and pineapples. . . .

"Until you take the plane, you are the guests of China," Wang told us as we departed. "In Hong Kong one of our men will welcome and take care of you. Don't be afraid to ask for whatever you want."

But we were fortunate enough in Hong Kong to meet a Greek. So we did not need to ask anything from the polite Chinese.

July 23. In the morning, on the Island of Hong Kong. Greedy eyes, ready to fleece and deceive you, women with tight clothes showing their legs, a repulsive air.

A lovable Greek, Gregory Sarafoglou, from Constantinople, a resident of Hong Kong, came to welcome us. I ordered a new suit.

We dined high at the Hotel Carlton. Exquisite site: Hong Kong, full of lights, multicolored, a sea of lights. Unforgettable.

July 24. In the morning at the hotel, the Greek-Canadian correspondent of *Time,* Paul Chourmouzis, came. We spoke of China and Greece. I told him what I had seen in China and the differences between the new and the old China. I told him that the dilemma has been stated badly: freedom—slavery. He who has a faith feels more free . . . so much is he a slave to his faith. Remember Saint Augustine: Lord, I am free only when I obey your will. Therefore, the unfaithful Westerners wrongly accuse the

Communist slaves. Their slavery begins when they stop believing.

In the afternoon, a ride in Gregory's car on the Island of Hong Kong. Superb view, green hills, a fishing village, Aberdeen, full of people, junks, fishermen live here, very interesting.

July 25. We circled Hong Kong in a car. Very beautiful view. A look of farewell. In the evening Gregory invited us to dinner at the Peninsula. Tomorrow we leave for Japan.

What was Hong Kong for us? A cordial welcome, a Greek "deus ex machina," who read in the newspaper that Nikos Kazantzakis and Chrysos Evelpides would arrive in Hong Kong and lifted his telephone to locate us. What delicious Turkish coffee, what excursions in his kingdom, what conversations, what feasts! And with what kindness his charming wife and the equally charming Mme. X. helped us to do our shopping in a jiffy. I say in a jiffy because everything is done that way here: in twenty-four hours the tailor has ready for you the most elegant man's or woman's suit, the shoemaker the finest shoes, and the shirtmaker the most beautiful shirt. . . .

Victoria, the small island of Hong Kong, with its spiral road and its hanging villas, looked to me like the shell of a big snail. It was occupied by the British in 1839 during the Opium War; it is only ninety square kilometers. And it is separated from Kowloon, the stretched arm of China, by only a mile of sea which looks as if it wanted to grab it in its hand again, but it is not in a hurry. And behind Kowloon is the whole New China. . . .

On these few kilometers, the most densely populated in the world, the British still rule, they even issue their own money. Red China seems to find it to her advantage to retain the status quo instead of devouring the British possession. It allows thousands of Chinese to go back and forth from Communist China to the British Empire, always loaded, always smiling as if there were no reason to worry.

"How do all these refugees from Red China find shelter?" we asked our Greek host.

"Don't ask me. No one of us knows. For a European to find a house is impossible. But the Chinese . . ."

He laughs.

"Is it cold in the winter?"

"Yes, and a very penetrating cold. And in the summer, terrible humidity. A climate that may kill even a bull."

"Inspite of that, you will stay. And you love Hong Kong. . . ."

"And we love it. Only to retain our senses, we must go away for a while every two or three years, because otherwise it may get to us."

TOKYO.

July 26. Plane, sea, we pass over Formosa, then over uninhabited enchanting small islands with sandy shores and turquoise waters.

Arrived in Tokyo at 5:00 P.M. Imperial Hotel. Tokyo is Americanized. Vast, endless streets, monotonous, banal buildings. One difference from my first trip: the women are more beautiful, no more crooked feet, they don't carry children on their backs, even their mouths are corrected.

The Japanese learned from the Americans to eat more vitamins. Their women have become taller, as the American women became taller at an earlier time. And because their lighting is better, they do not all wear glasses.

The Imperial Hotel looks like a temple of the Aztecs. It is the work of the famous American architect Frank Lloyd Wright. All red tile, spacious, with comfortable living rooms, with two internal gardens, with small streams and bridges, according to the tradition. There is an entire shopping center in the basement where the best shops of Tokyo are, and a post office that takes care of all your communication needs immediately.

In all the rooms they have Thermos here, as in China, but not with boiling water; here they have ice-cold water. You need a blanket for sleep, and a fur to wear in the dining room, but in the large hall and the other rooms, despite the electric fans, the heat is unbearable. The atmosphere is heavy and humid both inside and outside. The Japanese have arranged their air-conditioning this way so that you will not feel the terrible change in temperature as you step in. In Hong Kong the abrupt change of at least thirty degrees in temperature affected our breathing.

And another characteristic of the Imperial: the flowers. In every corner, in the corridors, in the stairways, in the hallways or in the dining room there is one vase with three to five flowers. Sometimes two branches and only one flower or a branch and two flowers. We looked at those bouquets with infinite admiration and jealousy, because we surely would not be able to arrange them ourselves. In Tokyo, they told us, there are still today over twenty thousand professors of ikebana, the art of arranging flowers. This art is not studied only by the idle noble young ladies or the florists but also by the poor female factory workers when they are not working.

We stand in front of a vase, and Kazantzakis tries to explain to me what he who arranges the bouquet should always bear in mind:

"You see," he says, "this branch which is taller than the two blossoms symbolizes the sky; the middle blossom symbolizes man, and the lower one the earth. And the three together form a triangle. Every bouquet must always form a triangle and be made with flowers of the season. It must also follow the strict rules of ikebana and at the same time it must always remind you of nature with all its diversity. . . ."

"Is it true that they never put big bouquets in their houses?"

"That's true. And they are careful that every bouquet harmonizes with the landscape: that is, one kind of bouquet in front of the window that looks at the sea, and another kind before a window that looks at the mountain. I remember twenty years ago I visited many Japanese houses. What delight, what tranquillity, what politeness reigns inside them! In the main room there is the tokonomano, where you will always see a vase with three or five flowers in front of the most beautiful picture of the house; the other rooms are empty. . . .

In the Imperial they maintain proper etiquette. They do not allow men to eat in the large dining room without a tie. Fortunately, there is another dining room in the basement where you find the finest items of European cuisine, and excellent fresh butter that we had not eaten anywhere in China.

July 27. Strolls; in the evening, to a popular nightclub, miserable. Indecencies. Cloudy sky, it sometimes rains. Sweltering heat.

The nightclub they recommended to us was brutal and disgusting. Big, half-naked American women wearing high boots were slapped and whipped on their buttocks and loins by a cowboy with a huge whip and they whinneyed like mares. At the end, a plump, delicate geisha came, stopped for a second, and then quickly took off her wooden sandals and her kimono and dove into the lake. The Japanese strip tease is purer than the European. No lasciviousness. We felt ashamed as if we had peeped at a girl going to take her bath.

July 28. Sunday. In the morning to the National Museum. Beautiful wooden statues, pots and jugs, golden Korean crowns, paintings, white antelopes in a golden background. In the afternoon to the *kabuki*. Charming geisha dances.

We saw many rare Chinese vases, cups, dishes and plates. The young Korean who accompanied us was pleased every time we admired a beautiful product of his country.

Kabuki: Exactly as it was twenty years ago. The performance begins at three in the afternoon and lasts until eleven in the evening. What can I add? Kazantzakis has said everything. The orchestra has been repaired after the war. It is all covered with red velvet. It looks entirely European. The stage is twenty-three meters wide and has great depth. The settings revolve. There is always, at the left, the famous corridor-bridge through which the most important heroes come and leave.

The actors study every movement and position of their bodies to complement the settings so that the total effect is that of a brilliant painting. Now and then we heard from the orchestra a wild, hoarse voice saying: Veligu! Veligu!, which surely is the American "very good!," and some short Japanese word that our ears did not make out.

During the time we wandered along Ginza, the Champs Élysées of Tokyo. Kazantzakis and Evelpides chatted with the Greeks who came to welcome them and with Japanese professors and journalists. In the evening, Kazantzakis in our room tried to explain to us the present situation of Japan:

"For three hundred years the Japanese succeeded in maintaining the same population, that is, thirty million. But when they stopped the horrible makibi, filling the nostrils of the newly born with tissue paper, then the population immediately began to increase. Today it surpasses ninety million. How will this population that annually increases, despite all the measures that the government has taken, be fed? To increase the agricultural production seems to me very difficult. Not a span of land has been left uncultivated. But what can they do with such poor land? Just think that only sixteen per cent of the area of Japan can be cultivated!"

"Do they have raw materials?"

"Only copper. Consequently, all the raw materials come from abroad—naturally, most from America."

"Surely the wages must be low enough to balance the expensive raw materials?"

"Before the war, I heard a thousand times, the Japanese industrial products were the cheapest in the world."

"Is it true that they dreamed of becoming the masters of Asia?"

"Their leaders and the Emperor did. But the simple people of any country do not ever want a war. The Japanese are very moderate; one handful of rice is enough for them. But as a French proverb says: eating brings an appetite: 1896, Formosa; 1911, Korea; 1932, Manchuria. . . ."

"Only Manchuria? Had they not reached as far as Peking?"

"They stayed in Peking for nine years. They had never planned to keep the whole of China forever; but they considered Manchuria definitely theirs. That's why everywhere else they stole, killed and destroyed, while in Manchuria they spent a lot of money building. . . . Then, they could export to all Asia. Now Korea boycotts them; Hong Kong does not want to do business with them; India, who used to buy from them all the cotton fabrics, now has become the main competitor; China, who once absorbed twenty per cent of the Japanese exports, now does not buy anything."

"And the Americans?"

"That's the question. How long will the Americans go

on helping them? During the Korean War, the Japanese made a lot of money. They earned eight hundred million dollars every year from their war industry. But today?"

"What did those who study the economic problems of Japan tell you?"

"They told us that the shipyards were doing well. They even paid us many compliments on the Greek shipowners who are their best customers. They also told us about the horrible and terrible capitalists—about the zaibatsu, which are big trusts that govern the economic life of all the country. Immediately after the war, the big monopolies were broken up, each into two or three hundred independent companies. But now the zaibatsu have raised their heads again; they come out in the light with their real names: Michubishi, Michui, Sumitomo, Yazunta. . . ."

"In other words, the American dream of making a democratic country out of Japan has not materialized?"

Kazantzakis seems to be thinking without responding. "How many countries have dreamed of democracy, fighting with America and not against America? How many countries of those that received aid from the Marshall Plan succeeded in establishing a healthy economy and a strong democracy?" As we went on, he spoke less and less, as if overcome by an inner vision.

We wandered around Tokyo. Alongside a lake in a large park, there is the Imperial Palace. Its iron gates open on the emperor's birthday and on the New Year. Now you see only the old pine trees behind the medieval walls.

The Americans bombed the palace on the first of May, 1945. Nothing was left except an iron fountain in the middle of the inner courtyard. As soon as the war was over, they proposed to Hirohito that they rebuild it, but he replied: "My country must be rebuilt first; I can wait."

Now the palace is rebuilt and big receptions take place on the third floor. Only on very solemn occasions, such as the coming of age of his son, does the Emperor wear his heavy historical uniform. Thousands have volunteered to keep the gardens clean.

From the airport to the hotel it took us over half an hour by car. We passed along big avenues, monotonous but beautiful, because the little houses were all low, wooden; here and there there were some two-story houses with charming balconies. They looked like doll's houses. There were also grocery and fruit stores, tea stores, restaurants, department stores, antique shops. Red, blue, yellow and white lanterns, beautiful signs . . .

On the green hills around Tokyo where the university is, there are beautiful houses for the well-to-do natives and foreigners. The more they are hidden by the trees the more they are liked by the Japanese who worship solitude and nature.

Here is how their great poet Basho Matsura sang three hundred years ago:

> *The bird sings of the spring that died*
> *And the eyes of the fish are filled with tears.*

> *The Magani River drew*
> *The burning sun into the sea.*

> *The spring night:*
> *Cherry trees! For the cherry trees the dawn is*
>   *fruitless.*

> *Wake up! Wake up!*
> *My sleeping butterfly, I'll make you my girl*
>   *friend!*

> *Grasshopper's voice,*
> *Your insistence pierces the rock.*

I saw the first snow.
That morning I forgot to wash my face. . . .

The center of Tokyo where the ministries and the big department stores are is abominable. Ugly skyscrapers next to booths, excavated sidewalks, mud, uncompleted buildings, a multitude of shapeless crowds moving in a hurry— only here and there is there an elegant Japanese woman in her national costume, wearing wooden sandals. The elevated trains pass every two minutes over your head and the whole street shakes.

Only on the vertical alleys, left and right of Ginza, can you enjoy the old Japan—porcelains, silk fabrics, umbrellas, wooden sandals, kimonos, doll's houses and window displays with genuine food, real paintings by Cézanne or Matisse. And wandering cooks, with hot noodles that remind you of the vermicelli of China . . .

The taxis are very impressive and their drivers very polite. And all are kamikazi. Yese! ("Yes, sir!") Whatever you tell them, Yese!—and a terrifying race begins. Who will surpass the other, all in the middle of the street? Holes, stones, ditches, pedestrians, cats—nothing can stop them. Yese! and by a miracle you find yourself still alive when you reach your destination. But then, what can the poor taxi driver do? Imagine a street whose numbers do not follow any logic; there are no odd and even numbers or even the system of the English squares—1, 2, 3. They say the house numbers agree with the birthday of every house. Next to 5 you have 967, then 234, and immediately next to it 48. How can you possibly find your number? And most streets do not even have numbers. Only when the hotel clerk illustrated on a paper the place where we wanted to go was our taxi driver able to find it without difficulty.

We had the same trouble with the telephone. I remem-

ber very well how I disturbed three hotel clerks who spent
the entire morning trying to make a telephone call to
Kazantzakis' Japanese publisher. At that time, I was upset
and I pitilessly insulted, in my mind, the poor hotel clerks.
Only later our friends explained to us that no one can find
a telephone number easily. The system of the telephone
directory in Japan is so complicated that you almost always have to make five or six other calls in order to get the
person you are seeking.

KYOTO.

July 30. At 9:00 A.M. we leave for Kyoto. Although we
travel second class, the railroad is clean and luxurious.
Green landscapes, rivers, little lakes, charming tiny wooden
houses.

A touring of the temples. Beautiful roofs, paintings. I
shall remember the horse with the golden adornments,
roosters with stretched wild wings, and under them the
dull chicken. The straw mats shine clean. Exquisite stone
lanterns.

The food in the dining car was cheap, plentiful and perfect. European cuisine. The Japanese seem to like the
roosters very much and now they have a species with very
long and beautiful tails.

I will not describe the Japanese temples we saw. Kazantzakis did it twenty years ago and they are exactly the same
today.

How beautiful Kyoto is! We passed through narrow
streets with doll's houses, looking as if they would fall
down if you blew on them. We climbed many broad stone
stairs, we saw many pagodas on our way, always inside
parks with old cedar and pine trees. Fog, coolness, and
down there, the city of Kyoto—dim and soft as velvet. At
the summit, the Miyomizu temple with a very beautiful
lightning rod and with very old and beautiful paintings

surrounding the ceiling of the veranda. It is built at the edge of the precipice. Waters flow down the rocks. At night on the terrace of our hotel we read "Chatting with the Stars" by Achuo Ogi, a contemporary poet:

CHATTING WITH THE STARS

Stars!
You are red fish that you shine pale.
Speak to me of the immeasurable depth of
chaos
Where you swim!

Stars!
I stop to stretch standing up in the desert plain,
At the endless night,
I stay there naked to hear your words better.

Stars!
With tears
I cleansed my shameful flesh that fell in love,
My heart remains naked and broken.

Stars!
All things and all living creatures taste sleep.
Tell me your secret slowly,
The hour has come!
O stars, the lights that spring up
How mute they are!

In Japan there are 81,700 Shinto temples and 73,500 Buddhist ones. Sometimes in the same building you find the one next to the other. The Japanese get married in Shinto ceremonies, but they also celebrate the Buddhist holiday when the dead come to visit the living.

According to the census of 1956, there were 77,780,327

Shintoists, 47,714,876 Buddhists, and only 500,000 Christians in Japan.

July 31. In the morning, to the Imperial Palace. Large courtyards, excellent paintings of pine trees.

I shall remember the Golden Pavilion with the wild golden bird on its top.

Inside the Imperial Palaces there are very beautiful gardens with old pine trees, cedar trees and hiding places. The Imperial Palaces are made of wood painted all gray, including their roofs, except for the ends of the round tiles on the roofs, which are painted white. The emperor used to eat, study, sleep, and receive his courtiers in different palaces. The largest of these palaces is the one opposite the central entrance-way. To the right of the front stairway there is a round-trimmed orange tree and to the left a cherry tree and beautiful stone lanterns.

The Golden Pavilion is reflected as truly gold on a light green lake. They say that its gardens are the most beautiful in Japan. Its last owner donated it for a temple.

The temple with the thousand Kannons is the largest one in Japan. The goddesses have forty arms and eleven heads. Behind the Kannons there are twenty-four disciples. A lot of money is thrown at their feet.

Unfortunately, temples and museums close at the most unsuitable hours; that is, at five and often at four in the afternoon. Even during the summer.

August 1. In the morning, we went by car from Kyoto to Nara. We passed through the Samprin temple. A miracle of coolness and simplicity, straw mats, paintings, an admirable garden.

An all-green world, charming hills, often covered with tea-plants. We pass through small villages and arrive in Nara; narrow archaic streets, the large park with the deer;

in a Shinto temple a beautiful girl does a hieratic dance and two young men crouch with crossed legs and play the *santouri*.

Red columns, red gates, centuries-old trees. A multitude of stone lanterns. Pilgrims ring the bells, then clasp their hands and cry and call on God, and then they hang a paper prayer on a tree. In the burning heat, we eat peaches and bananas.

Eating the juicy sweet peaches—which are really inexpensive—we remember the atom bombs and the fright of every Japanese who knows that the radioactivity in the fruits and the vegetables increases every now and then . . . We decide not to go to Hiroshima. I am especially afraid for Kazantzakis.

We were very fortunate to see a religious dance. Now we can understand better how the Chinese and Japanese theater was born.

In the afternoon in Kyoto, at a teahouse. A charming little house with a notable garden, water spurting. Then comes an ugly geisha wearing eyeglasses who serves us a thick green tea. I was not in a good mood, I remembered the ugly geisha who also wore glasses and served me twenty years before.

We left, walking slowly through the neighborhood among the trees where the geishas live. A man had climbed on a pine tree and was cleaning it, beautifying its leaves.

Nizo: The most beautiful Japanese castle in a big park. It is made of wood painted gray with a large veranda all around. All its walls are painted. In a golden background there is a gigantic pine tree. It springs from one corner and sprawls fifteen to twenty meters all over the wall to the other end. It has knotted branches and beautiful foliage. A little farther along are two storks. A tuft of bamboo, a white peacock. Two wild ducks. A cherry tree in bloom. A white lammergeier. Snow-clad mountains. Over every sliding door—all the doors are sliding—gilded peacocks, snakes, lotuses, dragons are carved on wood.

For hours we wandered in the cool half-dark rooms; our eyes had become accustomed to discern the details, and our feet enjoyed the cool, thick straw carpets.

We entered a small temple with many shining bronze vessels. And there were many small tables with rice, eggplants, melons and apples.

The guide burst out laughing when we asked him who ate them.

TOKYO.

August 2. We leave Kyoto by train; greenery, sweetness, light fog. On the train young American boys and girls, sixteen or seventeen years old, giggle and read comics. Terrifying, dangerous youth.

In the evening we go to the Ministry of Foreign Affairs: dinner in a large restaurant.

The dinner was given in one of the most beautiful restaurants of Tokyo, not in the large hall. Inside a park we passed a small bridge; we climbed a green hill; the moon rose behind the willow trees. We entered a pavilion and took off our shoes; three beautiful young geishas helped us sit on soft pillows. They put an electric fan under the table. We ate Japanese dishes, certainly not as delicious as the Chinese but served with the same politeness; we drank hot sake, an alcoholic drink made of rice. They naturally asked us about China. They know there is no other solution for Japan but a business agreement with China, the sooner the better.

Kokichi Mikimoto! Mikimoto! There is no man in Japan who doesn't know this name. There is no goldsmith in the world who does not do business with him. Mikimoto! The best cultured pearls. The only ones that are as worthy as the genuine ones.

But where and how did Mikimoto start out in order to reach what he is today? He has sixteen hundred companies and an annual income of ten million dollars.

Fifty years ago, he thought of cultivating pearls and began to do so for himself on a small scale in the Ango Bay. Today, this industry has expanded all over Japan. I don't think he invented the pearl cultivation, but he systematized it and brought it to absolute perfection, achieving the designs and colors he wanted. And their quality is superior to all other brands, Japanese, Korean, Indo-Chinese. Three years ago in Cannes they had shown us a short film: women from twenty to fifty years of age, wearing white kerchiefs to keep the sharks away, dive for one to three minutes to catch the oysters. They get oysters that are three years old because Mikimoto says that's their best age. They put them in big frames and select the right ones. Then other women place a tiny bead of ivory and a small piece of meat in every oyster. (I don't know exactly what kind of meat, but I think oyster meat.) The difficult thing is to know exactly how deep this bead is to be placed so that the oyster will not throw it out immediately; it cannot be put in too deeply, for it might hurt or kill the oyster. As soon as this surgical operation is over, other women take the oysters and put them in vats and lower them again quite deep into the sea. The vats are tied with wire and hang in the sea. The oysters must stay inside the water for three or four years to form a beautiful pearl. At regular intervals women dive, take out the oysters, clean off the seaweed and shellfish that are glued on them and put them back into the vats.

At the central stores of Mikimoto which are on the Ginza, we met not only many European, American and

English ladies, but also two Greek ladies who approached us with great politeness as soon as they heard us speaking Greek. They had come from Egypt.

At the time we were to take the train to return to Tokyo a terrible thunderstorm broke out; we missed the first train and the second was hit by lightning, so we reached Tokyo two hours later than scheduled. In the hotel we met three men—a publisher and two friends of his—and two very beautiful women—Mrs. K., who had bought Dassin's film He Who Must Die, and her daughter. In our confusion we thought that all of them were one party and we accepted an invitation for dinner from the ladies although we had accepted days ago a dinner invitation for that evening from the publisher. But the Japanese fortunately do not get angry and are not offended because of a misunderstanding; or if they are angry or offended, they do not show it. Smiling and good humored we all got into three cars and went to eat with Mrs. K. in a charming little Japanese restaurant, one of those we had admired on the Ginza. The restaurant eagerly waited for us. We had told them that we would be there by eight, but it was near eleven when we arrived. We ate many Japanese dishes. They always served us with great courtesy and explained to us what the dishes were made of and how we should eat them and kept filling our cups with sake. I will never forget those Japanese dinners eaten on a low table with an electric fan beneath it. We sat on soft pillows on the ground with crossed legs.

We talked again about the atom bomb. Mrs. K. and her daughter visit the Cannes Film Festival every year. Two years ago she had presented a tragic film about the atom bomb, What the Birds Don't Know, which the journalists found boring.

She told us that He Who Must Die would receive the first prize in Japan, and indeed her prediction was correct. The film based on Kazantzakis' novel Christ Recrucified or The Greek Passion did get the prize. It was the best film of the year.

Why should we have had to leave Japan when we had begun to meet some wonderful people? How many things we could have learned from them! How many more places we could have seen if we only had had a little more time at our disposal!

That day in our room we found a note saying: "Professor Kono called. If you could see him, he would be happy to visit you."

We finally came in contact with Professor Kono and told him that we would be very happy to see him.

We waited for Professor Kono in the reception room of a hotel that was full of Europeans with stiff collars and gold rings and big pearl necklaces, hats with feathers, veils and beautiful dogs. Two Japanese arrived dressed in modest black tunics, wearing wooden sandals and with the indispensable little bundle hung on their left arms: Dr. and Mrs. Kono. Japan, for the first time, opened like a big lotus for us to enter and harvest like bees the sweetest honey in its hearts. . . .

Professor Kono taught Ancient Greek and had received a letter from his friend, the Japanese ambassador in Athens, telling him to meet the two Greek travelers. He had read all the books by Kazantzakis that have been published. He had also read Japan-China and had a big question about a Japanese word which appeared in this book.

"What's the meaning of fudoshin? I keep thinking about it, but I don't understand it. . . ."

Mrs. Kono, who was also a professor, smiled, shook her head, but she also did not understand it.

Kazantzakis then explained to them how he learned this word on the ship that brought him to Japan twenty years ago and what a great impression this word made on him and what a great influence it had had on his life. Calmness and composure! Always keeping your soul immovable before happiness and misfortune!

Professor Kono takes out of his pocket paper and pencil, listens carefully, and puts down the three ideograms: Fu, Do, Shin; he shows them to his wife, they study them for some time, and suddenly he gets up full of joy and says:

"Oh, now I understand, yes, I understand! That is the Buddhist commandment: Fu ("denial"), Do ("movement"), Shin ("heart"). That is, to keep your heart immovable. Oh, how pleased I am that I understood it!"

He sits down again, smiles, slowly opens his bundle and puts a big long box on the table and says:

"This is a Japanese pastry. I hope you'll like it!"

We open the box quickly, full of curiosity, and we see a sort of yellow kandaif (the Greek and Turkish shredded cake with chopped nuts and honey), made of egg yolks, without any stuffing. We had eaten a pastry almost like it in Madrid. We bring forks and we share it with all our friends. Meanwhile, Mr. Komoi, the publisher, comes with the interpreter and his friends.

And as we eat and laugh and lick our lips, Mr. and Mrs. Kono open a small square box, with red, green, yellow and glistening blue square papers and both begin, without saying a word, to play a very childish game: they fold, fold again, unfold, twist, caress, fold, unfold, caress again, twist, untwist until the small square papers become minute balls in their fingers, and then slowly take on a form and sail on the marble table as if they were wild ducks in water, frogs, water lilies, Japanese lanterns, battleships, fishing boats. We applaud them and ask them to make more so that each one of us may take an entire series to Europe.

"And now tell me," I ask Nikos, "which one of our professors would condescend to 'play' like a child with strangers without being afraid that they would laugh at him? Isn't it a great virtue, this oriental naïveté?"

NIKKO.

August 3. I saw once more the huge trees, the red altars, the red bridge, the three monkeys. I saw the waterfall, the huge Buddha, the thousands of pilgrims. No special emotion.

Once upon a time, at the beginning of the seventeenth century, a pious youth respected and admired his grandfather, the great founder of the Tokugawa Dynasty, and he never allowed anyone to speak to him of his ancestor unless he wore his official uniform, and knelt and turned his eyes to the ground.

Besides the worship for his ancestors, Yemitsu seemed to love the beautiful colors, the right carvings, the flowers, the mythical birds and whatever else can fill the heart of a good man. And in order to glorify his grandfather, he brought the best artist of his time, gave him a lot of money, and left him free to become intoxicated in that thousand-year-old forest with its high trees, falling waters, rocks, green hills, birds and animals and to build the palaces of his Halima. After the completion of the temples and the mausoleum for his grandfather, Nikko became synonymous in the Japanese language with kekko, which means splendid, excellent.

What does it matter if we preferred the simple gray palaces with their gray roofs to the multicolored, gold sculptured altars, the beautiful red bridge that looks like a half moon, the exquisite castle gates including the famous one, with the three monkeys, which itself would have been enough to immortalize Hidari Yingoro? In Nikko, the Japanese rejoice that thousands of pilgrims from all over the world enjoy seeing them.

This artistic vision carved on wood cost twenty million yen at the time it was made. Yemitsu gave from his own treasures and his noble vassals were made to give even more.

Grandfather and grandson are now found next to each other in two simple bronze mausoleums.

The waterfall that Kazantzakis mentions is the Hidari Yingoro which falls from a height of one hundred meters; the lake to which we went on the mountain was very beautiful and was called Chuzenji.

KAMAKURA.

August 4. A horrible journey, heat, dust, thousands of cars. Thousands of pilgrims are in Kamakura. This gigantic Buddha is beautiful, but the Daibutsu of Nara is bigger.

But how beautiful was this Buddha with his half-closed eyes. He was not imprisoned in a dark temple, but free, under old trees! Typhoons and fires raged over Kamakura; the temples were burned down to the ground; the people became ashes. But Buddha, calm, has always smiled the same, since 1252, and perhaps he dreams behind his half-closed eyes of a future world better than ours. . . .

Here the red notebook stops. Here I, too, will end our journey. Only I'll ask you, dear reader, again to forgive me, for my duty was difficult and I'm afraid I've failed. I beg you to judge me as God would judge, that is, not according to my act but to my intention, always full of respect for the memory of Nikos Kazantzakis.

—Antibes, February 26, 1958.

TRANSLATOR'S

NOTE

■ A NOTE ON THE AUTHOR

■ Nikos Kazantzakis is the literary giant of modern Greece, and one of the greatest writers of the twentieth century. This is not only the opinion of his Greek admirers, but also that of men like Albert Schweitzer, Thomas Mann and Albert Camus. Greece found in him an author who could express the spirit and the heritage of all the periods of her long history, as well as the agony and the anguish of modern man. He has done this in many of his works, especially in most of his tragedies in verse. But Kazantzakis was not a writer of exclusively Greek themes. His thirst for knowledge and his desire to encompass the total experience of mankind in his world view led him a number of times to leave his country in search of new visions, impressions and experiences out of which he would select whatever would meet the needs or curiosities of his soul, which were almost limitless, and to transmute them into art.

He was fortunate enough to become aquainted with nearly all the leading spiritual, intellectual and political movements and leaders of our time: Orthodox and Roman Catholic Christianity, Bergson, Nietzsche, nationalism, liberalism, psychoanalysis, Buddhism, socialism, communism, Lenin, Mussolini, Schweitzer. Some of these movements and leaders had influenced him at one moment or another of his life, but they had never held him under their spell. Out of the host of varied and conflicting ideas with which he nourished his intellect, he formed his own

world view, which he so beautifully and powerfully presented in his novels, tragedies and travel books and more
directly in *The Saviors of God* and in his *Odyssey* (in the
eighteenth and twenty-first books of which he contrasted
it to Buddhism and Christianity). The summation of his
ideal is expressed in his motto, engraved on his tomb: "I
hope for nothing. I fear nothing. I am free." Thus freedom for him becomes the process of ridding himself of all
earthly bonds. His life was a constant struggle to achieve
that state and was a brilliant example of a complete dedication to a "noble passion."

He was born in Herakleion, Crete, on the eighteenth of
February, 1883. Despite his travels and his self-imposed
exile in his last twelve years, Crete remained his spiritual
home. The "spirit of place" never left him. He was proud
of his Cretan peasant origin. His father, who has been
idealized as Capitán-Michális in his *Freedom or Death*,
was a storekeeper and farmer. He was a man of great physical power and primitive instincts, unsociable and taciturn. Kazantzakis both admired and feared his father, but
loved his mother exceedingly, a pious, sweet and submis-
sive woman. The author attributed the ambivalence of his
will to the disparity of the character of his parents. He had
two sisters and a brother who died while he was an infant.
He attended school in his native town. During the Cretan
Revolt of 1897, many Cretans sent their families away to
the Cyclades Islands. The Kazantzakis family was sent to
the island of Naxos. There young Kazantzakis had the opportunity to attend for two years (1897-99) the French
School of the Holy Cross, which was administered by the
Franciscan monks. In this school he learned French, Latin
and Italian and became acquainted with the European, especially French, literature of the nineteenth century in the
marvelous library of that school. In the last two years of
his gymnasium studies, he studied English and German

by himself. His classmates still remember him for his unusual diligence and intelligence, and his Franciscan teachers felt that he would become a great man, probably a cardinal. From 1902 to 1906, he studied law at the University of Athens and graduated with high honors in December, 1906. In 1905 he worked as a columnist in the leading Athenian newspaper *Acropolis*, under the pen name of Akritas. There he met the great nationalist and demoticist leader Ion Dragoumis (-1920), who became his idol and whom he did not cease to admire throughout his life.

While he was a senior in the School of Law he published his first article, "The Sickness of Our Century," and under the pen name Kárma Nirvamé his first book, *Serpent and Lily* (a lyric narrative in the form of a diary of ninety-five small pages). This book was relatively well received by the columnists and critics of the time as the first attempt of a writer. It is the passionate story of a young artist who, unable to achieve a complete communication with his girl, commits suicide with her in a closed room filled with flowers where they spent their last night and succumbed to the intoxicating aroma of the lilies. The influence of Gabriele D'Annunzio's *Triumph of Death* is obvious in the first work of Kazantzakis.

In 1907 the committee that granted the awards in a drama contest praised his first play, *It Dawns*, a drama in three acts. The same play was presented in Athens and was thought rather controversial because it depicts in a sympathetic light the plight of a woman who is in love with her husband's brother and prefers to commit suicide instead of breaking up her marriage. In the same year he wrote two other plays, *Fasga* and *How Much Longer?* In 1909 an Egyptian magazine published his one-act tragedy entitled *Comedy* or *Requiem*.

Kazantzakis started on his travels in 1907, and there were only a few countries in Europe and Asia that he did

not visit. His father had promised him that he would pro-
vide for a trip to Italy after his graduation from the School
of Law. Kazantzakis took this trip in 1907 with his girl
friend and fellow student of arts and letters, Galatea Ale-
xiou (1886-1962), herself a writer. He was married to her
in 1911, despite his father's strong disapproval, and lived
with her (except for his long trips) until 1924. They were
divorced in 1926.

From 1907 to 1909 he studied in Paris, primarily under
the philosopher Henri Bergson, who influenced his thinking considerably. Bergson's *élan vital*, the life force that
can conquer matter, became in Kazantzakis' own philosophy the force that enables the dutiful and dedicated man
to transmute flesh into spirit.

After his physical similarity to Nietzsche was pointed
out to him by a Parisian girl, he made it his aim to study,
follow and emulate the German philosopher. In 1908 he
wrote his ninety-three page doctoral dissertation on *Frie-
drich Nietzsche and his Philosophy of Right* which was
accepted by the School of Law of the University of Athens
and was published in Herakleion in 1909. As P. Prevelakis
(his biographer and friend) pointed out, in this mono-
graph, Kazantzakis summarized those parts of Nietzsche's
philosophy which he himself had absorbed—ideas, pre-
cepts and utopias which, remarkably unchanged, are encountered throughout his work.

While in Paris he worked as the correspondent for Athenian newspapers and magazines, wrote a philosophical
essay, "Science Has Failed," published in an Athenian
magazine in 1909, and a dissertation in French on pragma-
tism, inspired by the theories of William James. This he
later destroyed.

In 1909-1910 the demoticist literary magazine *Noumás*
published, as a serial, his first novel, *Broken Souls*, under
his pen name Pétros Psiloreítis. This novel is the story of a
group of Greek students in Paris. Oréstes Asteriádes, the

hero, is an idealist with limited will power to materialize any of his noble dreams. His visionary and naïve fight against the realities of life causes his breakdown. His tragic end is shared by his kind but weak girl friend and by Professor Gorgías, an old man stricken by the glory of the past and its nostalgia. This symbolic novel was intended to be the first part of a trilogy that was never completed.

In the next year he received an award for his Nietzschean drama, *The Sacrifice*, inspired by one of the best-known Greek folk songs, "The Bridge of Arta." This play later became the libretto of the first opera of Manolis Kalomíris, under the new title of *The Masterbuilder*. This is the first work in which he expresses his theme that the dedicated man should be willing to sacrifice or reject his woman and his domestic happiness in order to advance his cause and accomplish what he set out to do.

He volunteered for service in the First Balkan War (1912-1913) and was assigned to the office of the prime minister (Eleutherios Venizelos) as special assistant to the latter's secretary. From 1911 to 1915 he worked at translating the most important works of William James, Nietzsche, Eckermann, Laisant, Maeterlinck, Darwin, Buchner, Bergson, and six of the dialogues of Plato for the Phexis publications and wrote with his wife a series of school readers under her name that brought them a considerable income.

In 1914 and 1915 he and his favorite friend and poet, Ángellos Sikelianós (1884-1951), undertook a systematic pilgrimage to the ancient and modern shrines of Greece. Both sought to saturate themselves with the Greek-Christian spirit so that they might reproduce it in their works.

Two years later, he unsuccessfully operated a mine near Mani with George Zorbas, whom he later made the personification of the life force of a man of action and thus immortalized him in his novel, *Zorba the Greek*. After his failure as a businessman, he spent two years in Zurich.

From May 1919 to November 1, 1920, as Director-General of Public Welfare, he successfully undertook the mission of repatriating the Greek refugees from Caucasus to their native land. At that time he became aware of the refugee problem which he touched in his *Greek Passion*.

He began his intensive study of Buddhism in Vienna in 1921. There he began the writing of his tragedy *Buddha*. (Prior to this, he had written *Odysseus, Christ,* and *Nikephoros Phokas*.) Buddha, although foreign to his peasant soul, remained throughout his life one of his beloved prophets and leaders of men.

The years 1922 through 1924 mark a turning point in Kazantzakis' life. The ardent nationalist was converted to socialism. It may well be that the horrible picture of a prostrate and starving Germany and of a bleeding Greece after its disaster in Asia Minor and the influence of his new friends played an important role in his ideological orientation. During the three years he spent in Berlin, Kazantzakis was the moving power in a circle of young Polish and German Jewish socialists and intellectuals. The young women of this group worshiped him as the theosophists worshiped Krishnamurti. (Most of these girls were either executed in the purges of the Stalinists in 1937 or died in the German concentration camps.) During this period, Kazantzakis developed his own theory of metacommunism (a society to go beyond communism). Although he admired Lenin as a prophet linked with the people, he intensely disliked his doctrine and the materialistic philosophy of Marxism in general. He strongly felt that Marxism ignored the metaphysical and spiritual needs of man. He was sickened by the Communist bureaucracy and its inhuman preoccupation with numbers and statistics. His theory of metacommunism as well as his belief that man's dedication to creative activity alone "saves God" were expressed in his *Saviors of God*, the spiritual exercises of an ascetic, which was originally published in the Greek periodical *Anagénnisi* in 1927 and in a revised version in 1945. Kazantzakis' world view was further developed into an unusual form of art, his great baroque epic, *The Odyssey: A Modern Sequel.* This poetic "monument of our age" superbly presents the agony of modern man, his search for god, and the drama of ideas in our world today. This long epic of 33,333 lines (of seventeen-syllable iambic verse) had been written in seven drafts before it reached its definitive version (Winter 1925— December 1938). During these thirteen years that Kazantzakis had been working on his *Odyssey* he wrote two novels in French (*Toda-Raba* and *Jardin des rochers*), four travel books, a number of tragedies, *Lidio-Lidia,* a play about an old prodigal cardinal, *Othello Returns,* a Pirandello-type *comédie,* most of his twenty-one cantos, four screenplays, about forty children's classics freely adapted into Greek, a few hundred articles for the Encyclopedical Lexicon of Eleutheroudákis, a number of articles for newspapers and magazines, and he translated Dante's *Divine Comedy,* Goethe's *Faust,* and poems of Juan Ramón Jiménez and other Spanish lyric poets.

After Kazantzakis finished his *Odyssey,* he felt somewhat relieved. He visited England in 1940 and spent nearly all the years of the occupation period in his retreat on the island of Aegina writing his picaresque novel, *Zorba the Greek* and four tragedies and translating Homer's *Iliad* (in collaboration with the brilliant classicist Professor John Kakrides), Machiavelli's *The Prince,* Jørgensen's *St. Francis,* and retranslating Dante's *Divine Comedy.*

After the liberation in 1945, he involved himself for a short period in politics by becoming minister without portfolio in the liberal government of Sophoulis in which he represented the small democratic and socialistic parties that did not collaborate with the Communists.

On November 11, 1945, he was married to his faithful companion and collaborator who had encouraged and helped him in the completion of his vast work, Heleni

Samios, the granddaughter of Professor Aphentoúlis, one of the most brilliant and enlightened Greek scientists and intellectuals of the last century.

On June 2, 1946 he left for England where he had been invited to visit by the British Council. He did not return to Greece before his death. For eleven months (May 1, 1947 to March 25, 1948) he was the director of the UNESCO Bureau of Translations. Finally in June 1948, he settled at the ancient Greek city of Antibes on the French Riviera and devoted all his energies for the rest of his life to his own writing. There in the Villa Manolita he wrote his traditional novels that made him famous all over the world: *The Greek Passion* (Christ Recrucified); *Freedom or Death*; *The Last Temptation of Christ*; *Saint Francis*, and his lyrical autobiography, *Report to Greco*.

In 1953 he fell seriously ill. For the rest of his life he suffered from leukemia and was treated by Professor Heilmeyer at the clinic in the University of Freiburg, Germany where he died on October 26, 1957 after his return from his trip to China and Japan.

The travel books of Kazantzakis made a great contribution to the development of modern Greek literature by the establishment of a new genre, the literary travel narrative including everything from a descriptive vignette to a philosophical essay about the great thinkers of a country. This type of literary writing has become very popular in Greece today. Many of the leading contemporary Greek writers have systematically and successfully cultivated it, but none has surpassed the beauty and depth of the Kazantzakis series of travel books. They made him known to the Greek public long before his first novel was published. His tragedies, his *Odyssey*, and his *Saviors of God* never attracted the Greek readers, but his travel books enchanted them with their thrilling descriptions, faithful representations of persons, places and incidents, concise profound thoughts, and unforgettable aphorisms. These books are permeated by the author's sincerity—his effort to understand the people with whom he came in contact and to try to find out the origin and development of their patterns of behavior and their way of life by tracing their history as far back as was relevant for his study.

In his travels, he also tried to find the invisible thread that binds mankind together regardless of nationality, state, religion and civilization. As he said, "One of the greatest joys of the human mind is to listen to both of the opposite views and to recognize the relative value of each one of the opposing views and to try, out of these fanatic inimical ideas, to create a perfect synthesis."

Kazantzakis craved for a better understanding among peoples and sought to find behind the multiplicity of the present-day societies the similarities of the human beings that comprise them.

His first travel book was published in Alexandria, Egypt in 1927 under the title *Traveling—Spain, Italy, Egypt, Mount Sinai*. It includes an interview with Mussolini and the author's impressions of the Mediterranean countries he visited in the previous year. This book—minus Spain, and with additional chapters on Jerusalem, Cyprus and Peloponnesus—was republished in 1961 in Athens. A French version of it came out in 1957 under the title *Du Mont Sinai à l'île de Venus*.

His four trips to the Soviet Union in the twenties inspired three books (two in Greek): *What I Saw in Russia* (1928); a two-volume *History of Russian Literature* (1930); and a novel in French, *Toda-Raba* (1931). *What I Saw in Russia* has been republished under the title *Traveling—Russia*.

In 1937, the chapters on Spain in his first travel book and "Viva la Muerte," a chronicle of the Spanish Civil War, were published under the title, *Traveling—Spain*, and are soon to be published in the United States.

The most popular of his travel books in Greece has been

Traveling—Japan/China, published for the first time in 1938. It includes his impressions from the trip to the Far East in 1935 (February 22–May 6).* Some of the beautiful descriptions of this book have passed, slightly altered, into *The Rock Garden*, a novel in French, written about 1937. In the fourth edition of *Japan/China* in 1958, a second part was added including the last writings of Kazantzakis, his notes for a book he planned to write about China under the title, "Twenty Years After." These notes have been comprehensively annotated by his wife who accompanied him and who gave us all the background information about his last trip to the Far East in 1957. A new edition of this book came out in 1962 in Athens.

The last of his travel books is *England*, also very successful in Greece. It presents England in its heroic effort during the critical hours of 1940.

Kazantzakis also wrote two articles about Crete in *Holiday* and a series of articles entitled *The Land of Greece*, published in a Greek magazine. The first of these articles, which is a very beautiful hymn to Greece, is included in the *Modern Greek Reader*, compiled by this translator. Most of the *Land of Greece*, somewhat revised, has been integrated into his *Report to Greco*.

Some of the main themes of his travel books are the psychology of peoples, the heroes of thought and action, the monuments and landscapes and their interrelation to the soul of the people, the mortality of civilizations, and the future of each country and of mankind in general.

In *Spain*, Kazantzakis vividly painted the passionate nature of the Spaniard and the two poles of his soul, passion and *nada*. In *England*, he beautifully illustrated the simple nature of the Englishman as opposed to that of the Spaniard and epigrammatically described the English *gen-*

---

* He went there, as a special correspondent of *Acropolis*, an Athenian newspaper and in order to see new landscapes, fauna, and flora for his descriptions in his *Odyssey*.

tleman, in control of himself and his instincts, with his wide perspective and global thinking. The *gentleman,* Magna Charta, and Shakespeare are three of the great victories won by man in the history of his evolution from ape to man. Kazantzakis' philosophy about the future of mankind is optimistic. He believes that man will develop into a species much more deserving the name of "man." In his concluding chapter in *China* he presents a few aspects of a future society. His fascination with the Orient is revealed in a letter he wrote to M. Renaud de Jouvenal on his return to Aegina from the Far East: "My eyes are still full of the Orient and my heart is breaking to pieces. Now everything in Europe seems to me insipid, tasteless, odorless, trivial and sad. I saw many beautiful things in Japan and many profound and very human ones in China."

Ideas did not concern him very much. He admired the individual who had a purpose in his life and was prepared to make sacrifices to defend it and advance it beyond his own powers. His heroes were the leaders of men who dedicated themselves completely to the purpose of their lives regardless of what this purpose was. His twenty-one cantos and most of his twelve tragedies depict the struggles of such heroes of action and thought as Christ, Buddha, Moses, Mohammed, Lenin, Dante, Nietzsche, Shakespeare, Leonardo Da Vinci, Columbus, Genghis Khan and Hideyoshi.

He was a very religious man but did not belong to any religion. He sought a God, or better, his *maestro* (master), his *duca* (leader), whom he encountered successively in Christ, Buddha, Lenin, Odysseus without adopting any one, always seeking to reconcile the irreconcilable. The leitmotiv of his work, as he said, was his struggle for the achievement of the various forms of freedom, political, religious and intellectual.

In this book the concept of freedom sometimes takes on a strange nuance. We may not always agree with Kazantzakis' challenging statements, but we always find them thought-provoking.

After he passed through the three stages of ideological orientation that Prevelakis has described: aristocratic nationalism, utopian socialism or metacommunism and heroic nihilism, he reached a new stage which we may call universal humanism and spiritual ascension. Every man must fight for his betterment as well as that of others so that mankind will be enabled to move uphill. All the potentialities and all the wealth of life must be cultivated and experienced. We can move upward only by fighting for a "noble passion." Our upward movement can knock us down, but it can also lead us to the realization of man's potentialities that have not yet been discovered. Kazantzakis, through his works, tried to help us discover hidden power within ourselves to follow the right path of life and fight our way uphill. Through the centuries to come, mankind will find in his writings inspiration and courage.

BIBLIOGRAPHY

Pandelis Prevelakis, *Nikos Kazantzakis and His Odyssey*. Translated by Philip Sherrard. Simon and Schuster. New York, 1961.

The special issues of the two leading Athenian literary magazines, *Nea Estia* (December 15, 1959) and *Nea Epoche* (Autumn, 1958), devoted to Nikos Kazantzakis.

G. K. Katsimpales, "The Unknown Kazantzakis" (*Nea Estia*, April 15, 1958).

Renaud de Jouvenal, "Nikos Kazantzakis" (*Nea Estia*, November 1, 1962).